Responsible Partisanship?

STUDIES IN GOVERNMENT
AND PUBLIC POLICY

Responsible Partisanship?

The Evolution of
American Political Parties
Since 1950

EDITORS
John C. Green
Paul S. Herrnson

 University Press of Kansas

Published by the University Press of Kansas (Lawrence, Kansas 66049), which was
organized by the Kansas Board of Regents and is operated and funded by Emporia
State University, Fort Hays State University, Kansas State University, Pittsburg State
University, the University of Kansas, and Wichita State University

Library of Congress Cataloging-in-Publication Data

Responsible partisanship? : the evolution of American political parties
since 1950 / editors, John C. Green, Paul S. Herrnson.
    p. cm. — (Studies in government and public policy)
  Includes bibliographical references and index.
    ISBN 0-7006-1216-5 (cloth : alk. paper) — ISBN 0-7006-1217-3 (pbk. :
alk. paper)
    1. Political parties—United States. 2. United States—Politics and
government—1945–1989. 3. United States—Politics and
government—1989– I. Green, John Clifford, 1953– II. Herrnson, Paul S.,
1958– III. Series.
JK2261 .R47 2002
324.273'09'045—dc21   2002009286

British Library Cataloguing in Publication Data is available.

Printed in the United States of America

10 9 8 7 6 5 4 3 2 1

To the Committee on Political Parties of the American Political Science
Association, 1946 to 1950—scholars committed to advancing political
science and serving the political process.

E. E. Schattschneider, Chair
Thomas S. Barclay
Clarence A. Berdahl
Hugh A. Bone
Franklin L. Burdette
Paul T. David
Merle Fainsod
Bertram M. Gross
E. Allen Helms
Evron M. Kirkpatrick
John W. Lederle
Fritz Morstein Marx
Louise Overacker
Howard Penniman
Kirk H. Porter
J. B. Shannon

Contents

Figures and Tables

FIGURES

TABLES

Acknowledgments

The Political Organizations and Parties (POP) organized section of the American Political Science Association (APSA) commissioned the essays in this book as part of the commemoration of the fiftieth anniversary of the publication of "Toward a More Responsible Two-Party System," the 1950 Report of the Committee on Political Parties of the APSA. We were honored to serve as cochairs of the committee charged with organizing the commemoration at the annual meeting of the APSA in 2000, where most of the chapters in this book were presented as papers. This project was the work of numerous people, and we gratefully acknowledge their contributions.

We would like to thank first the other members of the committee: Gerald Pomper, John Bibby, Sandy Maisel, Sheilah Mann, David Mayhew, Paul Beck, Diana Dwyre, John White, Robert Hauck, Ruth Jones, Frank Sorauf, and Jerome Mileur. John Coleman played an active role on the committee and deserves special recognition for creating a web site for the project.

Jeffrey Berry, the chair of the POP at the time of the events, deserves special recognition, as do its other officials, Secretary-Treasurer Diana Dwyre and council members David Farrell, Anna Harvey, Mary Coleman, Beth Leech, Marian Palley, Robert Harmel, and Laura Woliver. In this regard, two former chairs of the POP, John Bibby and Ruth Jones, began the planning for this event far in advance and are owed a special thanks, as is Charles Hadley, the longtime secretary-treasurer of the POP.

Other participants in the project included David Broder, James Burns, Nelson Polsby, Ralph Goldman, Jeane Kirkpatrick, Susan Scarrow, Herbert Kitschelt, Patrick Seyd, Paul Whiteley, Matthew Shugart, Eric Uslaner, E. J. Dionne, Donald Fowler, and Joseph Schlesinger. Our gratitude extends to Harold Scarrow, Daniel Shea, Philip Davies, Kenneth Janda, and William Crotty for their patient advice. And we would like to thank David Canon and Robin Kolodny for their thorough and helpful reviews of the initial manuscript.

We also thank these sponsors for providing the financial resources to carry out the project, including the publication of this book: the American Political Science Association; the Center for American Politics and Citizenship, University of Maryland; the Center for Congressional and Presidential Studies, American University; the Committee for Party Renewal; Jerome Mileur, University of Massachusetts at Amherst; and the Ray C. Bliss Institute of Applied Politics, University of Akron. This project was partially supported through grants from the Pew Charitable Trusts.

We are especially indebted to Fred Woodward and his associates at the University Press of Kansas, not only for their fine work on the book but also for their patience and fortitude. Special thanks go to Kimberly Haverkamp, Gail Garbrandt, and Janet Bolois of the Bliss Institute at the University of Akron for taking care of the logistics of the project, a duty shared by Peter Francia and David Clifford, associated with the Center for American Politics and Citizenship at the University of Maryland.

Responsible Partisanship?

1

The Search for Responsibility

John C. Green and Paul S. Herrnson

The year 2000 was an important milestone in American politics: the two hundredth anniversary of the first peaceful transfer of power from one political party to another. Politics has changed a great deal since 1800, but the United States has enjoyed an uninterrupted succession of fifty such transitions. As the controversies surrounding the 2000 presidential election reveal, such transfers of power have sometimes been strained. Nevertheless, this record is no small feat. Party scholars argue that it was not by accident that this pattern of partisan transition was peaceful rather than violent.

The year 2000 was also an important milestone in the scholarly study of political parties: the fiftieth anniversary of the publication of "Toward a More Responsible Two-Party System," the Report of the Committee on Political Parties of the American Political Science Association (Committee on Political Parties 1950a). Politics has also changed a great deal since 1950, but scholarly attention to political parties remains uninterrupted. Like particular elections, the role of parties has sometimes been strained. Nevertheless, political parties remain a critical part of American democracy.

Indeed, the Report is a landmark in a persistent quest to improve the political parties peculiar to the American system of government. Central to this quest has been a "search for responsibility" (Ranney 1954). Dating back to the origins of political science as a discipline and with roots in the founding of the Republic, all manner of observers have sought to make American parties better and more accountable instruments of government. Here political scientists have made two important contributions: a debate over what parties *should do* in the American system, and research on what parties *actually do* in politics. The intersection of these two contributions has produced numerous practical proposals for reforming the party system, of which the Report is a prominent example. Although its direct effect on political parties has been

1

modest, it has deeply influenced American party scholarship (see, for example, Pomper 2001, 162).

This book commemorates the Report in a fitting way, with new scholarship on American political parties. Taking the Report and its recommendations as a starting point, the authors of the eleven chapters in this collection chart the changes in the party system since 1950, searching for evidence of party responsibility and the conditions that foster or undermine it. The contributors do not all agree with the Report's normative stance or its empirical assumptions, but they share a deep appreciation of parties as political institutions. But before we introduce these chapters, a brief summary of the Report is in order.

ORIGINS AND CONTENTS OF THE REPORT

The Report was primarily a prescriptive document, the most prominent ever issued under the imprimatur of the American Political Science Association. It was the product of the Committee on Political Parties, a group of sixteen political scientists appointed by the APSA president in 1946. Such committees on political matters were common in that era before the "behavioral revolution"; other examples include the Committee on Citizenship Participation in Politics, Committee on Judicial Organization, and Committee on Congress (see *American Political Science Review [APSR]*, "News and Notes" 1947–1951). Indeed, the latter's work on congressional reform, which influenced the 1946 Legislative Reorganization Act, was the model for the Committee on Political Parties (Galloway 1946). The products of such committees sometimes appeared in print under the auspices of the APSA, such as the recommendations of a Special Committee on Congressional Reapportionment (Special Committee on Reapportionment 1951).

Although one of the most respected American party scholars of the day, E. E. Schattschneider, chaired the Committee on Political Parties, many of the key figures were not party specialists, including Fritz Morstein Marx, who chaired a five-member drafting committee and strongly influenced the Report's final text and tone. Indeed, the impetus for the appointment of the Committee on Political Parties came from a proposal for a study of political parties by Marx, Paul David, and Bernard Gross, all students of public administration then employed in federal government agencies (David 1992). Thus, the Report was both typical and unusual for its era (see chapters 2, 8, and 11 for more information on the origins of the report).

After several drafts, the Report was accepted by the APSA in 1950; it was included as a supplement to the *American Political Science Review* (Committee on Political Parties 1950a) and issued by a commercial publisher soon afterward (Committee on Political Parties 1950b), thus obtaining wide circulation. The document was a little more than one hundred pages long, including the foreword, which describes its purpose, thesis, the process by which it was written, and the authority by which it was issued.

Its purpose was "to bring about fuller public appreciation of a basic weakness in the American two-party system. In other words, this is not a research document aimed at professional readers only. It seeks the attention of every one interested in politics. It is therefore written without regard for the customary form in which scholars present their scientific findings" (Committee on Political Parties 1950a, v). According to its thesis:

> Historical and other factors have caused the American two-party system to operate as two loose associations of state and local organizations, with very little national machinery and very little national cohesion. As a result, either major party, when in power, is ill-equipped to organize its members in the legislature and the executive branches into a government held together and guided by a party program. Party responsibility at the polls thus tends to vanish. This is a very serious matter, for it affects the very heartbeat of American democracy [v].

The Report and its recommendations were distilled from information assembled from extensive interaction with numerous party scholars and a wide variety of political practitioners (vi–viii; David 1992). The Report's authority was thus described:

> Its conclusions stand solely on the professional judgment of the members of the Committee on Political Parties. The American Political Science Association, with its large membership, does not put itself on record as a body behind the findings agreed upon among groups of political scientists, including its own committees. The American Political Science Association, through its chosen organ, has approved the publication of this report as the work of its Committee on Political Parties. Such approval means no formal endorsement of the substance of the report [Committee on Political Parties 1950a, viii].

The foreword concludes, "In presenting this report, the Committee on Political Parties is impressed with its own limitations, with the areas that have remained inadequately illuminated, and with the rich opportunities for research that challenge the imagination of the students of political parties. . . . Nothing would be more satisfying to the whole committee membership than to know that its report has served as a starting point for constructive public debate, creative political action, and more intensive scientific studies" (ix).

The Report begins with an outline summary of its contents, including a list of almost four dozen proposals for reforming the party system (a number of others were implied in the text). It had three parts: a brief statement of the need for greater "party responsibility," a detailed discussion of the formal proposals, and a short discussion of the prospects for action.

In the first section, the Report identified the major political parties as "indispensable instruments of government." It noted both serious weaknesses and great potential for improvement. What the country needed, the committee argued, were more "democratic, responsible, and effective" parties (17). The Report defines party effectiveness first: "An effective party system requires, first, that the parties are able to bring forth programs to which they commit themselves and, second, that the parties possess sufficient internal cohesion to carry out these programs" (18–19). Effectiveness applied to the party in power, but an equally important feature was an effective "opposition party," as distinct from an intraparty, bipartisan, or nonpartisan opposition, because "when there are two parties identifiable by the kinds of action they propose, the voters have an actual choice" (18–19).

Such an effective two-party system required greater "integration" of the party components, partly to resist the pressure of allied interest groups and partly to develop loyalty among each party's leaders and followers. Better-integrated parties could produce more coherent programs and disciplined support for them. Here the Report's authors were careful to recognize the dangers of excessive "ideology" and polarization and argued that party discipline should be enforced primarily by the "positive means" of fostering "strong and general agreement on policies" (20–21).

The Report then defined "responsibility," offering two different standards (22–24). First, the major parties must be accountable to the general public "as enforced in elections." The authors note that such "external" responsibility required two competitive parties so that voters would have a choice and then argue that the "clarification of party policy" was likely to improve voter choices. Second, party leaders must be accountable to the "party membership, as enforced in primaries, caucuses and conventions." The authors note that intraparty conflict could be minimized if national, state, and local party leaders recognize a common responsibility to party members. The authors asserted that "the external and internal kinds of party responsibility need not conflict" and therefore strongly endorsed democracy *within* as well as *between* the major parties.

Having defined party effectiveness, responsibility, and democracy in terms of party programs, the Report outlined the inadequacies of the two-party system of its day (24–36). Three major problem areas were identified: parties were organized largely at the state and local levels, they lacked national leadership, and they had no clear definition of party membership. More specific deficiencies included weak national party organs, poorly articulated party platforms, a lack of intraparty democracy, and the absence of research by parties.

The Report's authors argued that such problems had become especially serious because of the "new demands upon party leadership," including the need for policy development and the rise of national issues. They recognize that many of these party problems were rooted in the U.S. Constitution, particularly federalism and separation of powers. However, they concluded that amending the Constitution to change these basic features was an impractical way to encourage more responsible parties and instead recommended party adaptation under the Constitution.

The second section of the Report is the well-known list of recommendations to foster such an adaptation (37–84). They fall under five headings (see chapters 3, 4, 7, and 8 for details of the proposals).

- National party organizations (proposals to strengthen the national committees and national conventions; the creation of a "party council" to govern party affairs)
- Party platforms (proposals for developing platform planks, interpreting them, and resolving national–state conflicts)
- Party organization in Congress (proposals to strengthen the party organization in the House of Representatives and the Senate, the operation of congressional committees, and the schedule of legislation)
- Political participation (proposals for fostering intraparty democracy, including a new concept of party membership focused on party principles; congressional and presidential nominations; the conduct of elections, including changes in the Electoral College, terms of members of Congress, campaign funds, apportionment, and redistricting; removing barriers to voting, such as changes in voter registration and access to the polls, removal of "undemocratic limitations" to voting, such as ending racial discrimination; and the institution of the short ballot)
- Research on political parties (proposals to increase the information available to parties, research done by parties, and new studies of parties)

The Report concluded with an assessment of the "prospects for action" on its recommendations (85–96). After a brief summary of likely opponents and proponents, the authors identified four dangers of inaction: instability in national policymaking, especially if the nation encountered an "explosive era"; overextending the presidency; the disintegration of the major parties; and polarization of party politics between the left and the right, resulting in an "unbridgeable political cleavage."

SCHOLARLY CONTROVERSY AND POLITICAL CHANGE

The Report was controversial from its inception (see chapters 8 and 11), arousing considerable disagreement even before its publication, when the Committee on Political Parties sought comment from political scientists and political leaders (David 1992). A brief summary of this controversy is relevant to the chapters in this book.

One important critique was normative: some scholars disagreed with the Report's definition of "responsibility." Ranney raised this issue soon after the Report's publication (1951, 1954; see also Pennock 1952). He noted the tension between external and internal responsibility and pointed out that Schattschneider, the chair of the Committee on Political Parties, had argued against intraparty democracy in his influential books (1942, 1948). Ranney also pointed out that the Report failed to define "party members" adequately, even though such a definition was essential to internal responsibility. Further, he highlighted the Report's strong preference for majority rule, a position that has been questioned from a number of perspectives (for a good summary, see Kirkpatrick 1971, 979–985). Thus, the question "what is responsibility?" continues to structure the debate over political parties, including that of the chapters in this book.

Another important critique was empirical: some scholars disagreed with the factual assumptions underlying the report. Turner opened this line of attack with his "dissent from the floor," also shortly after the publication of the Report (1951a, 1951b; see also Huntington 1950). Turner argued that the Report underestimated the degree of responsibility that already existed in the two-party system; furthermore, he believed that some of the Report's recommendations would worsen the party system's defects. Indeed, many of the leading party scholars of the era disagreed with the Report's assessment of the party system, including the wishes and desires of voters (for a good summary, see Kirkpatrick 1971, 971–976; Pennock 1972). Although such criticism of the Report itself lessened as the party system changed, debate over the relationship between the party structure and party responsibility continues to this day, as exemplified in the chapters in this book.

Yet another line of criticism of the Report pertained to political advocacy by political scientists in their professional capacity. The best example came on the twentieth anniversary of the Report's publication from a member of the original Committee on Political Parties, Evron Kirkpatrick (1971). He offered a thorough criticism on normative and empirical grounds, but his most salient complaint was that the Report represented poor "policy science." That is to say, it did not use the special knowledge of party scholars to make a credible case for its proposals. The Report was thus identified as a lesson of how not to conduct policy science. The appropriate role of political scientists in political advocacy has been a perennial topic in the discipline (for example, Wildavsky 1979). Interestingly, almost all of the extensive involvement of political scientists in party reform since 1950 has occurred outside professional associations (see chapter 2).

In the face of this barrage of criticism, the Report itself has had few defenders, although a number of scholars adopted a similar view of parties (for example, Bailey 1959; Burns 1963; Sundquist 1988). Even scholars actively engaged in the search for responsibility have not been particularly impressed with the Report (see Pomper 1971, 2001; White 1992; Baer and Bositis 1993).

What then accounts for the Report's influence on party scholarship? For one thing, its basic goal—more democratic, effective, and responsible parties—is widely shared by students of political parties. Despite its many limitations, the Report addressed questions central to the search for responsibility. Just as important, changes in American politics since its publication in 1950 have given these questions new relevance.

Indeed, some of the Report's concerns seemed prescient in the decades after its publication (for a good overview of these changes, see Shafer 1998). American politics did become more national in scope and more policy oriented, and many of the limitations on citizen participation have dissipated. Trends in party organization were toward stronger national organs, and interest groups have become more important in politics; likewise, party organization and party voting in Congress have been strengthened. And the Report's "dangers of inaction" were given credence by political events. The 1960s looked very much like an "explosive era" to scholars of that time, and in any event, maintaining stability in national policymaking has been frequently difficult. The major political parties have indeed experienced some serious problems over the last five decades, and the term "disintegration" seemed to apply. Moreover, there has been notable polarization of national politics, with notable concern about extremism at particular junctures.

There have also been developments that the Report's authors did not entirely anticipate. From the perspective of the party literature in 2000, surely the best example is the rise of "candidate-centered" politics, which has replaced the "party-centered" politics presumed by the Report (Bibby 1998; Herrnson 1988, 2000). The authors seemed unaware of this trend, which was under way when the Report was published. Indeed, some of the recommendations appeared to encourage it. For example, the Report endorsed direct primaries to nominate congressional and presidential candidates, a technique widely believed to encourage candidate-centered politics. The authors often stressed the role of individual politicians: "It is a remarkable comment on the present structure of both the major parties that such party leaders as Grover Cleveland, Theodore Roosevelt, William Jennings Bryan, Woodrow Wilson, Charles E. Hughes, Herbert Hoover, Alfred E. Smith, Robert M. La Follette, William Borah, Wendell L. Wilkie, Thomas E. Dewey, and Franklin D. Roosevelt never held an official party position" (Committee on Political Parties 1950a, 40–41). These "party leaders" made their names as candidates and officeholders; all aspired to and some achieved the presidency; and only a few actually held official party posts during their careers.

Candidate-centered politics has been accompanied by a raft of new phenomena that has fundamentally altered the party system since 1950 (see the following chapters). These phenomena include the advent of the electronic media, especially television; a decline in party loyalty and an increase in ticket-splitting among voters; a decay of traditional state and local party organizations; an expansion in the role of money in campaigns and the appearance of political consultants; the development of new, national "service" parties; and most important, the regular occurrence of divided government, with different parties controlling the White House and the houses of Congress. While the causal links among these phenomena are complex, each can significantly inhibit party responsibility (White and Shea 2000, chaps. 3, 4). Since 1950, independent candidates have replaced the independent state and local parties as objects of concern in the search for responsibility.

Perhaps the best example of the impact of candidate-centered politics on the party system is the presidency (Milkis 1993, 1999). The Report expressed a preference for a "parliamentary" presidency (Committee on Political Parties 1950a, 35) and a concern about the overextension of the office under the pressures of modern government (92). Since 1950, the presidency has come to dominate national politics to an unprecedented degree. Dubbed the "plebiscitarian presidency," the chief executive has developed an increasingly unmediated relationship with the public. This relationship often undermines effective deliberation within the major parties, disrupting regular linkages between party leaders and members. At the same time, the administrative capacity of the White House has grown dramatically, giving presidents an enormous capacity to act independently of their parties within and outside of government. The presidency also administers a vastly larger federal government than in the past—one that has expanded under both conservative and liberal presidents, albeit in different ways. Some scholars see the modern presidency as fraught with irresponsibility (Lowi 1985) while others are more sanguine about its prospects to contribute to responsible party government (Pomper 1999).

Another illustration of the impact of candidate-centered politics has been the increased activity of third or minor party candidates since 1950 (see Herrnson and Green 2001). The Report made only passing reference to minor parties. Although the authors note with favor the tendency of minor parties to have greater programmatic cohesion (Committee on Political Parties 1950a, 46), they seemed to regard minor parties as largely irrelevant to the operation of the political system: "When we speak of the parties without further qualification, we mean throughout our report the two major parties. The inference is not that we consider third or minor parties undesirable or ineffectual within their limited orbit. Rather, we feel that the minor parties in the longer run have failed to leave a lasting imprint upon both the two-party system and the basic processes of American government" (Committee on Political Parties 1950a, 18). However, since the Report's publication, there have been several significant minor party challenges to the major parties in presidential elections: George Wallace in 1968, John Anderson in 1980, and Ross Perot in 1992 and 1996. Other less successful campaigns, such as Eugene McCarthy in 1976 and Ralph Nader in 2000, nevertheless influenced major party politics. In some respects, these candidacies weakened the two-party system, disrupting major party coalitions without creating permanent alternative party organizations (see White 2001). But in other respects, they encouraged greater responsibility by giving the major parties incentives to adopt new policies and to absorb new constituencies (see Guth and Green 1996). In this sense, minor parties provide another avenue of accountability for the major parties. Indeed, some scholars have argued that the development of a multiparty system in the United States would produce a more responsible party system (Lowi 1998, 1999). Like other changes in the political system, these "presidential" developments have cast the Report's concern for more responsible parties in a new light.

PARTY RESPONSIBILITY FIFTY YEARS LATER

Like the Report itself, the chapters in this book offer a mixed assessment of the two-party system from the perspective of party responsibility. In some respects, the major political parties have moved closer to the Report's recommendations, especially in terms of the strength of national party organs and party organization in Congress. Although the Report had little direct impact on these developments, many of its specific recommendations have come to pass. A chief reason is the steady nationalization of American politics. At the same time, however, many of the Report's recommendations remain elusive, and in some respects the parties have moved away from its goals. A chief culprit is candidate-centered politics. Thus, the parties are in many respects stronger at the national level than in 1950 but not necessarily more responsible.

The book begins by setting the Report in political context. In chapter 2, John White and Jerome Mileur argue that the Committee on Political Parties wrote "in the spirit of their times," reflecting both the legacy of the Progressive movement and the more recent experience of the New Deal. After a review of the Report's origins, the authors discuss the impact of presidents Woodrow Wilson and Franklin Delano Roosevelt on the American party system and party responsibility. They then describe two subsequent attempts at party reform that were influenced by the Report: the McGovern-Fraser Commission of the early 1970s and the Committee for Party Renewal in the 1980s and 1990s. White and Mileur conclude that the enduring importance of the Report stems from the critical questions it raised rather than from the specific answers it offered.

In chapter 3, John Green and Paul Herrnson consider the adaptations of party organizations to changes in the early, mid-, and late twentieth centuries, using criteria for responsible parties abstracted from the Report. The biggest moves toward the model occurred at the national level and involved expanded institutional capacity, campaign resources and electoral activities, as well as increased representativeness and participation within party organizations. The biggest moves away from the model involved party platforms, party membership, state and local organizations, and citizen participation. Green and Herrnson conclude that a century of party development may well have laid the foundations for responsible party government, but this goal is yet to be achieved.

The Report recommended a number of changes in the institutional context in which the major political parties operated. In chapter 4, Sandy Maisel and John Bibby consider these and other changes, including innovations in election laws, court rulings, and party rules and practices. They find that some of these changes have moved the party system toward the Report's goal of more responsible parties. Good examples are the lowering of barriers to voting, the strengthening of political parties in constitutional law, and the nationalization and integration of the major party structures. However, other changes have made parties less responsible, especially those that have fostered candidate-centered politics. Maisel and Bibby conclude by noting the great capacity of American parties to adapt to changing circumstances.

The key to the expanded influence of national party organs organizations since 1950 was a dramatic increase in financial resources. In chapter 5, Frank Sorauf describes the origin and consequences of this new wealth. He notes that historically, campaign finance regulation has often hampered parties and that the post-Watergate campaign finance reforms were no exception. However, the national parties successfully adapted to the new rules and eventually exploited additional opportunities, such as "soft money," "issue advocacy," and "independent expenditures." By 2000, the parties had become dominant in campaign finance. Yet, Sorauf notes that financially strong parties are not necessarily responsible ones. Accordingly, he argues for new regulation of party finance and concludes that "the search for a more responsible two-party system goes on."

Many members of Congress, most notably Senators John McCain (R-Ariz.) and Russell Feingold (D-Wis.) and Congressmen Chris Shays (R-Conn.) and Martin Meehan (D-Mass.) share Sorauf's assessment of the need for campaign finance reform. Largely as a result of these legislators' efforts, Congress passed and the president signed into law the Bipartisan Campaign Reform Act of 2002 (BCRA). The BCRA restricts soft money in a fashion consistent with Sorauf's arguments. National party organizations, including the congressional and senatorial campaign committees, are prohibited from raising or spending soft money. State and local party committees are limited to a maximum of ten thousand dollars in soft money from a single source, if permitted by state law, and required to spend such funds only on generic voter registration and get-out-the-vote drives. In addition, the law prohibits parties from spending soft money on so-called "issue advocacy advertising," and it prohibits interest groups from engaging in such expenditures thirty days before a federal primary and sixty days before a general election. The BCRA also raises the existing hard dollar limits that individuals can contribute to candidates and parties. At this writing, the BCRA is the subject of several lawsuits. Many observers believe the law's soft money regulations are likely to withstand constitutional scrutiny. However, other provisions may be found unconstitutional, including the limits on interest-group issue-advocacy advertising. Though controversial in some circles, the increased hard dollar limits are not at issue in the lawsuits.

One important feature of the candidate-centered politics is the rise of professional campaign consultants. In chapter 6, David Magleby, Kelly Patterson, and James Thurber consider the impact of consultants on the party system and the prospects for responsible party government. Making use of principal-agent theory, the authors describe the ways responsibility can be defined among parties, candidates, consultants, and voters. Then they use the results of a national survey of campaign consultants to investigate the role that consultants might play in these relationships. On the one hand, they find that consultants have different goals from those of the parties, and on the other hand, they are far more committed to issues and ideology than most party organizations.

The Report made extensive recommendations regarding the party organizations in Congress, which Barbara Sinclair reviews in chapter 7. She describes the increasing importance of congressional parties in the latter half of the century, especially in the House of Representatives. She notes that they are better organized, more involved in setting the political agenda and in promoting party messages, and in coordinating legislative activity than in 1950. Further, there is much more party cohesion on roll-call votes—a fact that is widely celebrated as evidence of increased party responsibility. Sinclair agrees that in many respects the congressional parties of 2000 represent a "dream fulfilled" from the point of view of the Report. The lack of coordination between the president and the Congress is still a serious problem, however, even when the same party controls both the executive and the legislative branches.

In chapter 8, Charles Jones looks at the presidency from the point of view of party responsibility. He points out that the Report is vague and ambiguous with regard to the parties and the presidency, although the chief advocates of responsible party government see the president's leadership as pivotal. The root of the problem, Jones argues, is that notions of responsibility must take into account the impact of separation of powers. In this respect, he suggests that scholars should be less concerned with "party government" than with a "government of parties." Indeed, he argues that a good way to commemorate the Report is to alter the mission of reform-oriented party scholars to an exploration of how a "government of parties" can be made to work more effectively.

The Report frequently referred to voters, but their role in party responsibility was not entirely clear. At some points, the authors stressed loyal partisans but in other places noted the importance of independent or swing voters. In chapter 9, Herbert Weisberg clarifies the role of voters by considering party in the electorate as a basis for more responsible parties. He begins by noting the seminal works in voting behavior that introduced the concept, nearly all of which were published after the Report was completed. He then reviews data from the National Elections Studies (1952–2000) on mass partisan identification, partisan balance, and ideology. Weisberg concludes that the party in the electorate can be an important basis for more responsible parties in a fashion consistent with the Report's goals.

Gerald Pomper and Marc Weiner offer a similar argument in chapter 10, finding a "more responsible two-party voter" in their use of National Election Studies. In the 1950s, shortly after the Report was published, partisanship was generally affectual, based largely on family and other social attachments and thus not conducive to party responsibility. However, by the 1990s, partisanship was more cognitive, based largely on issues and ideology. The apparent source of this change, clearer policy differences among party elites, would surely please the Report's authors. Pomper and Weiner conclude that the electorate can now contribute to party responsibility.

Leon Epstein brings the book to a close in chapter 11. Drawing on his long career as a party scholar, he evaluates the Report and its impact on party scholarship. Epstein wonders if the twenty-first century will see some diminution of the "persistent quest" for party responsibility as a new generation of scholars brings new approaches to the old problems of improving parties and democratic government. One suspects that the original Committee on Political Parties would honor the spirit of such innovation, much as this book honors theirs. The search for a fuller realization of American democracy is a responsibility that every generation bears.

2

In the Spirit of Their Times

"Toward a More Responsible Two-Party System" and Party Politics

John Kenneth White and Jerome M. Mileur

Americans have always regarded political parties as suspect, and with the exception of several decades in the nineteenth century, they have abided parties more than embraced them. Parties were present but unpopular before the Revolution (Main 1973; Patterson 1973), and parties arose following the ratification of a Constitution that Richard Hofstadter once described as being "against parties" (Hofstadter 1972, chap. 2). James Madison's fret about "factions" in *Federalist* no. 10 is familiar to all students of the subject (Madison 1987, 122–128), as is George Washington's farewell warning against the "baneful effects of the spirit of party" (Washington 1958, 169–175). The American founders worshiped at the altar of unity, believing that a nation born in revolution would be best served by a nonpartisan regime acting in the national interest, rather than responding to what Alexander Hamilton called the "little arts of popularity" (Hamilton 1961, 414). But to govern is to choose, and by 1796 the founders moved into two warring camps that became organized into political parties (Chambers 1963; Charles 1956).

It was left to Martin Van Buren, more than a quarter century later, to praise parties: "It has always struck me as more honorable and manly and more in harmony with the character of our people and of our institutions to deal with the subject of political parties in a sincerer and wiser spirit—to recognize their necessity, to prove and to elevate the principles and objects to our own party and to support it faithfully" (quoted in Price 1984, 97).

The kind of party system that Van Buren espoused was grounded in patronage jobs and spectacular grassroots campaigns. Despite linking citizens to their government more effectively than any system before or since, patronage parties provoked a flood of criticism, reflecting historic suspicion of parties as well as their own shortcomings. Although the patronage parties were frequently characterized by clear policy differences, critics complained about the lack of

13

strong and consistent party programs. Party leaders, especially the local bosses, were routinely accused of corruption and undemocratic practices. By the end of the nineteenth century, these criticisms came together in the Progressive movement's full-scale attack on the patronage party system.

"Toward a More Responsible Two-Party System," the Report of the Committee on Political Parties of the American Political Science Association (Committee on Political Parties 1950a) was concerned with reforming political institutions to manage political conflict more effectively and thus to foster more efficient and accountable government (Schattschneider 1975, 15). But unlike many reformers, the Report's authors saw great value in parties, arguing that greater party responsibility was a potent tool for improving American government without fundamentally altering the U.S. Constitution. Indeed, the Report owes its enduring significance as much to the questions it raised about the appropriate role of parties in the American system as to the specific answers it recommended. Its authors wrote in the spirit of their times, reflecting progressive ideals and the more recent example of party politics during the New Deal era. In this chapter, we place the Report in a larger political context, exploring its place in the public life of the nation then and now.

ORIGINS OF THE REPORT

The Committee on National Parties and Elections was established by the Executive Council of the American Political Science Association in December 1946. Its charge was to study "the organization and operation of national political parties and elections with a view to suggesting changes that might enable the parties and the voters to fulfill their responsibilities more effectively." Specific areas of study included improving the party machinery as it affects legislative-executive relationships; remaking political parties into more effective instruments for making public policy; securing more competent, representative, and responsible personnel in the top political and governmental posts; strengthening control of the electorate over the parties and party machinery; and improving elections and the electorate (*American Political Science Review* 1947, 123). The APSA president was authorized to appoint a Committee on Political Parties, and a "substantial" budget was proposed, although it was hoped that additional funding could be raised from private sources.

Members of the Committee on National Parties and Elections were formally appointed in April 1947, and Elmer E. Schattschneider was chosen to be its chair. One year later, Schattschneider reported that the committee had met seven times, exchanged memorandums, and made "substantial progress" in clarifying and perfecting its proposals (*American Political Science Review* 1949, 121–122). Interest in the committee ran high; its panel "The Future of the Parties" was the best attended at the APSA's annual conference. Reporting to the Executive

Council, Schattschneider indicated that the committee had issued a statement, "Outline of a Proposed Program for Party Responsibility: A Preliminary Draft for Discussion," which had been widely circulated (*American Political Science Review* 1950, 160). The final Report was published as a supplement to the September 1950 issue of the *American Political Science Review* (Committee on Political Parties 1950a). At the Executive Council luncheon that year, APSA's President James K. Pollock read a letter from Harry S Truman that welcomed the association's advice pertaining to voter turnout and to increasing citizen participation in government (*American Political Science Review* 1951, 165).[1]

The thesis of the Report was stated succinctly in its opening pages: "Historical and other factors have caused the American two-party system to operate as two loose associations of state and local organizations, with very little national machinery and very little national cohesion. As a result, either major party, when in power, is ill equipped to organize its members in the legislative and the executive branches into a government held together and guided by the party program. Party responsibility at the polls thus tends to vanish" (Committee on Political Parties 1950a, v). The committee warned that unless the party system was reformed, the consequences could be onerous. First, there might be a shift of "excessive responsibility to the President," who would be left to build support for his program "through his personal effort without benefit of party." Second, the "disintegration" of the major parties, caused by a growing estrangement of a large segment of the electorate from party leaders, could provide "a great incentive for voters to dispose of parties as intermediaries between themselves and the government." Third, the government might become deadlocked and "set in motion more extreme tendencies to the political left and the political right" (92–96).

The Report's call for more "responsible parties" was not original. Such pleas were heard among political scientists from the discipline's earliest days. In 1900, Frank A. Goodnow argued, "The individual candidate must be sunk to a large extent in the party. Individual responsibility must give place to party responsibility" (Ranney 1954, 96). But it was E. E. Schattschneider who popularized the concept in his influential textbook, *Party Government* (1942). The idea of responsible parties informed debates over politics during the first half of the twentieth century, either explicitly, as was the case with Woodrow Wilson, or implicitly, as with Franklin Roosevelt. But thanks in large measure to the Report, this debate has continued from the postwar period to the present.

The Report reflected the spirit of its times. In its reformist impulse, it was thoroughly at home with the key elements of the Progressive movement, still a dominant influence among intellectuals. It also mirrored the growing role of social science in public affairs. Following World War II, Americans were giving greater attention to political science as an academic discipline, believing that the solutions to the problems of war and governance could be found in the academy. An April 1949 Roper poll, for example, reported that 14 percent thought political science should be a required subject for male college students; 9 percent believed that girls should take it as well.[2] And the Report reflected the frustrations and ambitions of New Dealers (David 1992). In a series of speeches given at the University of Maryland in 1948, Schattschneider spoke of the enormous new burdens placed on government after the end of the war: "As a nation we have had little opportunity to prepare ourselves for the realization that *it is now necessary for the government to act as it has never acted before. The essence of the governmental crisis consists of a deficiency of the power to create, adopt, and execute, a comprehensive plan of action* in advance of a predictable catastrophe in time to prevent and minimize it" (Schattschneider 1948). The Report recommended reforming the major parties so they would foster these ends, drawing on the Progressive legacy of party regulation, the wisdom of social science, and the uses (and limits) of presidential leadership during the New Deal era.

PROGRESSIVISM AND THE REGULATION OF PARTIES

American political parties began as private associations. Neither mentioned in the Constitution nor regulated by federal or state law, they were extra-constitutional and extralegal institutions and remained so until after the Civil War.[3] But a growing population and the rise of strong patronage-oriented party organizations meant a greater role for state and federal regulators. In 1883, Congress passed the Pendleton Act, which created a merit-based civil service that delivered the first of many fatal blows to party patronage. Civil service reform spread to state governments, most of which had adopted the merit principle by the turn of the twentieth century. The long-term effect of the merit system was to erode the importance of patronage as an incentive to partisan activity.

States also began to adopt the Australian ballot system, under which they, not the political parties, prepared official ballots for elections. By 1900, all states had some version of the state-prepared ballot. This required a statutory definition of what was meant by a qualified party, usually a stipulation that candidates receive a minimum number of votes in the prior election for certain offices (typically governor and president). The new laws encouraged a change in the relationship between parties and voters: parties found it less important to educate voters between elections as to why they should affiliate and more important to frame campaign appeals to attract votes. Moreover, minor parties found it necessary to expend more time and money to obtain the number of signatures needed to be on the ballot. The collective effect of these laws was to make the major parties more secure from minor party challenges but more vulnerable to populist and progressive reforms advanced in the name of the people.

The regulation of political parties quickly spread in the first decade of the twentieth century. Several states followed Wisconsin's example and adopted state-run primaries that nominated party candidates for state and congressional offices and included the expression of a presidential preference. This new system made it relatively easy for candidates to pursue office from outside formal party structures. Nonpartisan forms of local government, especially the commission and city manager, also became more popular. Moreover, in the name of direct citizen democracy and obviating the "corrupting" effects of party government, Progressives won adoption of the initiative, referendum, and recall in a number of states and obtained legislative victories aimed at regulating the role of campaign money and political lobbying. Progressives also won passage of the Seventeenth Amendment, providing for the direct election of U.S. senators. This wrenched control over senatorial selection away from state parties and severed the formal connection between political parties in Congress and those in the states.

Taken together, these election reforms radically altered the legal environment in which political parties operated. Their collective effect was to teach citizens to vote "the person," not "the party." A century later, 44 percent of Americans think of themselves as individuals when they enter the voting booth; just 29 percent see themselves as partisans.[4]

But progressives were not of a single mind in their view of American parties. Nearly all progressives saw the existing political parties as corrupted by patronage and big money, but one group sided with Herbert Croly, who wanted to abandon parties altogether in favor of direct democracy and other nonpartisan forms (Croly 1988). Another faction agreed with Henry Jones Ford, who wanted to strengthen political parties, believing that Croly's "cure" would cripple the deliberative processes essential to democracy (Ford 1967). These two factions were actively involved in the three-way fight for the presidency in 1912. Each of the candidates gave voice to one of these factions, and each posed different solutions to the party problem. The third party candidacy of Theodore Roosevelt posed the most formidable challenge to the two major parties. TR's commitment to direct democracy became the centerpiece of the Progressive Party campaign in 1912, and it aimed at drastically reducing the influence of party organizations in government and politics.

In his "confession of faith," made in accepting the Progressive Party's nomination for president, Roosevelt launched an extended attack on the old parties. He decried them as "husks with no real soul . . . divided on artificial lines, boss-ridden and privilege-controlled, each a jumble of incongruous elements, and neither daring to speak out wisely and fearlessly" (Roosevelt 1994). Advocating the initiative, referendum, recall, and other mechanisms of direct democracy, Roosevelt wanted "a larger opportunity for the people themselves directly to participate in government and to control their governmental agents" (1994). He derided the need for intermediary institutions, including political parties, believing that voters inherently would act with moderation and restraint.

Republican nominee William Howard Taft struck back at Roosevelt, charging that Roosevelt would fundamentally change the republican character of government erected by the Constitution's craftsmen. He accused the Progressive Bull Moosers of proposing to "utterly tear down all the checks and balances of a well-adjusted, democratic, constitutional, representative government" and of destroying "the limitations on executive and legislative power as between the majority and the minority" (quoted in Milkis 1999, 56). He was particularly incensed over Roosevelt's suggestion that the initiative, referendum, and recall be applied to judges. Although scathing in his critique of Roosevelt, Taft was no apologist for the existing party system. He applauded those people who called public attention to the corrupting ties between corporate trusts and party machines. However, he also saw responsible political parties as critical to the success of representative government: "In a proper system of party government, the members of each party must agree on certain main doctrines in respect to governmental policy and yield their views on the important ones, in order that they may have united action, and in order that these main and controlling doctrines, when the party is successful at the election and controls the Government, may furnish the guide for governmental action" (Taft 1913, 29).

Taft blamed the parties' shortcomings on voters' collective failure to use the system properly (Burton 1988, 120). In Taft's view, Americans had demonstrated that "they are far better able to select candidates than they are to pass upon complicated questions of legislation" (Taft 1913, 54; 1921). If the electorate was capable of the latter, he argued, it was also capable of remaking political parties into better agencies of popular representation. Although he objected to initiative, referendum, and recall, he approved of some modest party regulation, arguing that "the direct primary in local elections with certain limitations is a practical step to oust the boss and destroy the machine of patronage and corruption." Yet he acknowledged that "no plan can avoid the effect of corruption" (1913, 120). Thus, while he offered a spirited defense of the party system as essential to the peculiar nature of the American constitutional system, he offered no plan to restore the parties as institutions of popular representation.

Woodrow Wilson was the Progressive candidate with a party plan. The Democratic candidate agreed with Taft that popular government in a constitutional democracy required a representative system whereby voters could monitor those individuals who held public office in their name. This did not necessarily mean a direct role in governance; rather, it meant that citizens would have mechanisms in place that allowed them to avoid being misgoverned. Voters, in other words, could throw the rascals out. But the problem with popular control was that the Constitution's separated and divided powers fractured sovereignty, leaving it unclear where responsibility resided. Unlike Britain, where responsibility rested clearly with the House of Commons, there was no single locus of authority in the American regime, thereby making it difficult to ascertain who the rascals were.

For Wilson, the political party was the most promising institution upon which to build programmatic leadership and accountability into American national government and politics. The major parties, which cut across the several branches and levels of government, were, he believed, "absolutely necessary to hold things thus disconnected and dispersed together and give some coherence to the action of political forces" (Wilson 1908, 217). Without parties, he believed that "it would hardly have been possible for the voters of the country to be united in truly national judgments upon national questions" (1908, 217).

The Report's writers shared with the Progressives certain beliefs that informed their recommendations:

- Politics should be organized by issues, not patronage.
- Special interests would corrupt democracy if unchecked.
- Ideal citizens were those actively engaged with the policy questions of their time.
- Representative democracy must be tempered by a more direct role for citizens in their own governance.
- Public opinion should be a positive guide to governance, not just a check upon it.
- The Constitution, as an organic document, should be adapted to the new needs of a democratic politics but not changed in its institutional design.

For these reasons, the Report's authors largely accepted the progressive regulation of parties, particularly the direct primary, with only modest alterations. Although they generally agreed with Roosevelt's critique of the reality of party politics, they also shared Taft's appreciation of the potential value of political parties. Not surprisingly, they were most impressed by Wilson's plan for party reform and party government.

As a scholar, Wilson thought Congress, especially the House of Representatives with its strong committee system, was the most promising institution for an American "cabinet" that could be a locus of responsibility within the constitutional framework, though he had reservations about its excessive parochialism and partisanship. But as president, he saw his office as the essential ingredient needed to ensure party responsibility: "We have grown more and more inclined from generation to generation to look to the President as the unifying force in our complex system, the leader both of his party and of the nation" (Wilson 1908, 60). In his first term, he provided a model of responsible party governance, declaring in his Inaugural Address: "There has been a change of government. . . . No one can mistake the purpose for which the Nation now seeks to use the Democratic Party" (1913). He worked closely with the Democratic majority to enact the "New Freedom" reforms upon which he had campaigned—

even traveling the short distance to Capitol Hill to lobby for support. But Wilson's leadership was more personal than institutional, and nothing in his program dealt directly with the party system as such. Yet his success as president gave credence to a conception of party government that so impressed Assistant Secretary of the Navy Franklin Delano Roosevelt that he drew upon it while serving as governor of New York and later as president of the United States.

THE NEW DEAL AND THE FRACTURING OF THE AMERICAN PARTY SYSTEM

Franklin Roosevelt's New Deal administration revolutionized the American party system. It triggered a partisan realignment that gave the Democrats majority-party status until the Cold War and the disintegration of a social and cultural consensus restored the Republicans to the White House (White 1998). By recasting the presidency as the "vital center" of American politics, the New Deal fractured the major parties at the national level, dividing them into presidential and congressional wings, thus creating a "four-party system" that has persisted for the remainder of the century (Burns 1963). These changes both increased and decreased the prospects for party responsibility (Milkis 1999).

Franklin Roosevelt entered the White House a strong party man. Everything in his experience had taught him that leading a government and serving as party leader were synonymous. In 1921, after losing his bid for the vice-presidency, FDR turned his attention to party reform. Writing to thousands of state and local party officials and activists, he solicited their ideas for strengthening the party machinery, including the creation of a party council that would give rank-and-file Democrats a larger role in intraparty decision making. After the disastrous 1924 convention that saw John W. Davis nominated on the 104th ballot, followed by the Democratic Party's worst defeat ever in a presidential contest, Roosevelt campaigned by letterbox for reform. He lamented that the national headquarters consisted of "two ladies occupying one room in a Washington office building," adding, "we have no money, no publicity, no nothing!" (quoted in Burns 1956, 95). According to James MacGregor Burns, Roosevelt "wanted the party to unite more closely, to get rid of its 'factionalism' and 'localism,' to do a better publicity job, to get on a firmer financial basis" (99). Roosevelt's warnings were generally ignored, but they served to keep his name before the public—a tactic that would pay off eight years later when he won the Democratic presidential nomination.

Seeking the governorship of New York in 1928, Roosevelt relied heavily on the party organization, as he had in his first campaign for the state senate in 1908. But he also sought to broaden his appeal, and he sent his wife and her female friends out on the hustings to seek support from newly enfranchised women in upstate cities and towns. With a narrow victory—25,000 votes out of 2 million cast—Roosevelt almost immediately found himself trying to cope with the Great Depression. In so doing, he developed a liberal program that anticipated the New Deal and became a model for presidential leadership in national politics.

Roosevelt understood the frustrations of party leadership. He began his political life as a reformer by challenging Tammany Hall over the election of a Democrat to the U.S. Senate. He took the bosses on again in 1912, when he backed New Jersey governor Woodrow Wilson for president against Tammany-supported House Speaker Champ Clark. FDR paid a price two years later when Tammany blocked his bid for a U.S. Senate seat. After that bitter experience, he sought better relations with the New York City machine and was rewarded by being chosen as the featured speaker at their Fourth of July celebration a few years later. Roosevelt's pragmatism led him to defer to Tammany when he had to, and he eventually came to admire many of its sons—especially Al Smith, Robert Wagner, and Ed Flynn—for their dedication to improving the social and economic conditions of their working class and poor constituents.

Roosevelt knew from experience the difficulty of reforming his party nationally. Historically, the Democrats had been the party of Jefferson and of the South, where states' rights was a fundamental tenet of party doctrine. Although the South had been losing influence in the selection of the party's presidential candidates, it remained a cornerstone of the national party. Its conservatism was counterbalanced by the liberalism of the urban Democrats, who looked to the national government more for patronage than for programs. In the end, Roosevelt clashed with southern and northern conservatives in his pursuit of a more liberal national party.

When he first ran for president, FDR thought he could maneuver big city northerners and rural southerners into remaking the Democrats into a new liberal party—a cause he advocated through the lean years of the 1920s. Election results were encouraging. In 1932, he won his party's nomination for president with strong southern and conservative support. Four years later he won forty-six of the forty-eight states, with the enthusiastic support of northern and western liberals as well as the South. Democrats rode into office on FDR's coattails. When Congress convened in 1937, there were just eighty-eight Republicans in the House and seventeen in the Senate. Fifty-three percent of people responding to a 1937 Gallup poll said they were dissatisfied with the leadership of the Republican Party.[5]

Like Wilson, Roosevelt believed that a political party should be organized around a coherent viewpoint and a governing program. It should embody a clear public philosophy; it must champion policies and programs consistent with its larger beliefs; and it must organize a coalition whose members shared these convictions and would follow through on them if elected. FDR held to the view that the American party system should offer a clear choice between a predominantly liberal party and an opposing conservative one. This often meant that the president should take the lead in shaping the political debate and work with congressional leaders to implement the party program. At the same time, FDR's view of party was tempered by the practical lessons taught by Tammany, that a party must win before it could govern and that, to continue in office, its programs must be translated into laws that produced tangible results.

As president, Roosevelt attempted to apply these lessons. Working closely with Democratic National Chairman James Farley, FDR courted urban bosses, southern agrarians, and western progressives, involving them in the administration of federal programs and rewarding them with the traditional patronage. "His strategy for enlisting them was to create programs that brought tangible benefits to their constituents in the belief that policies that improved people's lives would translate into voter loyalty" (McJimsey 2000, 131). Roosevelt also worked closely with his party's congressional leaders. He undertook numerous legislative initiatives after hearing a wide range of expert opinions drawn from Congress, the administration, interest groups, and the academy.

The legislative successes of the first and second New Deals were based in Roosevelt's collectivist style of leadership. But his legislative prowess did not translate into a successful reconstruction of the Democrats into the nation's liberal party. Opposition grew during his first term, as southerners balked at legislation reforming labor-management and working conditions. Conservative northerners, including former presidential nominees Al Smith and John W. Davis, joined the anti–New Deal American Liberty League, even as populist Democrats, especially Huey Long, attacked from the left. Moreover, a conservative Supreme Court invalidated much of the New Deal, including the National Industrial Recovery Act and the Agricultural Adjustment Act, the cornerstones of FDR's recovery program.

Roosevelt's successes at the polls in 1932, 1934, and 1936 documented his great popularity. Yet while the public saw a triumphant and confident president, party insiders, especially after 1936, saw a lame duck. Congressional Democrats grew less cooperative, and FDR shied away from the collaborative leadership style he had developed during his first term. In 1937, he introduced a court-packing plan to allow him to appoint another justice for every one over the age of seventy. A bitter battle ensued, and many recalcitrant Democrats joined with conservative Republicans to defeat the proposal. The second term also saw the defeat of Roosevelt's Executive Reorganization Act, which many people thought gave the president too much power. With his time in office appearing to be short and the goal of a liberal Democratic Party slipping away, Roosevelt sought to defeat conservative Democratic members of Congress in the primaries. Early polling showed some support for his move: 47 percent said it was a good idea that old party lines be abandoned in favor of a united liberal party— however, only 30 percent thought this would happen.[6]

Despite a few successes—most notably denying renomination to anti–New Deal New York congressman John O'Connor, chair of the House Rules Committee—FDR was beaten in major contests across the South. The attempted purge attracted little public support, largely because voters saw FDR as over-reaching and did not like the idea that their representative might be ousted. A 1938 Roper poll found 46 percent saying it was "a good thing" that the senators opposed by FDR won renomination; only 11 percent said it was "a bad thing."[7]

From 1938 to 1940, Roosevelt fell back on his two most valuable assets: himself and the presidency. Eventually, he won passage of a reorganization plan that strengthened the administrative capacity and power of the executive office of the president and made it the focal point of responsibility in national affairs. He had also attracted new forces into the ranks of the Democratic Party. Union members, Jews, African Americans, and other recent immigrants became the nucleus for the liberal party Roosevelt desired. Thus, the New Deal, George McJimsey argues, moved away "from 'national' solutions toward 'group' solutions and to a definition of citizenship that included identification with a social group" (McJimsey 2000, 85). FDR relied on securing the New Deal through an expanded regulatory state and an expanded system of federally guaranteed rights. The Wagner Act gave procedural rights to union members in organizing and bargaining with management; Social Security established a range of entitlements for children, families, and the elderly; the Fair Labor Standards Act did the same for workers. These laws encouraged ordinary citizens to look to the executive branch and to the president, not to the party, as their benefactor and protector. Millions of Americans boasted that it was Roosevelt who "saved my job" or "saved my home." The New Deal also eroded the patronage system that had been so important to Democratic Party organizations in both the urban North and the one-party South.[8]

Roosevelt linked the Democrats to his new liberalism by calling for an economic bill of rights and enunciating the Four Freedoms. This broadened the American conception of rights to include positive guarantees as well as negative ones, thereby providing a new rationale for the expansion of the federal government. By prosecuting World War II in the name of liberty and freedom, he opened the door to women, African Americans, and other groups to press their claims to share equally in the blessings of liberty in the postwar era. From this, there emerged a Democratic presidential party that was at once liberal and national in its approach to governing arrayed against a congressional party that was more conservative and localist. Republicans also saw a sharper executive-legislative division in their national party, with a moderate and internationalist faction dominant in presidential politics and a more conservative, rural, and small town–based wing dominant in Congress.

Roosevelt's failure to recast the Democrats into a "responsible" liberal party is instructive. The authors of the Report were strongly influenced by the Roosevelt experiences of the 1930s. They understood that the programmatic end of their recommendation was to expand the size and reach of the federal government (Ladd 1992, 34). But the efforts of Schattschneider and his colleagues to mold public opinion in the support of responsible parties largely failed. Although the Report has strongly influenced the study of political parties for two generations of academics, neither the public nor party activists pay it much mind. The Report may well have been twenty years late. Had it been written in 1926, it might have been used by Franklin Roosevelt to transform the party system by employing its recommendations. Although influenced by its time, the Report was strangely out of its time. The five decades since its publication have shown that its recommendations have been approached in some respects, but hardly in the manner envisioned by its authors.

RESPONSIBLE PARTIES AND POSTWAR THINKING IN CONTEXT

Franklin D. Roosevelt's experiences illustrate the importance of thinking about party reforms in the context of the times in which they are implemented. Just as the reasoning behind Roosevelt's reform proposals was twenty years late when the Committee on Political Parties took up the concept of party reform from 1946 to 1950, future party tinkerers likewise found themselves acting in the context of their times—and not always wisely. Following publication of the Report, the next significant effort to reform and strengthen the party system was the one advocated by the McGovern-Fraser Commission, after the disastrous Democratic National Convention in 1968 (Commission on Party Structure and Delegate Selection 1970). It, too, was limited by a fundamental misunderstanding of how the upheavals of the 1960s had affected the American party system and the institutions of government in which it operated.

The McGovern-Fraser Commission: "Reform or Else"

In the four decades since the 1968 Democratic conclave in Chicago, time may have healed some wounds, but the smell of tear gas and the shouting of the antiwar demonstrators still linger in the minds of those who lived through that turbulent era. So searing were these memories that Democrats did not reconvene in Chicago until 1996, when Bill Clinton was renominated in an era of unprecedented prosperity and worldwide tranquillity.

The calm setting of the 1996 Democratic Convention was a stark contrast to that of 1968. That year, two conventions were held: one controlled by the so-called party regulars, the other a street gathering whose ranks were filled with antiwar protestors locked out of the convention proceedings. It was this latter "convention" that amplified an already widespread belief that American democracy had become unhinged. Indeed, the street protestors were angered by what they saw as the autocratic actions of Chicago mayor Richard J. Daley, who refused to issue a permit so that the Vietnam War protestors could gather in the city's largest park. The antiwar movement believed it represented the feelings of the Democratic Party's base, since its candidates Eugene McCarthy and Robert Kennedy had won the state primaries over stand-ins for Lyndon Johnson and Hubert H. Humphrey.[9] Moreover, the party's nominee, Vice-President Humphrey, had not competed in a single primary. The party bosses, led by Daley, supported Humphrey and made him their nominee, even as Daley's police attacked the demonstrators with clubs and tear gas, creating what authorities subsequently described as a "police riot." Presidential chronicler Theodore H. White described how Humphrey had been "nominated in a sea of blood" (White 1969, 376).

The 1968 saga began when Minnesota senator Eugene McCarthy challenged Lyndon Johnson for the Democratic nomination. McCarthy's strong second-place finish in New Hampshire provided clear evidence of Johnson's electoral vulnerability. Shortly after this poor showing, Johnson withdrew, and New York senator Robert F. Kennedy immediately jumped into the race. Moments after Kennedy claimed victory over McCarthy in the California primary, he was assassinated. South Dakota senator George McGovern then announced his candidacy, which was initially designed to provide a home to the distraught Kennedy supporters. But as the convention unfolded, McGovern became convinced that the antidemocratic spirit of the Democratic Party regulars would inevitably lead to the party's demise: "Many of the most active supporters of Gene McCarthy and Bobby Kennedy and later of me, believed that the Democratic presidential nominating process was dominated by party wheel horses, entrenched office-holders, and local bosses. They believed that despite the strong popular showing of McCarthy and Kennedy in the primaries, a majority of the convention delegates were selected in a manner that favored the so-called 'establishment' candidates" (McGovern 1977, 130). The McGovern-Fraser Commission later arrived at a similar conclusion: "If we are not an open party, if we do not represent the demands of change, then the danger is not that the people will go to the Republican Party; it is that there will no longer be a way for people committed to orderly change to fulfill their needs and desires within our traditional system. It is that they will turn to third and fourth party politics, or the anti-politics of the street" (Commission on Party Structure and Delegate Selection, 1970).

It was this widespread belief that American democracy was on the precipice of collapse that provided the major impetus to the McGovern-Fraser reforms. Such thinking was supported by the events of the time. In 1968, Lyndon Johnson could hardly move about the country, the sole exception being military bases where the Secret Service felt it could guarantee his physical safety. A Louis Harris survey conducted in June 1968 found 59 percent believing that the American political system "is failing when the President can't announce where he is going for security reasons."[10] Those people who protested the Vietnam War and who hated Johnson believed the political system had become totally unresponsive to their needs. This concern was shared by a generally disaffected and alienated public. In 1970, 63 percent told the Gallup Organization that the political system "does not respond quickly enough to meet the needs of the people."[11] The McGovern-Fraser Commission reflected the prevalent public perspective that American democracy was out of whack and in need of drastic reform. Its recommendations included:

- A reaffirming of the abolition of the unit rule, an action that had already been approved by the 1968 Democratic Convention
- Refusing to seat delegates chosen in back rooms
- Prohibiting certain public or party officeholders from serving as delegates to county, state, and national conventions by virtue of their official position
- Banning proxy voting, a practice used by party bosses to cast votes on behalf of absent delegates, often without their knowledge
- Ordering states to choose delegates during the calendar year in which the convention is held
- Requiring states to post public notices announcing the selection of a delegate slate that would be committed to a particular candidate and inviting the rank and file to participate in the selection process
- Creating a Compliance Review Division within the Democratic National Committee to ensure that states obeyed the McGovern-Fraser recommendations

In some ways, the McGovern-Fraser reforms paralleled the recommendations of the Report. Both called for greater participation by rank-and-file Democrats and for midterm party conferences. But the spirit of the McGovern reformers had more in common with the antiparty elements of the progressive tradition associated with Theodore Roosevelt and Herbert Croly than with the "responsible party" tradition of Woodrow Wilson and the Report itself. In effect, the McGovern-Fraser Commission told the Democratic Party establishment to "reform or else." In its view, the nominating process must be more "open, timely, and representative" and, unless changes were made, the Democratic Party would become as extinct as the dodo bird. As McGovern later recalled, "In public statements, speeches, and interviews, I drove home the contention that the Democratic Party had but two choices: reform or death. In the past, I noted, political parties, when confronted with the need for change chose death rather than change. I did not want the Democratic Party to die. I wanted our party to choose the path of change and vitality. That was the function of the reforms" (McGovern 1977, 130).

Despite the bloodshed on the streets of Chicago, McGovern's contention that the Democratic Party needed life support now seems vastly overstated. Political parties have remained powerful and enduring forces, despite the enormous demographic and political changes that have affected American society in the decades since the 1960s. Whether it is dealing with an unpopular war, presidential scandals, or coping with enormous social and demographic changes within the United States, the legitimacy of the party system continues to have widespread public acceptance. The virtual tie produced following the 2000 election, which tested our constitutional structures once more, serves to reaffirm this point. Although Al Gore vigorously contested the Florida result, he accepted George W. Bush's legitimacy as president following the Supreme Court's intervention. So, too, did a majority of Americans. When pollster John Zogby asked, "If you define legitimacy as the will of the people, do you consider a George W. Bush presidency legitimate or not legitimate?" 59 percent said they accepted Bush as the country's legitimate president; 37 percent did not. Moreover, 59 percent said Bush's loss of the popular vote would not lessen his legitimacy as president.[12]

McGovern's belief that the Democratic Party would die without reforming itself runs counter to recent history. No political party has expired since the Whigs died out during the 1850s. As the historian Henry Adams said of the Whigs at the time, "Of all the parties that have existed in the United States, the famous Whig Party was the most feeble in ideas" (quoted in Schlesinger 1949, 17). One reason for this endurance is that the parties are now woven into the legal fabric, which gives them a certain degree of protection from the public's desires to weaken them. Thus, when California Democrats (and Libertarians) protested that state's restrictive laws prohibiting them from making party endorsements as a violation of their free speech rights, the Supreme Court sided with parties and added to the legal doctrine of the "right of association." Speaking for a unanimous Court, Justice Thurgood Marshall declared, "Freedom of association means not only that an individual voter has the right to associate with the political party of her choice, but also that a political party has a right to identify the people who constitute the association, and to select a standard-bearer who best represents the party's ideologies and preferences" (*Eu v. San Francisco County Democratic Central Committee*, 489 U.S. 214 [1990]). No wonder, then, that the political scientist Leon Epstein likens parties to public utilities, since both are embedded in the laws and are duly regulated by government (Epstein 1986, 155–199).

The primary motivation for the McGovern-Fraser Commission's reforms may not have been to save American democracy per se but to reorder the power structures within the Democratic Party. Simply put, the changes in the party nomination procedures advocated by the commission amounted to a power grab that succeeded brilliantly. "Old Democrats"—mostly white, middle-aged, establishment types who supported the Vietnam War—were replaced with "New Politics Democrats," who tended to be younger, professional, female, and black, and whose policy preferences were decidedly antiwar, antiestablishment, and antiparty. In 1968, just 14 percent of the delegates were women, two percent were under age thirty, and only 5 percent were black. Following the institution of the McGovern-Fraser reforms, women numbered 36 percent of the delegates; those under age thirty, 23 percent; blacks, 14 percent. Given the number of antiestablishment-minded delegates attending the 1972 convention, it was not surprising that Mayor Daley was ejected from the convention hall while George McGovern emerged with his party's presidential nomination in hand. Indeed, Democrats were so desirous to ensure that their nominating system was representative that a virtual quota system became the modus operandi, with the result that many longtime party workers in state and local organizations were excluded from its calculus. As McGovern himself admitted, "Whatever the commission originally intended, in administering the guidelines on minorities, women, and young people, it eventually moved very close to adopting a de facto quota system" (1977, 148).

Caught in the crossfire were the state Democratic Parties that did not desire much change in their own nominating procedures. To avoid running afoul of the national party, states hastily adopted the primary system for choosing presidential candidates. This change affected Republicans as well as Democrats, since many state legislatures at the time were controlled by Democrats who wanted to avoid having their state delegations challenged at their national convention. To apply an old aphorism, many Democratic legislators felt that "what was good for the goose was good for the gander," and when they decided to institute state presidential primaries, they did so for both parties. For Republicans, the institution of a primary system greatly facilitated the conservative takeover of the GOP, already begun by Barry Goldwater in 1964 and given renewed impetus by Ronald Reagan a decade later.

Another effect of the McGovern-Fraser reforms was to remove individual delegate discretion and judgment and in doing so to deinstitutionalize party responsibility. Today's conventions no longer exercise the slightest semblance of deliberation, as delegates are accountable to the candidates and not to the party—and the candidates want good television performances, nothing more. Indeed, the McGovern-Fraser reforms were a final step in the full emergence of "candidate-centered" rather than "party-centered" politics.

The Committee for Party Renewal: A Personal Memoir

A second attempt at party reform centered on the efforts of a group of approximately two hundred political scientists, as well as a number of party and public officials, who came together after 1976 to form the Committee for Party Renewal.[13] Although the committee had some impact at the elite level, particularly among Republicans who were receptive to its intellectual arguments to strengthen political parties, its influence was limited largely to the academic community. Still, the Committee for Party Renewal is important because its view of how the American party system should operate was widely held during its existence. In many respects, the committee represented an academic backlash to the McGovern-Fraser reforms. Like the writers of the Report, members of the Committee for Party Renewal believed that parties were essential to American democracy and that their weakening, which accelerated after 1968 and during the Watergate debacle, had many deleterious effects on the successful governance of the nation. Though its efforts toward party reform were designed to rejuvenate parties, the committee, like its predecessors, was a prisoner of its own time.

Like the McGovern-Fraser Commission, the Committee for Party Renewal was a direct response to the perceived failures of the party system. Motivating the committee was a series of presidential failures, the most notorious being the resignation of Richard Nixon in 1974. To the political scientists who formed the backbone of the committee, led by the indefatigable James MacGregor Burns, Watergate represented more than Richard Nixon's character flaws—it was the direct result of a party system so weakened that it could be captured by personal organizations like the Committee to Reelect the President (Nixon's 1972 reelection committee).

The Committee for Party Renewal sounded the alarm in its founding document, titled "Declaration of Principles," issued on the steps of the Jefferson Memorial in 1977: "Without parties there can be no organized and coherent politics. When politics lacks coherence, there can be no accountable democracy. The stakes are no less than that" (Committee for Party Renewal 1977). The committee warned that the costs to American democracy of a permanently weakened party system were enormous: "What would take the place of parties? A politics of celebrities, of excessive media influence, or political fad-of-the-month clubs, of massive private financing by various 'fat cats' of state and congressional campaigns, of gun-for-hire campaign managers, of heightened interest in 'personalities' and lowered concern for policy, of manipulation and maneuver and management by self-chosen political elites."

At the time the committee issued its declaration, there was a widespread belief that political parties had become so dysfunctional that their continued existence was imperiled. David Broder wrote a popular book, *The Party's Over,* which captured this imminent sense of party demise. In it, Broder linked the decline of parties with the failure of government: "The governmental system is not working because the political parties are not working" (1972, 1). Thinking that the failure of parties inevitably led to all sorts of democratic dilemmas, political scientists bemoaned the lack of voter turnout, the rise of candidate-centered campaigns, conventions that had become television shows instead of deliberative bodies, and the prevalence of divided party control of the presidency and Congress. Political scientists saw "dealignment" as the term that best described an alienated electorate, which, in turn, was the inevitable consequence of party decay. "Drift," "wandering," and "decay" were words commonly used to describe the American party system. Meanwhile, officeholders used their resources to create an "incumbent party" that proved to be immune to most democratic impulses. In 1980, Gerald Pomper, the longtime cochair of the Committee for Party Renewal, expressed the view shared by most political scientists: "We must either acknowledge the mutual reliance of our parties and our democracy—or lose both" (Pomper 1980, 5).

Until the committee ceased to exist in 1998, its members enunciated the view that party reforms must strengthen the parties, both organizationally and in government. Encouraging party responsibility, it was believed, would ultimately strengthen the parties electorally, as voters would become increasingly aware of the different messages conveyed to them by Democrats and Republicans. Over the years, the committee adopted several position papers that reflected these beliefs. Not surprisingly, many of its recommendations echoed those contained in the Report but also added new ones, including public financing, midterm conventions for both major parties, and reversing the trend toward more and more primaries (Committee for Party Renewal 1977). Behind these suggested reforms were several underlying normative principles. In a 1984 position paper, "Principles of Strong Party Organization," the committee outlined the functions parties must undertake in order to ensure a more responsible party system:

- *Political parties should govern themselves.* As private associations with public responsibilities, parties should be as free as possible from state and federal regulation to determine their own structure and function. . . . Parties should define their organization and powers formally and publicly through party constitutions or charters and by-laws, so that all who affiliate with them may know the rules of party governance.
- *Political parties should use caucuses and conventions to draft platforms and endorse candidates.* Caucuses and conventions are avenues of general participation in party affairs that encourage dialogue and peer review of party programs and candidates. The quantity of participation in them may not be as large as in primaries, but the quality of participation is much higher.
- *Political party organizations should be open and broadly based at the local level.* Local politics is a basic testing ground for candidates and the principal arena of direct citizen participation in politics. Strong local party committees should be the foundation upon which state and national party structures are built. They should be the principal party instrument for defining membership, registering voters, recruiting candidates, and conducting campaigns. They should also be central to the development of a party platform and to public education with respect to party programs for government.
- *Political parties should advance a public agenda.* Parties are the most broadly-based organizations in our democratic system and thus best able to define priorities for government and to develop programs that serve general interests. They serve the public interest best by developing and defining a broad philosophy of governance that differentiates

one party from another and giving voters a reasonable choice in the direction of government.

- *Political parties should endorse candidates for public office.* If parties are to present voters with a choice of policy alternatives and if they are to be accountable for governance, they must have a measure of control over who runs for office in their name. . . . Checks may be legislated on party endorsement processes to ensure full and fair participation of party members, but the ultimate check will and should be whether a party's program for and performance in government merit the support of the general electorate.

- *Political parties should be effective campaign organizations.* Parties will be strong insofar as candidates depend upon them for election and insofar as they are key to the success of those who seek election in their name. To this end, parties should recruit candidates who share their philosophy and should provide them with training and expert advice and direction in the organization and conduct of their campaigns, with research on the district and the opponent, and with polling, media, and other state-of-the-art campaign services. Parties should also endeavor to coordinate campaigns of all party candidates in a given election to minimize conflicts and to maximize resources.

- *Political parties should be a major financier of candidate campaigns.* No service to candidates is more important than the provision of money, and there should be few restraints on the ability of parties to raise and spend money in campaigns. . . . Parties themselves should be able to make unlimited contributions to the campaigns of their candidates for offices at all levels of government.

- *Political parties should be the principal instruments of governance.* Parties should be instruments of collegial governance which broaden and unite leadership in the different branches and levels of government and by means of which specific programs may be developed to implement party platforms. . . . Equally important, the opposition party(s) should be institutionalized, through question periods or in other ways, so as to provide a more effective check on specific policy decisions of the government.

- *Political parties should maintain regular internal communications.* Parties at all levels should keep members informed of activities, decisions, and plans through newsletters or other house organs. This is another avenue of accountability and also one of participation, for it facilitates an exchange of ideas, positions, and analyses about the party and politics of the moment.

- *Election law should encourage strong political parties.* More than other forms of political organization, parties have served egalitarian and majoritarian values and encouraged widespread citizen participation in American politics. They are our most democratic institutions and should be sustained and encouraged by public policy. . . . By law, parties should have a privileged position in our political system. They should be given advantages over special interest groups and over individual candidates (Committee for Party Renewal, 1984).

Throughout its existence, the committee stuck to these basic principles. Like the authors of the Report, the committee members publicly advocated their views in the belief that good citizenship, scholarship, and public advocacy went hand in hand. Republicans were more welcoming to the committee's message largely because, as one later admitted, the scholarly rationale for strengthening political parties coincided with the larger aims of the party at the time. Democratic officeholders, however, were either passive or downright hostile when it came to supporting reforms that would strengthen the party institutions. One confrontation occurred in 1991 when John Kenneth White, then the executive director of the committee, had an exchange with Democrat Sam Gejdenson, then chair of the House Task Force on Campaign Finance Reform:

> *Gejdenson:* Why would it be our responsibility to help these parties move forward? It seems to me, if parties stood for something, or if they did things, they on their own would do fine. . . . Why should we rig the [campaign finance] rules to strengthen the parties? Isn't that the parties' own business? The problem gets to be, as a lot of us here, both Democrat and Republican, know, is that the parties want to be nurtured. Should we also be nurturing the Communist Party? . . . If the parties stand for something, they'll survive; if they don't stand for anything, maybe they shouldn't survive.
>
> *White:* Well, I believe that political parties will survive, largely because they are so ingrained in the minds of Americans. After all, millions vote for only the Democratic or Republican candidate, not for a third-party candidate. I think there is a larger purpose involved generically with political parties, period, which is that they mobilize people to act. No other single interest group does that the way the parties do.
>
> *Gejdenson:* Maybe they should. I don't know if they do. But why should they do it with taxpayer dollars?
>
> *White:* Let me just say—You know, you mentioned what your obligation was to political parties. Let me just offer that the Democratic Party in Connecticut tendered you their nomination, as did the Democratic—
>
> *Gejdenson:* No, no. That's not how it happened. They tendered the nomination to somebody else. I went out and got the people's support, and then I . . . won the nomination in primary. . . . But why should the taxpayers, or why should the government, give [the parties] free television time to strengthen or weaken their hold? Why should it be their business? (White 1991)

Over time, the Committee for Party Renewal collapsed—partly due to inertia and partially to a general feeling among younger political scientists that the need to publish meant that there were fewer reasons to become active in the public sphere. Adding to this reluctance to become public advocates was a transformation within the discipline that emphasized the scientific component of political science. The result was an elaborate creation of rational choice models and the extended dominance of such thinking in journals like the *American Political Science Review,* which had initially published the Report as an addendum. These mathematical models may have enhanced our understanding of the operations of government, but they have little or no bearing on the making of public policy. Such reasoning was a stark contrast to the civic-mindedness that underlay the Report and whose authors welcomed the opportunity to change public thinking about parties. E. E. Schattschneider, chair of the Committee on Political Parties, believed that the academic and governing communities needed to rely more closely on one another. For his part, that meant an active public role. As Schattschneider boasted shortly before his death in 1971, "I suppose the most important thing I have done in my field is that I have talked longer and harder and more persistently and enthusiastically about political parties than anyone else alive" (quoted in Epstein 1986, 32). As the political science community in general and the APSA in particular moved away from public advocacy, the academic foundations underlying the Committee for Party Renewal eroded, and in 1998 it expired. Still, the committee's basic beliefs in a strong party system that would encourage responsible party government continues to form a consensus in the party scholarship.

LIKE WAITING FOR GODOT: THE IDEAL OF RESPONSIBLE PARTIES

For scholars interested in greater party responsibility, the fifty years since the Report's publication have been reminiscent of Samuel Beckett's play, *Waiting for Godot:* the prospect for more responsible parties is tantalizingly close, yet still remote. On the one hand, the strengthening of national party organizations and the clearer ideological separation of party elites and candidates appear to fulfill many of the Report's recommendations. These developments make the major parties more likely to offer voters clear choices and more capable of responding responsibly once such choices are made. On the other hand, party differences are often obscured by a politics of spin that emphasizes harsh and bitter personal attacks fueled by large sums of cold hard cash. Money and special interests seem more important than at any time since the early twentieth century. The frail public support for parties, the dominance of candidate-centered politics, the Supreme Court's endorsement of a radically individualized politics, and a news media committed to attacking the parties hardly make for a strong party system that might induce a new sense of responsibility into politics and government.

Yet it is worth remembering that at the close of the nineteenth century the powerful patronage-oriented party system seemed impervious to change, despite a flood of criticism. But the Progressive movement succeeded in replacing this system, creating an opening for strong presidents, such as Woodrow Wilson and FDR, to bring something like party government into being for short but productive periods of time. The current challenges posed by the American party system differ from those faced by past reformers and the authors of the Report. However, the questions they present—the meaning of democratic citizenship and of popular government, the vitality of the public and the quality of community, the representative character and responsibility of the political system—are much the same.

This reality should remind us that the work of democracy is never done, its arrangements never settled, and that the strength of democracy lies in the questions it poses, not in the answers given. It reminds us, too, of the wisdom of those individuals in our past who have been unsettled by settled circumstances, of Thomas Paine's admonition that "the long habit of not thinking something wrong gives it the appearance of being right," and of Lincoln's call upon us "to think anew . . . to act anew . . . to disenthrall ourselves" from the practices of a flawed present. Indeed, the enduring significance of the Report owes much to the fact that it asked these kinds of questions, and did so in the tradition of those prepared to challenge the present in the interests of a better tomorrow. The Report's authors have been limited by the spirit of their time, but the concerns they raised are timeless.

NOTES

1. The committee continued in existence for several more years, under the chairmanships of Bertram Gross and V. O. Key Jr. It issued some additional reports but none to rival the significance of its original Report.

2. Roper poll, April 1949. Text of question: "In grade school, almost all students are required to study subjects like arithmetic, spelling, and geography. Now, in college, are there any subjects you think all boys [and girls] should be required to study, no matter what they are going to do afterwards?"

3. States did enact laws in the early nineteenth century requiring voter registration, and permissive legislation regarding the use of party primaries for nominating candidates became increasingly common around the time of the Civil War (Merriam and Overacker 1928).

4. Louis Harris poll, September 8–17, 2000. Text of question: "When it comes to politics and voting, to what extent do you think of yourself as (READ LIST)—a lot, some, or not at all?" Percentage answering a lot: a man/woman, 44 percent; a supporter of one political party, 29 percent; a person in a particular age group, 26 percent; a member of one religion, 24 percent; a person from a particular city, town, or state, 21 percent; a member of one race or ethnic group, 20 percent; a person with a health problem

or disability, 15 percent; a member of a labor union or union family, 12 percent. Results adds to more than 100 percent due to multiple responses.

5. Gallup poll, November 14–19, 1937. Text of question: "Are you satisfied with the present leadership of the Republican party?" Yes, 32 percent; no, 53 percent; no opinion, 15 percent.

6. Roper poll, August 1938. Text of question: "In a recent fireside talk, President Roosevelt proposed that old party lines be disregarded and that the liberals of all parties unite to support liberal candidates for Congress. Do you think this is a good or bad idea?" Good, 47 percent; bad, 24 percent; don't know, 29 percent. Second question: "Do you think this is likely to happen?" Yes, 30 percent; no, 34 percent; don't know, 35 percent.

7. Roper poll, November 1938. Text of question: "Do you think it was a good thing or a bad thing that certain Senators who were recently opposed by President [Franklin] Roosevelt in his so-called purge attempt were renominated?" Good thing, 46 percent; bad thing, 11 percent; don't know or don't care (volunteered), 42 percent.

8. The Ramspeck Act (1940) extended civil service coverage to many New Dealers throughout the executive branch, in addition to which the Hatch Acts restricted the political activity of civil servants. New federal welfare programs also put the government into competition with the political party as a dispenser of social services.

9. For a different perspective, see Richard M. Scammon and Ben J. Wattenberg, *The Real Majority* (New York: Coward-McCann, 1970), pp. 142–146.

10. Louis Harris and Associates, poll, June 12–16, 1968. Text of question: "Let me read you some statements. For each, tell me if you tend to agree or disagree with that statement. . . . Our political system is failing when the President can't announce where he is going for security reasons." Agree, 59 percent; disagree, 31 percent; not sure, 10 percent.

11. Gallup Organization, poll, December 3–8, 1970. Text of question: "Some people say that the American political system does not respond quickly enough to meet the needs of the people. Do you agree or disagree?" Agree, 63 percent; disagree, 27 percent; no opinion, 9 percent.

12. NBC News/*Wall Street Journal,* poll, December 7–10, 2000. Text of question: "If George W. Bush is elected, he will have won the electoral vote but not the popular vote. Do you think that this would or would not lessen his legitimacy as president?" Would lessen his legitimacy as president, 34 percent; would not, 59 percent; not sure, 7 percent.

13. Both John Kenneth White and Jerome M. Mileur served as executive directors of the Committee for Party Renewal.

3

Party Development in the Twentieth Century

Laying the Foundations for Responsible Party Government?

John C. Green and Paul S. Herrnson

The influence of party organizations in American politics has waxed and waned over the twentieth century, but concern over their impact on national government has been a constant. Central to this concern has been a long and often frustrating quest for "responsible party government" (Ranney 1954). The best-known milestone in this quest is the Report of the Committee on Political Parties of the American Political Science Association, "Toward a More Responsible Two-Party System" (Committee on Political Parties 1950a). As far as party organizations are concerned, this quest has not been entirely in vain.

In this chapter we explore the development of major party organizations between 1900 and 2000 from the perspective of the responsible party model. First, we abstract a set of criteria for responsible party organizations from the Report's recommendations, and then we apply these criteria to party organizations in the early, mid-, and late twentieth century. By the end of the twentieth century, the major party organizations have met many but not all of these criteria. The biggest achievements occurred at the national level and involved expanded institutional capacity, campaign resources and electoral activities, and increased representativeness and participation within party organizations. The biggest shortcomings concerned party platforms, membership, state and local organizations, and citizen involvement in politics. We conclude that a century of party development may well have laid the foundations for responsible party government, but it has not yet become a permanent reality in American politics.

PARTY ORGANIZATIONS AND PARTY RESPONSIBILITY

American party organizations are concerned primarily with controlling the government by winning elections (Epstein 1967, 9; Schlesinger 1991). Politicians created party organizations for this purpose (Aldrich 1995) and have altered them over time to improve their own electoral prospects (Herrnson 1993; Klinkner 1994; Kolodny 1998a, 169, 175–181). Such organizations exist outside of formal governmental institutions, although they are often subject to government regulation, and elected government officials are usually involved in their management and activities (Epstein 1986, chap. 6). Traditionally, party organizations have been deeply involved in a number of critical electoral tasks, including the recruitment and nomination of candidates, the amassing of campaign resources, the development of platforms and campaign themes, the coordination of party committees, and the conduct of campaigns.

The Report's recommendations covered all these tasks but especially emphasized the development of platforms. The Report advocated that the parties develop detailed programs for public policy and make them central to the nomination of candidates, conduct of campaigns, and coordination of party committees. Its authors argued that such programs would give voters more meaningful choices in elections, make government more coherent and policy focused, and thus allow voters to hold the party in power responsible for its actions.

To make party organizations more "responsible" (i.e., more programmatic), the Report recommended that they become more centralized, representative, institutionalized, and participatory. This last feature was especially important: the Report envisioned a democratic process by which the mass of individual party members actively communicated their policy preferences to local, state, and national party leaders, who then distilled such preferences into a national party platform. This vision underlies the Report's recommendations regarding nominations, campaigns, and internal coordination.

The Report's authors harbored few illusions about the major party organizations in this regard. They noted that the institutional and political environment of American parties presented enormous obstacles to responsible behavior, not the least of which was the U.S. Constitution. But following a long American tradition, they argued that key improvements in party organizations could help overcome these obstacles (Milkis 1999). Thus, the Report can be read as a list of the perceived weaknesses of party organizations at midcentury. But its recommendations also reveal a set of criteria for responsible party organizations. A threefold division captures both of these features: national party organizations, state and local party organizations, and party activities.[1]

National Party Organizations

The Report argued that strong national party organizations were essential for party responsibility. It emphasized the desirability of influential national conventions, party councils, and committees. It was at the national level that the Report's authors saw the greatest weakness in the parties of their day.

The Report recognized the national party conventions as the ultimate governing body of the parties. They were to be held biennially, with the primary purpose of enacting the national party platforms. They were also to conduct other party business, including the seating of delegates and appointing some members to the national party council and national committee. The Report recommended that conventions have six hundred delegates, few enough to allow for genuine deliberation but large enough to represent the diversity of party constituencies. The delegates were to be apportioned to represent party strength across the states, with a substantial number elected through primaries and the remaining appointed by a national party council and other party organizations. The authority of the national committees implied a uniform set of party rules that could be enforced.

The Report proposed the creation of national party councils, formal coordinating bodies that would meet quarterly between the national conventions. Their primary tasks would be to develop a proposed party platform for the national conventions and, once a platform was enacted, to interpret and enforce its provisions with regard to party officials and candidates. Further, the party councils would coordinate and integrate party activities, screen and endorse potential presidential and congressional candidates, and appoint some national convention delegates. The party councils were to comprise fifty key leaders representing all the elements of the party (including the president and vice-president if the party were in power or the presidential and vice-presidential nominees if not), appointed by the national convention and other party organizations.

The Report advocated that the national committees play a major role in party operations. They were to maintain a permanent national headquarters with a specialized professional staff and adequate financial resources. The professional staffs would conduct research and support the work of the national conventions and party councils. Moreover, the staffs were to have the institutional capacity and resources with which to wage effective general election campaigns. The national committee members would be apportioned to represent party strength and be appointed by the national convention and other party organizations. The Report also recommended that the federal government provide financial and in-kind subsidies to the national committees. These recommendations applied to the national or "presidential" committees but not to the congressional and senatorial campaign committees, which were clearly to be subordinate to the national committees. However, many of the recommendations related to the capacity of national committees could logically apply to the congressional and senatorial committees.

State and Local Party Organizations

The Report expected state and local party organizations to perform many of the same tasks as the national organizations and in much the same fashion. However, it did not offer detailed recommendations for state and local organizations, in part out of deference to federalism and in part because it recognized special tasks for subnational organizations. It was at the state and local levels that the Report's authors saw the greatest strength in the parties of their day.

The Report recommended that state and local parties should hold frequent, participatory, and issue-oriented meetings. Presumably, it was at this level that the rank-and-file party membership would participate in platform writing and other party business. Subnational parties were also to hold regular, regional party conferences. State and local parties were expected to produce state and local platforms, which would be consistent with the national platform on national issues. Furthermore, state and local parties were given special tasks, including the integration of allied interest groups into party campaign activities (in part to resist interest-group pressures) and the maintenance of professional campaign machinery for general election campaigns. Consistent with its underlying assumptions, the Report called on parties to develop and maintain a formal mass base of dues-paying, issue-oriented, and active party members.

Party Activities

The Report's recommendations also addressed the electoral activities of national, state, and local party organizations. Such recommendations were largely complementary to those directed at party organizations themselves. They stress the areas in which the Report's authors saw significant problems.

The critical activity of party organizations was issuing biennial national platforms. All elements of the party were to participate in generating the platforms, but the Report's authors put special stress on the active participation of members of Congress and other elected officials. The platforms were to include statements of general party principles as well as specific policies and programs.

The Report advocated that party organizations play a major role in nominations, including issuing preprimary endorsements of candidates seeking nominations. A substantial number of national convention delegates were to be elected by direct primary. They would join delegates appointed by party organizations to choose the presidential and vice-presidential nominees at the national conventions. Congressional candidates were to be chosen in participatory primaries. The Report strongly endorsed closed primaries over open, blanket, or fusion primaries.

The Report's authors argued that party organizations of all sorts should play a more significant role in the conduct of general election campaigns, and in particular, that national organizations become a major force, including the provision of campaign funds. In this regard, there were to be no unreasonable legal restrictions on national party spending. All campaigns were to be waged on the basis of party platforms rather than on candidates' personalities or promises of patronage. Moreover, parties were to compete in all parts of the country and encourage high levels of participation among all citizens.

For a summary of this presentation of the Report's recommendations, which we will use as criteria for an evaluation of the development of party organizations from 1900 to 2000, see Table 3.1. Following a custom in the literature (Pomper 1971, 2001; Ranney 1975; Herrnson 1992; Baer and Bositis 1993), we also show on the table the degree to which these recommendations were met in the early, mid-, and late twentieth century, patterns we will consider later in this chapter.

PARTY DEVELOPMENT IN THE EARLY TWENTIETH CENTURY

Complaints about traditional, patronage-oriented party organizations were legion as the twentieth century began. These organizations still dominated electoral politics in 1900 (White and Shea 2000, 48–52; Mayhew 1986) and served as a point of departure for responsible party advocates. Despite the vitality of these parties and their ability to engage the public, they had three serious flaws (Merriam 1922; Schattschneider 1942). First, traditional party organizations were weak at the national level. The national conventions and committees were essentially temporary coordinating devices for managing presidential nominations and campaigns. They rarely survived beyond election day and had little influence on policymaking. Most institutional strength was located at the state and especially at local levels, where efficiency and honesty were frequently in short supply.

Second, traditional party organizations were largely unrepresentative, often nonparticipatory, and notoriously nonprogrammatic. Third, they fell short of the common expectations with regard to election activities. Party platforms were largely campaign documents that stated general party principles, but they were rarely useful guidelines for policymaking. Nominations were regularly settled in smoke-filled rooms, with a minimum of popular input. And although national organizations played a role in presidential campaigns, the bulk of the campaign resources and activities was in the hands of state and local organizations. Further, traditional parties did not compete in all parts of the country, nor did they always encourage high levels of citizen participation.

These shortcomings contributed to a torrent of reform between 1900 and the mid-1920s. Growing out of the Progressive movement, some of the reforms had a direct impact on party organizations; others influenced parties indirectly (Key 1964; McSeveney 1994). These reforms combined with a host of demographic and technological changes to alter the strength, influence, and operation of party organizations (Herring 1965).

National Party Organizations

The Progressive reforms had little direct impact on national party conventions, which already performed some of the functions assigned to them by the responsible party model, although perhaps not especially well (Merriam 1922).

Table 3.1. Party Organizations and the Responsible Party Model

	EARLY TWENTIETH CENTURY		MID-TWENTIETH CENTURY		LATE TWENTIETH CENTURY	
	Democrats	Republicans	Democrats	Republicans	Democrats	Republicans
National party organizations						
National Conventions						
The national party conventions:						
Held biennially	N	N	N	N	T	N
Enact platform, other party business, seat delegates	E	E	E	E	E	E
Appoint some members of party council and national committee	N	N	N	N	N	N
National party convention delegates:						
Moderate number, few enough for deliberation	O	O	O	O	O	O
Apportioned by party strength	N	T	N	Z	M	M
Some elected via primaries, others appointed	M	M	M	M	A	A
National Party Council						
Create a national party council:	S	T	T	T	N	N
Meets quarterly, governs between conventions	N	N	N	N	N	N
Develops and proposes platform to convention	S	T	T	T	P	P
Interprets/enforces party platform	S	T	N	N	N	N
Appoints some national convention delegates	N	N	N	N	N	N
Coordinates and integrates the party activities	N	N	N	N	P	P
Screens presidential and congressional candidates	N	N	T	T	N	N
Small group appointed by convention, other committees	S	T	T	T	N	N

Table 3.1. Party Organizations and the Responsible Party Model, *continued*

	EARLY TWENTIETH CENTURY		MID-TWENTIETH CENTURY		LATE TWENTIETH CENTURY	
	Democrats	Republicans	Democrats	Republicans	Democrats	Republicans
National Committees						
The national committee:						
Maintains national headquarters	M	M	A	A	E	E
Supervises professional staff	M	M	M	M	A	A
Raises adequate funds	O	O	O	O	A	A
National committee apportioned by party strength	N	N	M	M	A	M
Members appointed by convention, other committees						
Federal government provides financial, in-kind subsidies	S	S	S	S	M	M
State and local party organization						
State and Local Party Organizations						
Hold frequent participatory issue-oriented meetings	N	N	N	N	M	M
Hold regular, regional party conferences	N	N	N	T	N	N
Develop state/local platforms	O	O	N	N	M	M
Integrate allied interest groups	N	N			M	M
Maintain professional campaign machinery	O	O	O	O	M	M
Party members						
Dues-paying, issue-oriented, and active membership	N	N	N	N	N	N

Table 3.1. Party Organizations and the Responsible Party Model, *continued*

	EARLY TWENTIETH CENTURY		MID-TWENTIETH CENTURY		LATE TWENTIETH CENTURY	
	Democrats	Republicans	Democrats	Republicans	Democrats	Republicans
Party activities						
Party platforms:						
National party platforms are issued biennially	N	N	N	N	T	M
Elected officials participate in platform writing	N	N	O	O	M	M
Focus on general party principles and policies	T	T	M	M	M	M
Nominations:						
Party organizations issue preprimary endorsements	T	T	T	T	N	T
Primaries central to presidential nominations	M	M	M	M	A	A
Primaries central to congressional nominations	A	A	E	E	E	E
Primaries are closed; blanket and fusion ballots prohibited	M	M	O	O	O	O
General election campaign activities:						
National parties play a significant role in campaigns	O	O	O	O	M	M
National parties provide significant campaign funds	O	O	O	O	M	M
No unreasonable restrictions on funds	N	N	O	O	M	M
Campaigns are waged on the basis of platform	T	T	T	T	M	M
Parties compete throughout the country	O	O	M	M	M	M
Parties encourage citizen participation	O	O	M	M	O	O

Source: Committee on Political Parties, American Political Science Assocation, "Toward a Responsible Two-Party System," *American Political Science Review*, supp. 44 (1950).

Legend: A = Achieved; N = No significant change; E = Aready in effect; M = Movement toward; S = Suggested and discussed; O = Movement away; T = Achieved temporary, revoked.

However, there was some modest movement that anticipated the Report's recommendations. For instance, an increasing number of convention delegates were selected through direct primaries. By 1912, twelve states used primaries, so that approximately one-third of both parties' delegates were elected rather than appointed; and by 1920, twenty states used the direct primary to select two-fifths of Republican and more than one-half of the Democratic delegates.

In other respects, the conventions continued to deviate from the model. Both parties' delegates were apportioned by state population rather than by party strength. The Republicans partially addressed this situation by reapportioning their delegates in 1916 and 1924 (Merriam and Gosnell 1929, 277–279). Neither party instituted biennial conventions, and they had few uniform, enforceable rules. The number of delegates was of moderate size but still too numerous for genuine deliberation. The numbers increased slightly from less than one thousand in 1900 to eleven hundred by 1932. Yet, the national conventions did deliberate on key matters, including requiring numerous ballots to pick the presidential nominees. The best known of these struggles were in 1912, when it took the Democrats 46 ballots to nominate Woodrow Wilson, and in 1924, when they needed 104 ballots to nominate John W. Davis.

There was some experimentation with party councils. Wilson proposed a council in 1916 for the Democrats. The Republicans established one in 1919 to make recommendations for their platform, but it was disbanded a few years later. The national committees also expanded their organizational resources. The Republican National Committee established a permanent national headquarters under Chairman Will Hays in 1918. The Democratic National Committee eventually followed suit under Chairman John J. Raskob in 1929 (Merriam and Gosnell 1929, 226–227). Although the parties received no direct federal subsidies, President Theodore Roosevelt proposed the public financing of presidential campaigns in 1907 (Mutch 1988).

State and Local Party Organizations

The Progressive reforms had their greatest impact on state and local party organizations. The direct primary led to the demise of state and local conventions as decision-making bodies. On balance, traditional party meetings declined and were not replaced by issue-oriented meetings, nor did regional party conferences develop. These changes caused a marked decline in the frequency of state and local party platforms (Merriam 1924). As a result of the reforms, state-level machines had largely disappeared by the late 1920s, although local parties, especially the urban machines, adapted more effectively (Mayhew 1986). Generally, state and local campaign machinery was not modernized. A new set of interest-group organizations began to exercise increased influence in politics in the wake of party decline, often in direct opposition to traditional parties (Clemens 1997).

After 1900, the combined effects of ballot reform and direct primary legislation produced a legal measure of party affiliation in most states: voluntary party registration (Epstein 1986; Rusk 1970). Party registration was widely used to determine eligibility to vote in primaries, thus allowing more widespread and diverse participation in one element of party decision making. Meanwhile, the steady implementation of civil service laws slowly reduced the number of patronage-oriented party activists. The advent of Progressivism may have briefly interjected a greater level of programmatic interest among some partisans, but formal party membership fell far short of the responsible party model.

Party Activities

The national conventions continued to enact platforms resembling those from 1900 in tone and form. Some platforms, however, such as Wilson's New Freedom program in 1912, came much closer to those envisioned by the responsible party advocates (Milkis 1993). Elected officials, including members of Congress, helped shape the platform in their capacity as convention delegates, but officeholders had no special role.

By the 1920s, direct primary nominations represented the most common means of nominating congressional candidates. Primaries also were a significant factor in the politics of presidential nominations between 1908 and 1917 but declined in the 1920s (Epstein 1986, 89–94). During this period, most primaries were closed, although some states allowed open, blanket, or fusion primaries. Informal preprimary endorsements by party leaders became commonplace in many states and localities, and formal endorsements appeared in some states. There was serious discussion of formalizing endorsements at the national level in 1902 and 1921 (Merriam and Gosnell 1929, 358). Some informal endorsements occurred at the federal level. For example, in 1918 Wilson launched a controversial and largely unsuccessful attempt to defeat Democratic members of Congress in primaries who had not supported his program (Herring 1965, 219–220).

State and local party organizations were still central to the conduct of general election campaigns during this period. As in 1900, the national committees continued to coordinate presidential campaigns and to provide financial resources (Overacker 1932), and the congressional campaign committees began expanding their efforts in the 1920s (Kolodny 1998a). For example, in 1924 the national committees (including the congressional and senatorial committees) of both parties spent a total of $4.4 million (Pollock 1926, 27–31). The national party committees were first subjected to national campaign finance regulations during this period, but no "unreasonable" restrictions were placed on party spending (Mutch 1988). One impact of primaries was that candidates below the presidential level began playing a bigger role in conducting and financing their own campaigns.

The Progressive reforms did not encourage the extension of party competition to all regions of the country. Indeed, much of the country became less competitive between 1900 and 1928. Moreover, the restrictive rules that governed some primaries disenfranchised African Americans and other minorities (McSeveney 1994). And there was a dramatic decline in voter turnout among northern working-class men in the 1920s (Wiebe 1967).

Party Organizations and Responsible Party Government

What impact did party organizations have on responsible party government in the early twentieth century? The operation of the national government approximated the responsible party ideal on several occasions during this period, most notably during Wilson's first term. Other less dramatic approximations of party government occurred during the Republican administrations of Theodore Roosevelt, William Taft, and Herbert Hoover. Party organizations may well have contributed to these brief approximations of party government. For example, the advent of primaries may have aided these efforts by weakening state and local parties' grip on nominations, allowing presidents and other national leaders to intervene in congressional nominations.

However, party organizations fell so far short of the responsible party model that it is hard to credit them with promoting party government. The absence of strong, permanent, and effective national party organizations hampered presidents' abilities to develop a sustained party program. Yet, presidential leadership in party policymaking was in many respects the antithesis of the responsible party model. Moreover, the rise of primaries gave individual candidates more independence. Indeed, these weaknesses spurred on the quest for party responsibility. One must look elsewhere for the primary sources for programmatic party government during this period. Nevertheless, the embattled traditional party organizations provided one key factor often associated with party government: unified party control of the executive and legislative branches.

PARTY DEVELOPMENT IN THE MID-TWENTIETH CENTURY

In the late 1920s, party organizations were subject to many of the same criticisms as in 1900, despite the continuing impact of the Progressive reforms. These concerns became stronger during the New Deal and postwar eras. The Progressive reforms, combined with continued demographic and technological changes, had an important indirect impact on the development of party organizations, including the decline of state and local organizations, the rise of candidate-centered politics, and the continued expansion of interest groups (Bibby 1994).

President Franklin Roosevelt imposed his program on the Democratic Party and then used the party to build public support for it. Roosevelt had somewhat greater success in implementing his program than did Wilson, but FDR faced similar obstacles (Milkis 1999). Roosevelt's personal appeal transcended Democratic Party organizations, providing a candidate-centered model for his successors and other candidates in the postwar period (Milkis 1993). Indeed, Roosevelt's experience was a prime motivation for the Report and its recommendations (see chapter 2).

By 1950, when the Report was issued, the development of candidate-centered politics was well under way. Presidential and congressional candidates were increasingly self-recruited, winning nomination by their own efforts and organizing their own general election campaigns (Bibby 1998,153–154; Strahan 1998). This trend came to a head with the 1972 McGovern-Fraser Commission reforms, which formalized candidate-centered politics in presidential nominations (Ceaser 1979). Although national party strength increased over this period, party organizations, especially at the state and local levels, became more and more peripheral to the conduct of congressional election campaigns (Herrnson 1988, 18–29).

National Party Organizations

During this period, the national conventions changed in ways that both contradicted and accommodated the Report's recommendations. The number of convention delegates increased substantially, from 1,100 for both parties in 1932 to 2,622 for the Democrats and 1,331 for the Republicans in 1968. Presidential aspirants became increasingly adept at mobilizing delegates on their own behalf, especially those chosen by primary. These candidate activities eventually reduced the scope of convention deliberation: 1952 (Republicans) and 1948 (Democrats) were the last national conventions where the nominees were not chosen on the first ballot. Neither party instituted biennial conventions.

There were important changes in convention rules, however, that made them more representative of party strength. The Democrats abolished the two-thirds rule for presidential nominations in 1932, and the Republicans began to develop a detailed body of written party rules in 1936 (Merriam and Gosnell 1929). In 1972, the McGovern-Fraser Commission reforms dramatically altered delegate selection for the Democrats, and many of these changes were eventually extended to the Republicans in the 1970s and 1980s by state law (Polsby 1983; Crotty 1983). One result was greater reliance on primaries to choose delegates and thus the increased influence of presidential candidates in the conventions; another was the development of centralized party rules, which were eventually backed by the federal courts (Ranney 1978).

This period also witnessed continued experimentation with party councils. The Republicans formed a "program committee" (1938–1940) to develop platform proposals in response to the New Deal (Merriam and Gosnell 1929), and a "coordinating committee" (1964–1968) to help them recover from their 1964 defeat (Bibby 1994). The Democrats formed an "advisory committee" (1956–1960) following their defeat in 1956 (Roberts 1994).

The national committees experienced some changes as well. In 1952, the Republicans added to the national committee state chairs from states where the GOP had been successful in the previous election; in 1968, all state party chairs were included. The Democrats followed suit in 1970. Democratic Chairmen James Farley (1932–1939) and Paul Butler (1955–1960) made some improvements in their national committee staffs (Roberts 1994). The Republicans made important organizational gains under Chairmen John Hamilton (1937–1940) and Ray Bliss (1965–1969) (Bibby 1994). The national party committees began experimenting with direct-mail fund-raising in the mid-1960s, and this helped expand their financial resources. Public subsidies to the parties were debated as part of the overall discussion of campaign finance reform.

State and Local Party Organizations

The initial impact of the New Deal was to strengthen Democratic state and local party organizations. The New Deal programs provided a new source of patronage for urban machines and southern party organizations. However, the new patronage was reduced with the 1939 Hatch Act, and the New Deal social programs eventually contributed to the decline of urban machines (Epstein 1986). Similarly, the labor movement provided Democrats with a powerful ally but one that often competed with local party organizations for power. Policies set in motion by the New Deal eventually gave rise to the Civil Rights movement, which ended the Democratic solid South.

By 1950, most state and local organizations were weak, having failed to adapt to changes in technology, the increased influence of candidate organizations, and the growing prominence of interest groups (Sorauf 1980; Bibby 1998; Ware 1985; Mayhew 1986). These subnational organizations did not regularly conduct issue-oriented meetings, hold regional conferences, or issue programmatic party platforms. Few were able to modernize their campaign machinery.

The parties did not develop dues-paying, issue-oriented memberships and continued to rely on voluntary voter registration to determine primary participants. Cadres of liberal and conservative activists began to appear in party politics in the postwar period (McClosky, Hoffman, and O'Hara 1960). By the 1960s, issue-oriented activists had a greater hold in some local positions, leading to tensions between them and traditional party volunteers (Wilson 1960; Eldersveld 1964), a trend that continued into the 1970s and 1980s (Kirkpatrick 1976). In some respects, this development paralleled the rise in prominence of interest groups.

Party Activities

The national party platforms became somewhat more programmatic during the New Deal and again during the 1960s (Pomper and Lederman 1980). Officeholders continued to have only a limited voice in platform writing, which was increasingly conducted by convention delegates under the instruction of presidential candidates. Traditional disputes between the White House and Congress over policy development spread to party organizations, with the leaders of congressional campaign committees arguing that they, and not the national committees, should be the prime source of policy (Bibby 1998; Milkis 1993). These disputes were regular enough for observers to describe the situation as "four-party politics," with each party having a presidential and congressional wing at odds with one another (Burns 1963).

The role of primaries in selecting nominees changed during this period. Prior to 1950, primaries played a modest role in selecting national convention delegates, and most congressional candidates were nominated in closed primaries. After 1950, presidential candidates revived the custom of competing in non-binding primaries to demonstrate public support. As time passed, primaries became more important to delegate selection, and the number of open primaries grew more common. Many state and local parties continued to engage in formal or informal preprimary endorsements, and there were some continued experiments at the national level. The most famous was Roosevelt's attempt to purge anti–New Deal members of Congress in Democratic primaries in 1938. Like Wilson's efforts in 1918, the purge was quite controversial and produced mixed results (Herring 1965, 221–223).

The national committees continued to play a role in coordinating presidential campaigns, including the raising of campaign funds. For example, in 1956 the national committees (including the congressional and senatorial committees) of both parties spent $12 million (Heard 1960, 377). The 1940 Hatch Act set a $3 million limit on the amount of money national party committees could raise and spend in campaigns, a provision that was judged by the Report's authors as an "unreasonable" restriction. The parties responded by shifting funds to state committees; such limitations probably delayed the further development of strong national organizations (Mutch 1988). During this period, two-party competition spread to more regions. Citizen participation increased initially, reaching a high point in the 1960s but declining steadily thereafter (Mayer 1998).

Party Organizations and Responsible Party Government

The New Deal era witnessed one of the closest approximations to party government in American history. Roosevelt's efforts resembled Wilson's New Freedom program in many respects but was of longer duration and had greater impact. One major difference was that the New Deal evolved after 1932 and was first fully presented to the Democratic Party and the electorate in 1936; the New Freedom was presented to voters prior to Wilson's election. Other Democratic presidents offered similar programs during this period, including Harry Truman's Fair Deal, John Kennedy's New Frontier, and Lyndon Johnson's Great Society. The Republicans presented their most ideologically cohesive and programmatic platform during Barry Goldwater's 1964 presidential campaign; George McGovern's liberal platform in 1972 was similar in this regard.

Party organizations may have contributed something to these approximations to responsible party government. For example, the New Deal revitalized many Democratic organizations, and Roosevelt was able to use them to advance his program in elections and government. Direct primaries made many party organizations more open and receptive to public response to the New Deal. The presence of permanent national committee headquarters aided in the defense of—and opposition to—the New Deal programs. The national committees helped integrate and centralize party efforts on occasion.

Nevertheless, party organizations were not strong enough to sustain responsible party government. Roosevelt and his successors spent considerable effort struggling against state and local party organizations, a struggle that influenced the Report. Even more significant was the final decline of traditional party organizations and the rise of candidate-centered politics. The chief result of these trends was that unified party control of the executive and legislative branches became rare. This situation meant that presidents needed to devote more time to persuading self-recruited officeholders and members of the opposition party to support their programs. Missing was an overarching organization, like a party council, that could hold candidates—even presidents—accountable to the party platform.

PARTY DEVELOPMENT IN THE LATE TWENTIETH CENTURY

The late twentieth century was a period of dramatic renewal of party organizations, particularly at the national level (Cotter et al. 1984). The leading edge of this development concerned the expanded organizational capacity and finances of the national committees, including the senatorial and congressional committees, which remained separate and potent organizations (Herrnson 1988; Frantzich 1989). The national committees became institutionalized, adapting successfully to candidate-centered politics and technological innovation. National party organizations became a valuable source of campaign services, and in the process, forged stronger ties with many candidates, interest groups, and voters than their counterparts had done at midcentury. By century's end, national party organizations were playing a critical role in coordinating the efforts of their affiliates and their candidates and contributing to campaigns (Bibby 1999b). The parties were more programmatic than in the past (Pomper 1999), with many of their candidates campaigning on common themes and issue agendas (Herrnson, Patterson, and Pitney 1996; Little 1997). This trend extended to measures of governing, such as voting in Congress (Rohde 1991), and even became more responsive to party cues (Bartels 2000). If the 2000 election was any guide, this phase of party development has not yet run its course.

In many respects, late twentieth-century party organizations matched the recommendations of the Report. However, the parties did not become sufficiently programmatic to be labeled as "responsible." As in previous eras, some changes moved party organizations toward and others away from the responsible party model (see chapter 4).

National Party Organizations

National party conventions continued to develop in ways that both countered and conformed to the Report's recommendations. They ceased to be deliberative bodies, and they continued to grow in size. In 2000, the Democrats had 4,336 delegates and the Republicans 2,066, more than one-half larger than in 1968 (Cook 2000). More important, conventions have become dominated by the campaigns of presidential candidates, who substantially recruited and elected the delegates. The conventions became symbolic events, designed to kick off the general election campaign with good media coverage. Ironically, conventions had become so carefully choreographed by 2000 that the major network broadcasters regarded them as not being newsworthy and thus afforded them only limited coverage.

Yet the conventions also became more representative of party strength. The reform process implemented by the McGovern-Fraser Commission continued with some modifications. Most delegates were chosen by primary, and some were appointed by party organizations; the best example of the latter was the Democratic "super delegates" chosen from among Democratic officeholders. Delegate selection was largely governed by national party rules, which were affirmed by the federal courts (Epstein 1999). The Democrats experimented with something like a biennial convention in 1974 (Pomper 1980; Baer and Bositis 1993).

The parties did not create national councils during this period of revitalization, but the national committees began to perform some of the tasks the Report assigned to a party council. Formal party rules and the concentration of money at the national level allowed a small number of key party leaders considerable ability to coordinate nomination rules, platform development, and campaign activities. The national parties' institutionalization resulted in their becoming major centers of political resources, and this dramatically altered the flow of power within the major parties (Bibby 1981, 1999a; Herrnson 1988, 2000).

The major change in this period was the institutionalization of the national committees, including the congressional and senatorial campaign committees.

Much as the Report recommended, these national organizations maintained sophisticated national headquarters, employed larger professional staffs, and had extensive financial resources. Abundant money was a key to this success, including extensive hard money accounts and, in the 1990s, extensive soft money accounts, raised and spent in cooperation with their state party affiliates (Dwyre 1996).

Party fund-raising was deeply influenced by campaign finance reforms enacted in 1974, 1976, and 1979. On the one hand, these reforms were antiparty, funneling most funds through candidate committees, giving interest groups special recognition through political action committees, and setting limits on the financial role of parties (although not overall spending levels). Perhaps the biggest loss pertained to presidential campaigns, where parties were given no role in financing nominations and only a very limited role in financing general election campaigns. Public funds largely went directly to candidates. There were, however, some benefits to parties. Public financing of presidential campaigns lifted a major financial burden from the national committees, although the law did contain some special roles for parties (especially the 1979 legislation, which opened up soft money fund-raising), and there was a modest subsidy for the national conventions (Mutch 1988). During this period, fourteen states directly subsidized party campaign activities (Malbin and Gais 1998, 52–53). The development of soft money gave the national committees considerable influence over state parties and candidates.

The institutionalization of the national committees also led to the reapportioning of national committee membership. The Democrats were more extreme in this regard, dramatically expanding committee membership to represent a combination of party strength, geography, and key constituencies. The Republicans largely maintained equal apportionment by state but have allowed ex officio membership of various party groups (Bibby 2000, 107–110).

State and Local Party Organizations

Party renewal extended to many state and local party organizations as well (Bibby 1999b). Most state parties developed permanent headquarters, and legislative campaign committees appeared in many states to carry out functions that parallel those of the congressional and senatorial campaign committees (Gierzynski 1992; Shea 1995). Although local parties are not as strong as they were at the turn of the century, many are stronger than at the time the Report was written (Cotter et al. 1984, 61–80; Bibby 1999a; Friendreis and Gitelson 1999).

Neither party developed a formal membership base of dues-paying, issue-oriented, and active citizens. Voter registration rolls continued to be the operational definition of party affiliation for the purposes of voting in primaries, a practice that became increasingly problematic with the decline of party registration and the spread of open primaries. A large base of direct-mail donors to the parties had some of the characteristics of party membership, but such donors had no direct role in party decision making. Ideologically oriented activists became more involved in party activities (Jackson, Brown, and Bositis 1982; Green, Jackson, and Clayton 1999) and have become so prominent in presidential campaigns that one set of scholars dubbed their approach "advocacy politics" (Bruce, Clark, and Kessel 1991). Such activists were influential in a series of reform commissions that followed the McGovern-Fraser reforms and in the experiment with midterm conventions. At the same time, the expanded number and resources of interest groups make them a major factor in party and national politics (Bibby 1999b).

Party Activities

Party platforms continued to emphasize general party principles and helped differentiate the major parties (Pomper and Lederman 1980; Pomper 1999, 256–260). They remained moderate in tenor but became modestly more programmatic. Members of Congress have become significantly more involved in writing national platforms, and midterm policy documents that resemble platforms have become more common. These include the House Republicans' Contract with America and issue handbooks and policy papers prepared by both parties' House members (Herrnson, Patterson, and Pitney 1996). There has been a resurgence of state party platforms as well. For example, Republican parties in twenty-nine states emulated the contract (Little 1997).

In formal terms, nominations conform to the Report's recommendations. Most state parties use primaries to select delegates to the presidential nominating convention. However, the Report's authors would most likely have objected to the influence of presidential candidates on the selection of delegates. Direct primaries also are used to select congressional candidates. Open and blanket primaries became more common, but the Supreme Court ruled the latter to be unconstitutional in 2000 (*California Democratic Party et al. v. Jones,* 530 U.S. 567 [2000]). Ten states continue to allow fusion tickets in primaries (Spitzer 1997, 129). Experimentation with preprimary endorsements continued during this period, but these occasionally resulted in significant intraparty squabbles at the congressional level and became less common (Herrnson 1998). In only twelve states did one or both parties use conventions to make preprimary endorsements (Jewell and Morehouse 1999).

National party activity in general elections increased dramatically during this period. For example, in the 2000 election, the national, congressional, and senatorial committees of both parties spent a total of $1.26 billion, including $495 million in soft money (Federal Election Commission 2000). In fact, the soft money expenditures by the national parties exceeded the spending by their presidential nominees, a dramatic change from 1950, when the Report was written. Although there were legal restrictions on party spending, in practice they do not represent unreasonable limitations. Indeed, rulings by the federal courts and the Federal Election Commission allowed for essentially unlimited party expenditures.

Thus, by the 2000 campaign, expanded financial resources allowed the national party committees to exercise unprecedented influence in national politics (see chapter 5). The national committees were working to set a national campaign agenda, aggressively recruiting candidates, and providing candidates in competitive races with assistance in aspects of electioneering requiring technical expertise or in-depth research. They also helped these candidates attract money and campaign assistance from political action committees (PACs), political consultants, and other groups that participate in politics. Moreover, parties began to make independent expenditures and issue advocacy advertisements. National party funding also was critical to the massive voter-mobilization efforts conducted by state and local parties. Most of this assistance was delivered to help federal candidates, though others benefited from it as well (Bibby 1999b; Herrnson 2000, 93–115). Platforms became somewhat more important in the campaigns of this era.

Two-party competition at the presidential level spread to all regions as the century drew to a close. Party recruitment and campaign assistance contributed to this trend, especially in the South, where Democratic hegemony gave way to two-party competition in some places and Republican dominance in others. Nevertheless, party efforts did not increase voter turnout. Only slightly more than one-half of all eligible voters went to the polls in 2000.

Party Organizations and Responsible Party Government

Did the renewal of national party organizations contribute to responsible party government? Some scholars believe so, pointing to the correlation between the increased strength of party organizations and the clearer programs of the parties in government (for example, see Pomper 1999). The events surrounding the 1994 election and the 104th Congress reveal the strengths and weaknesses of these arguments.

On the surface, the House Republicans' efforts bore a close resemblance to the model of responsible party government. First, the Republican Party developed something like a party platform, the Contract with America, before the election. Then the National Republican Congressional Committee (NRCC), Republican National Committee (RNC), GOP political consultants, and allied interest groups worked with the House Republican leadership to develop and disseminate the contract, which presented a stark alternative to the Democrats' agenda (Gimpel 1996; West and Loomis 1998, 114–117). Through their Victory '94 program, Republican national party organizations transferred more than $14 million to state and local GOP committees for party building, campaign advertising, voter-list development, and voter-mobilization efforts. This effort dovetailed with the NRCC's recruitment of a record number of exceptionally talented congressional challengers, and it helped them raise record amounts of money (Herrnson 2000, 43).

When the Republicans won a dramatic victory in 1994, taking over control of both houses of Congress for the first time in forty years, they claimed a mandate to pursue the contract and took steps to enact it into law. The NRCC held training sessions to teach lawmakers and their staffs how to use mass media, town meetings, and other communications to sell contract-related legislation. They distributed television and radio commentaries extolling the contract's virtues to cable and broadcast stations. National chairman Haley Barbour routinely met with Republican House and Senate leaders to coordinate the GOP message and to discuss political and legislative strategy. These efforts, combined with the measures House Republican leaders took to centralize power under Speaker Newt Gingrich, helped the House Republicans pass nine of the contract's ten points in less than one hundred days (Gimpel 1996, 36–40, 115–117; Sinclair 1997, 175–216). Then, in the next election, Republican Party organizations defended House members who supported the contract from attacks by Democrats, unions, and other liberal groups. They worked with local party activists and Washington-based interest-group leaders to orchestrate op-ed pieces, letters to the editor, and TV ads praising these legislators; and they provided candidates in close races with significant election support (Herrnson 1998, 97–102).

Although this effort was quite impressive by historical standards, it fell short of the Report's expectations in a number of important respects. The contract was conceived and developed by a small group of party insiders, with very little input from other party officials, Senate candidates, or party activists, let alone rank-and-file party members. Only a limited number of House candidates explicitly campaigned on the contract in 1994, and most of those drew only on those planks that conformed to their individual campaign platforms (Gimpel 1996, 22–26; Kolodny 1998a, 204–205). Indeed, after the 1994 election, only 35 percent of all voters had even heard of the contract (Koopman 1996, 147). The shallowness of the contract's roots helps explain why many Senate Republicans did not embrace it and why President Clinton felt free to veto key components that reached his desk. Perhaps most revealing is the fact that the House Republicans did not run on the contract or on a similar platform in 1996.

This episode reveals the potential value of strong party organizations in achieving responsible party government as well as the value of the Report's vision for party organizations. Without the increased institutionalization of national organizations, something like the Contract with America would not have been possible, its limitations notwithstanding. Indeed, such efforts have been attempted by popular presidents only in the twentieth century. But without public support, grassroots participation, and coordination with other party organizations and elected officials, elements of the contract could not be enacted into law or sustained over time. And as in the past, the late-century increase in partisanship in government may reflect factors other than the impact of party organizations.[2] Thus, while institutionalized national party organizations may have contributed to these moves toward party government, the goal was not fully realized. Put another way, institutional resources may be a prerequisite for party government, but the existence of such resources does not guarantee that parties will behave responsibly.

RESPONSIBLE PARTIES AND A CENTURY OF PARTY DEVELOPMENT

Generally, party organizations have met many but not all of the criteria for responsible parties suggested by the Report (see Table 3.1).[3] The biggest gains occurred at the national level and involved expanded institutional capacity, campaign resources, and electoral activities, with increased representativeness and participation within the party organization. The major shortcomings concerned party platforms, membership, state and local organizations, and citizen involvement in politics. In sum, a century of party developments may have laid the foundations for responsible party government, but it has not yet become a permanent reality in American politics.

Surely the biggest disappointment has been the national conventions. From the Progressive era forward, the conventions have become less influential in party politics. Contrary to the responsible party model, they have steadily become less deliberative and less involved in generating programmatic party platforms. In 1900, the conventions were dominated by the agents of state and local party organizations; and in 2000, they were dominated by the agents of candidate and interest-group organizations. Neither situation encouraged genuine deliberation, although the former was more deliberative, and the latter was more consistently issue-oriented. This last point results from a trend toward the Report's recommendations: conventions have become more representative and participatory over the century and more governed by centralized party rules. It is indeed ironic that as the conventions became more democratic institutions, they became less effective instruments of democratic government (Schattschneider 1975).

Despite numerous experiments, the parties have not created party councils and thus have failed to meet one of the major criteria for responsible parties. However, by the end of the century, some of a council's coordinating tasks were conducted by the national committees, by virtue of increased institutional capacity. Indeed, the institutionalization of the national committees, including the congressional and senatorial committees, represents the most dramatic move toward the responsible party model to date. Most of these gains occurred in the late twentieth century, but they were the culmination of century-long trends.

State and local party organizations experienced a very different pattern over time. The initial movement toward the responsible party model during the Progressive era initiated a steady decline in the influence of state and local parties. By midcentury, subnational party organizations had ceased to be the central actors in campaigns. Although they also experienced some institutionalization in the late twentieth century, paralleling the national committees, they have not become the participatory, issue-oriented, platform-writing organizations the Report envisioned. Indeed, they may well be further from this criterion in 2000 than in 1900—although surely closer than in 1950.

Another major weakness is the failure of the parties to develop a mass base of dues-paying, issue-oriented, and active members. Over the century, an ideologically oriented activist corps and a cadre of direct-mail campaign contributors have replaced a patronage-oriented activist corps. This development has made party politics more issue-oriented but has fallen short of the kind of mass membership the Report envisioned.

Party platforms also show a mixed pattern. Programmatic platforms occurred at various points in the century, typically tied to popular presidents. On balance, platforms had become more programmatic by 2000, and elected officials were somewhat more involved in platform writing. Yet these gains were not tied to grassroots participation and were heavily dependent on the interests of candidates.

One area where party organizations closely resemble the Report's recommendations is in regard to nominations. Primaries have become the norm in choosing convention delegates for presidential campaigns and congressional candidates. The century began with an emphasis on closed primaries, moved toward open primaries and other alternatives, and back again toward closed primaries at the end. Experiments with preprimary endorsements also occurred over time but never became common. Ironically, the expansion of primaries may well have become a chief obstacle to responsible parties (Polsby 1983).

The overall role of parties in campaigns has also fluctuated, but the influence of national organizations has steadily increased, becoming substantial by the end of the century. This trend was particularly strong with regard to campaign funds, where the legal regime has varied over time. Platforms have been the basis of campaigns from time to time and were fairly important toward the century's end. On a bright note, two-party competition steadily spread to all regions of the country; but on a darker note, the level of citizen participation reached its peak just after midcentury and has declined since.

Clearly, the major party organizations were incapable of sustaining responsible party government in the early and mid-twentieth centuries, although ironically, some of the closest approximations to party government occurred in those periods. The capacity to sustain party government has increased over time, particularly by 2000. However, this capacity is not yet fully developed, and thus the quest for responsible party government has yet to be fulfilled. But as far as party organizations are concerned, this quest has not been entirely in vain.

NOTES

1. Unless otherwise noted, the criteria for responsible party organizations are drawn from the Report's formal recommendations as well as from recommendations implied in its text. Thus, our rendering of the Report's recommendations is more expansive than that presented by most commentators.

2. Alternative explanations for the high levels of party-line voting exhibited by House Republicans during the 104th Congress include the ideological sorting out of the two parties' congressional caucuses (Rohde 1991, 23–24), the election of seventy-three new Republican House members who had no experience with the decentralized style of leadership that had prevailed under the Democrats, and the predisposition of many new and senior members to support the centralization of power under Gingrich, who had orchestrated the GOP takeover. Also, GOP legislators recognized that part of the reason for their ascendance on Capitol Hill stemmed from the public's frustration with government gridlock, and they understood that a failure to achieve any significant legislative accomplishments could cost them their party's slim majority.

3. It is worth noting the similar patterns for the Republican and Democratic parties in Table 3.1. This similarity results in part from the lengthy time periods covered. One or another party was frequently ahead of the other in particular party developments. However, in the long term, both parties tend to resemble each other organizationally, as suggested in Table 3.1. This may reflect similar responses to the same environmental conditions and the effects of party competition.

4
Election Laws, Court Rulings, Party Rules and Practices

Steps Toward and Away from a Stronger Party Role

L. Sandy Maisel and John F. Bibby

The political scientists who wrote "Toward a More Responsible Two-Party System," the Report of the Committee on Political Parties (1950a), would in all likelihood react with mixed emotions to the status of American parties fifty years after their seminal effort at prescriptive political science. They would be pleased with changes in party rules and practices that have strengthened the national party organizations, enabling them to take a more active role in federal elections, and with judicial decisions that have protected the two-party system and recognized the associational rights of parties. Heightened integration of national and state organizations would surely be seen as a positive development, as would the removal of legal barriers to voting. However, it is also likely that the Report's authors would be deeply disappointed in the present-day status of parties, particularly with the trends toward a candidate-centered system in which party organizations operate in service to their candidates (Aldrich 1995, 269–274). They would also be bothered by the role that big money contributions have played in strengthening party organizations and in increasing national–state party integration.

The net impact of fifty years of changes in election law, court rulings, and party rules and practices has been to maintain a strong party role in American politics, but not the role the Report's authors envisioned. In some respects, the role of parties has moved substantially closer to the Report's model, but at the same time it has been pushed away from the reformers' responsible parties ideal in significant ways. The experience of the past fifty years suggests that legislation, court rulings, and party rules and practices will continue to follow these two seemingly contradictory patterns. These changes in the institutional environment of political parties can be summarized as removing barriers to voting, strengthening parties in constitutional law, nationalizing and integrating the party structure, and expanding candidate-centered politics.

REMOVING BARRIERS TO VOTING

Concerned about the low levels of turnout in the 1940s, the Report's authors called for removal of obstacles to voting in order to increase the number of persons exercising the franchise and thus to give greater legitimacy to elected officials and their decisions. Much has been accomplished in this regard by means of constitutional amendments and federal and state legislation.

Constitutional Amendments

Three constitutional amendments have been implemented since the Report was issued. The Twenty-third Amendment (ratified in 1961) extended the right to vote for president and vice-president to citizens in the District of Columbia, granting them the right to elect three presidential electors, that is, the number equal to the least populous state.

In February 1964, the Twenty-fourth Amendment was ratified, imposing a ban on poll taxes or the payment of other taxes as a qualification for voting in federal elections. Two years later, in the case of *Harper v. Virginia State Board of Elections* (33 U.S. 663 [1966]), the Supreme Court extended this ban to any election in the United States.

Eighteen-year-olds were made eligible to vote through ratification of the Twenty-sixth Amendment in 1971. This followed a Supreme Court decision in *Oregon v. Mitchell* (400 U.S. 112 [1970]), which struck down a provision in the Voting Rights Act of 1970 that had made eighteen-year-olds eligible to vote in all federal, state, and local elections.

Two of the amendments extended the franchise without addressing low turnout by those already enfranchised, a problem that the Report dealt with by calling upon public bodies supervising elections to be responsible for ensuring that voters had every opportunity to vote (Committee on Political Parties 1950a, 76–77). This problem has been addressed in federal civil rights legislation, laws on voter registration, and the process of voting.

Federal Civil Rights Legislation

In the Civil Rights Act of 1957, Congress gave the Civil Rights Commission power to investigate voting-rights violations and to suggest appropriate remedies. The Civil Rights Act of 1960 went further by empowering federal courts to appoint referees to help blacks register in areas in which discrimination had been found. Like the Supreme Court ruling in *Smith v. Allwright* (321 U.S. 649 [1944]) that had banned the whites only primary elections common in many southern states, these attempts to remove the effects of Jim Crow met with limited success. In 1964, only 6.7 percent of blacks of voting age in Mississippi, 19.3 percent of those in Alabama, 27.4 percent of those in Georgia, and a total of 33.2 percent of blacks living in the states of the old Confederacy were registered to vote (Maisel 1999, Table 4.1, 97). Literacy tests, strategic placing of polling places, timing of registration, poll taxes, and especially social pressure continued to depress black participation in the electoral process.

The Voting Rights Act of 1965 addressed these issues directly by suspending the use of literacy tests and by empowering federal registrars to replace local or state officials as the people who registered voters in areas that had used literacy tests in the 1964 election or where fewer than half of those eligible to be registered were in fact registered for that election. The result of this legislative initiative was dramatic. By 1968, black registration had jumped nearly tenfold in Mississippi, tripled in Alabama, nearly doubled in Virginia, and increased over 30 percent overall in the states covered by the law (Maisel 1999, 94–96).

Congress strengthened voting rights through amendments in 1975 by applying provisions of the act to foreign-language minorities. The 1982 amendments to the act extended its key provisions through 2007 and strengthened enforcement by overturning the Supreme Court's decision in *Mobile v. Bolden*, 446 U.S. 55 (1980), which required plaintiffs to prove that an election law provision has discriminatory intent rather than discriminatory effect.

Changes in Registration Procedures

Though barriers to black registration have been removed and voting has increased dramatically, particularly in southern states, the problem of low turnout nationally has remained a concern. With the mobility of the population long thought to be a significant barrier to voting, the Voting Rights Act of 1970 established a thirty-day maximum residency requirement for voting in federal elections. Subsequently, the Supreme Court ruled in *Dunn v. Blumstein*, 405 U.S. 330 (1972), that the thirty-day residency limit should be used for all elections. The 1970 act also called for uniform minimum state standards regarding absentee ballots. Four states—Maine, Minnesota, Oregon, and Wisconsin—have had long-standing policies that allow election-day registration at the polls; and Idaho, New Hampshire, and Wyoming have added similar provisions to their election codes in recent years.

After much partisan skirmishing in 1990 and 1992, which included a Republican-led filibuster of a House-passed bill and a presidential veto, the National Voter Registration Act (NVRA), often referred to as the motor voter bill, was signed into law in 1993. This act sought to increase registration by requiring states to make voter registration possible when citizens apply for a motor vehicle license, to permit voters to mail in their voter registrations, and to have registration forms available at certain public assistance offices. The Federal Election Commission (FEC) reported that the act has been successful in increasing voter registration numbers. In states covered by the law, voter registration increased 3.7 percent between 1994 and 1998, to the highest level in an off-year election since 1970 (Federal Election Commission 1999).[1] However, the impact of the law in terms of actually increasing turnout at the polls has been far from impressive (Martinez and Hill 1999).

Easing the Process of Voting

Although the motor voter law sought to increase the number of registered voters, approximately one-half of the states have developed liberal absentee-ballot rules. Generally, they will send an absentee ballot to any voter who simply requests that option, with no excuses or notarization needed (Busch 1996, 24; Romano 1998, A1). Wisconsin statutes even permit voters to request that their absentee ballots be sent to them by e-mail or fax; and in Michigan, voters over sixty automatically receive absentee ballots in some counties (Wayne 2000, A11). Beginning in 1995, Oregon conducted the first statewide primary completely by mail, and the state has now eliminated the polling booth entirely, using mail-in ballots. Seventeen other states have also used mail-in ballots for local, county, and special elections in an effort to reduce costs and boost turnout.

According to Curtis Gans, the director of the Committee for the Study of the American Electorate, thirteen states now allow early voting, permitting residents to vote seventeen to twenty-one days prior to election day. This procedure, which individualizes and extends the voting process over a number of weeks, has been shown to have considerable public appeal. In Dallas, over sixty thousand persons cast their ballots during the first week of early voting in 2000; and in Washington state, where 12 percent of the vote was cast with absentee ballots in 1980, nearly one-third of the 1.7 million ballots cast in 2000 came from absentee ballots (Wayne 2000; Sanchez 2000). Gans had predicted that over one-quarter of the 2000 presidential vote would be cast by nontraditional methods. However, although these nontraditional ways of voting seem to be gaining popularity, there is limited evidence that they are also increasing turnout (Wayne 2000). The people most likely to choose to vote early are already highly motivated to participate in the political process (Karp and Banducci 2001). Moreover, the increasing use of mail-in and absentee voting tends to increase the parties' and candidates' costs of campaigning (Romano 1998).

Political parties have been deeply involved in absentee and early voting campaigns, as the controversies over voting practices in the 2000 presidential election in Florida amply illustrated. It is also clear that party officials' strategic assumptions must be reexamined when the voting timetable changes (Romano 1998). The act of voting is being transformed, and much will depend on the parties' abilities to increase turnout and to mobilize their supporters in the new twenty-first-century order of voting. Mail-in voting and expanded use of absentee and early voting also made counting the votes more time consuming. For example, it took two weeks to tally the Washington Senate contest in 2000 and another week to do the recount (Gorman 2000, 3725).

The most recent innovation aimed at increasing voter turnout deals with Internet voting, which has been used on occasion in a few districts in remote sections of Alaska. However, the use of Internet voting by Arizona Democrats in their March 2000 presidential primary was the first use of this system that gained national attention in an election. Basic issues of fairness and access were immediately raised, and it is difficult to evaluate the result, based upon one noncompetitive primary. Nevertheless, turnout was over the traditional or expected number. A potential problem, according to a task force studying Internet voting in California, is the need for tight security, which could make the process cumbersome and could discourage participation. Yet, it is possible that Internet voting may be used more extensively as technology advances and more citizens gain access to the system (Gorman 2000, 3725; Sostek 2000).

STRENGTHENING PARTIES IN CONSTITUTIONAL LAW

Since the Constitution does not mention political parties either in the original document or in subsequent amendments, it provides little direct guidance concerning the status of parties within the political system. Nonetheless, the courts have had to wrestle with the constitutional status of parties as the national government and the state have sought to regulate the popularly perceived evils of the party system and the parties have sought to maximize their freedom of action under the law. The basic issue is whether parties are private associations having all the protections of other private organizations, or quasi-public organizations because of their crucial role in the electoral process. And if they are quasi-public, are they then entitled to more protection from government regulation than private groups, or does their quasi-public status legitimize state regulations that would not be appropriate for private groups (Peltason 1999, 9–10)?

In dealing with these issues, the Supreme Court has sought to protect the right of individuals "to associate with the political party of one's choice and with others for the common advancement of political beliefs and ideas" (*Eu v. San Francisco Democratic Committee*, 489 U.S. 214 [1989]). The Court has also sought to free parties from excessive state regulation by insisting that regulations imposing "severe burdens" on parties must meet the test of "a compelling state interest" to pass constitutional muster (Peltason 1999, 10–11). Moreover, the thrust of post-1950 decisions has been to strengthen the national party organizations at the expense of state party units.

Presidential Electors as Party Agents

The Constitution's framers clearly expected that presidential electors would be free agents. However, in the aftermath of the 1948 elections, in which Alabama's Democratic electors voted for the States' Rights ticket of Strom Thurmond and

Fielding Wright, the Court upheld the power of the states' Democratic Party under authority of state law to withhold certification of presidential electors who did not pledge support for the nominees of the Democratic National Convention (*Ray v. Blair*, 343 U.S. 214 [1952]). Interestingly, in their dissents, Justices William O. Douglas and Robert H. Jackson voiced objection to this decision, arguing that it effectively enhanced national party influence by permitting state law to reinforce national party actions. In 2000, a bare majority of the states (twenty-six) had laws binding electors to support their party's nominee.

National Party Rules Take Precedence over State Laws and State Party Rules

Following the national Democratic Party's massive rules reform effort after the 1968 convention, the Court came down firmly on the side of national party rules when those rules are in conflict either with state laws or state party rules governing selection of national convention delegates. Thus, in *Cousins v. Wigoda* (419 U.S. 477 [1975]), the Court upheld the power of the 1972 Democratic National Convention to deny seating to Illinois delegates chosen under Illinois laws that violated national Democratic Party rules. The parties' First Amendment rights of association were again invoked in *Democratic Party of the U.S. v. Wisconsin* (450 U.S. 107 [1981]), where the Court held that national Democratic rules banning open presidential primaries took precedence over Wisconsin's law, which provided for open primaries to select national convention delegates. Since the Wisconsin case not only strengthened the role of the national parties but also struck a blow for the parties' right to ban open primaries, it probably would have been warmly welcomed by the Report's authors.

Freeing Parties from Excessive Burdens of State Regulation

Because the states are responsible for the administration and integrity of their electoral processes, they regulate the political parties extensively. However, because First Amendment protection for the right of political association has been accorded to parties, state regulations that burden the parties' ability to operate in a manner consistent with their own beliefs and that cannot be shown to serve a compelling state interest have been struck down.

In a landmark case, *Eu v. San Francisco Democratic Committee* (489 U.S. 214 [1989]), the Court invalidated a California law that forbade official party units from engaging in preprimary endorsements, made it a misdemeanor for a candidate to claim an official party endorsement, required the chairs of state central committees to be rotated between northern and southern California, and mandated parties to establish county-level governing bodies. These provisions were declared unconstitutional on the grounds that they violated the associational rights of parties and that the state had failed to demonstrate that its regulations were justified in order to promote stable government and to protect voters from confusion and influence (see analysis by Peltason 1999, 16–18).

The *Eu* decision followed close on the heels of a prior case that had demonstrated the Court's inclination to allow parties to determine their own internal procedures. In 1986, it had upheld the Connecticut Republican Party's decision to open its primary to independent voters even though state law provided for a closed primary system in which only registered party voters were allowed to vote in partisan primaries (see *Republican Party of Connecticut v. Tashjian,* 479.U.S. 208 [1986]). Justices rejected Connecticut's claim that its closed primary law was needed to avoid voter confusion and to prevent opposition-party voters from crossing party lines and engaging in primary raiding. The Court observed that the state was substituting its judgment for the party's in deciding how to protect the party's integrity (Epstein 1999, 58–59).

Few state parties have actually taken advantage of the *Tashjian* decision and opened their primaries in an effort to increase citizen interest in the parties (Epstein 1989, 260–270). In one instance, opening a state party's primary proved a colossal blunder for its sponsors. In Michigan, Governor John Engler led a move within the GOP to open the state's 2000 presidential primary to Independents and Democrats in an effort to assist George W. Bush and fend off challenges from his more conservative rivals, Gary Bauer, Steven Forbes, and Senator Orin Hatch (R-Utah). Instead, it led to an infusion of voters into the Republican primary supporting the candidacy of Senator John McCain (R-Ariz.) and to Bush's losing the Michigan primary.

Interestingly, the *Tashjian* precedent was not successfully invoked by state parties seeking to close their primaries until California's Republican and Democratic Parties, along with two minor parties, challenged the state's blanket primary law, which was adopted through a ballot initiative in 1996. In a seven-to-two decision, the Supreme Court in 2000 declared that California's blanket primary constituted a "stark repudiation of political association" that denied parties the power to control their own nomination processes and to define their own identities (*California Democratic Party v. Jones,* 530 U.S. 567 [2000]). In taking this position, the Court adopted a view of the party as a mainly private rather than a public association. Writing for the majority, Justice Anton Scalia stated, "In no area is the political association's right to exclude more important than in the process of selecting nominees." Scalia further declared that the state's interest in opening up the nominating process could be better served constitutionally by adopting a "nonpartisan" primary similar to that used in Louisiana. In response to this decision, the California legislature promptly enacted a semiclosed form of primary to replace the blanket primary. Under this new semiclosed primary statute (2000 *Cal ALS* 898; 2000 *Cal SB* 28), voters registered as partisans receive their party's ballot on primary election day; unaffiliated voters are free to choose in which party's primary they will vote, provided the party's rules permit unaffiliated voters to participate. California, therefore, is following the formula set forth in *Tashjian*.

The California blanket primary case left open the question of whether or not open primaries are constitutional, since Scalia noted that the Court was not required to deal with that issue in the California case. But the dissenting justices, John Paul Stevens and Ruth Bader Ginsberg, said the majority decision cast serious doubt on the constitutionality of other forms of the open primary. It is not clear, however, that either the states or the Court is prepared to throw out traditional open primary systems that have become established parts of states' political cultures.

Through cases according parties associational rights, and in the California blanket primary case in particular, the Court acted in accord with the views of parties contained in the Report, which advocated stronger party organizations, parties with distinct policy positions, and abolition of the blanket primary.

Protecting the State Parties from Raiding and Sore Losers

In a series of cases in the 1970s, the Court upheld state laws discouraging cross-party raiding in primary elections. In *Rosario v. Rockefeller* (410 U.S. 752 [1973]), it upheld a New York statute that required voters to be registered in the party of their choice thirty days prior to the general election on the grounds that it was a reasonable means to prevent raiding. However, later that year the Court threw out an Illinois law that prohibited a person from voting in the primary of one party if that individual had voted in another party's primary within the preceding twenty-three months (*Kusper v. Pontikes* 414 U.S. 51 [1973]). In the Illinois case, the Court held that the state was preventing voters from participating in the next primary of their most recent choice; in the New York case, the state had required voters to meet only one deadline (see Peltason 1999, 19).

The Court has also endorsed state attempts to limit the ability of candidates who have lost a party primary to then run as Independents in the general election. In upholding a California "sore loser" statute (which banned losing candidates in primary elections from then running as Independents in the general election), the Court noted that the states have a legitimate interest in preventing "splintered parties and unrestrained factionalism" within their borders (*Storer v. Brown*, 414 U.S. 737 [1974]). The Court also upheld a California "disaffiliation" statute that prohibited persons from running as Independents if they had been registered with a party during the year preceding the primary.

Maintaining the Two-Party System

The Supreme Court has taken the position that neither Congress nor the states are forbidden from adopting measures that promote a two-party system on the grounds that dualism promotes political stability. Yet the Court has also asserted that the two-party system need not consist of any particular set of parties such as the Republicans and Democrats (*Anderson v.Celebrezze*, 460 U.S. 780 [1983]).

Clearly, the Federal Election Campaign Act (FECA) affords special advantages to the two major parties by providing them with substantially higher levels of public funding for their conventions and presidential candidates than is available to minor or new parties. In upholding a challenge to the FECA, the Court noted that third parties have not constituted a credible threat to the major parties since 1856 and 1860, and that being aware of this fact of political life, Congress was justified in giving full funding to major parties and only a percentage of the major parties' funding level to minor parties. Furthermore, it held that Congress had a legitimate interest in not creating artificial incentives for splintered parties and heightened factionalism (*Buckley v. Valeo*, 424 U.S. 1[1976]; Peltason 1999, 21–23).

A particularly significant decision putting the Court squarely on the side of promoting two-party politics came in *Timmons v. Twin Cities Area New Party* (520 U.S. 351 [1997]), upholding a Minnesota law that banned "fusion candidates" or "cross-filing," that is, running as the nominee of more than one party simultaneously. Writing for the Court, Chief Justice William Rehnquist acknowledged that parties have associational rights to select their own candidates but asserted that states also have the constitutional right to regulate elections. He noted that "the Constitution permits the Minnesota Legislature to decide that political stability is best served through a healthy two-party system." Rehnquist also stated that the ban on fusion tickets imposed only an insignificant burden on a minor party and left it "free to spread its message to all who will listen." Clearly, this decision was a major blow to minor parties that believe a route to influence is through alliances with major parties, as has been demonstrated by the New York Conservative and Liberal Parties, which have taken full advantage of that state's laws permitting cross-filing (see Scarrow 1983, 55–79).

Although the Court has been quite willing to accept the states' right to promote "two-partyism," it has also been protective of citizens' constitutional right to create and develop new parties. In accordance with this doctrine, it has struck down those state ballot access laws that grant the major parties virtual monopoly status; laws that prevent third parties from serving as agents of political protest and disseminators of ideas have also been rejected. In what Peltason has called the foundation case in this area, the Court threw out an Ohio law that required new parties to place their candidates for presidential elector on the ballot ninety days before the election and to present petitions with signatures equal to 15 percent of the vote in the last gubernatorial election, yet established parties were required to have received only 10 percent of the gubernatorial vote in the prior election (*Williams v. Rhodes*, 393 U.S. 23 [1968]; see Peltason 1999, 24–31).

NATIONALIZING AND INTEGRATING THE PARTY STRUCTURE

Since 1950 there has been a series of developments in party rules and practices that have resulted in a more nationalized and integrated party structure, one of the goals of the Report.

National Party Rules Enforcement

Following the 1968 divisive Democratic National Convention, the national party embarked on a major rules reform effort that lasted through the 1980s (Maisel 1999, 266–280). This reform process was carried out by a series of commissions whose recommendations were later promulgated by the Democratic National Committee (DNC).[2] The resulting party rules provided for binding mandates upon states and state parties in the selection of national convention delegates, the composition of the national committee, and the creation of a party charter. The DNC has also created a mechanism to monitor enforcement of its national party rules.

As we have seen, the Supreme Court upheld the primacy of the Democratic Party's national rules governing delegate selection over state laws and state party rules. The significance of the post-1968 Democratic rules, which have been reinforced by the courts, was highlighted by Austin Ranney, who observed that the new rules "constitute the first increase in the power of a party's *national* organizations since the heyday of presidential nominations by congressional caucuses from 1800 to 1824. . . . Everywhere the states now turn, they are hedged by these rules. The new rules have stuck and stuck hard" (1978, 226–227).

The Republican Party has followed a quite different course from that of the Democrats in that it has not sought to impose restrictive mandates upon the states and state parties regarding the delegate selection process. Nor has it sought to make changes in delegate selection procedures between elections. Its rules authorize the national party to make rules changes (including delegate selection rules) only at national conventions and not between elections, as has been done by the DNC. Most important, the Republicans have consistently demonstrated a preference for maintaining the confederate nature of their party's legal and representational structure. Thus, while the Democrats mandated detailed rules upon their state affiliates, the Republicans have retained highly permissive delegate selection rules at the national level (Bibby 1981, 102–107).

Further, the Republicans have not moved as far as the Democrats in expanding the size of their national committee. Membership on the Republican National Committee is based on the principle of state equality, with each state, the District of Columbia, Puerto Rico, and territories being represented by a national committeeman and woman and the state chair. The GOP state chairs were added to the RNC in the 1960s, and the Democrats took similar action in the 1970s. The RNC does, however, accord ex-officio representation to various affiliated groups, including Republican elected officials and the National Federation of Republican Women. The DNC membership, by contrast, is much larger. Its representational scheme takes into account state population and reflects the geographic strength of the party and its constituent groups, making it much more consistent than the Republican apportionment system with the recommendations of the Report, which called for national committee membership to "reflect the actual strength of the party in the areas [members] represent" (Committee on Political Parties 1950a, 39). It should be noted that both national committees remain too large to function as effective decision-making bodies. Their actions are directed largely by the national chairs, smaller executive committees, and professional staffs; therefore, changes in the representational schemes of the committees are less meaningful than might appear at first glance (Bibby 2000, 107–110; Maisel 1999, 80–83).

Party Nationalization Through Providing Services to State Parties

The expanded professional staffs of the national committees and the congressional and senatorial campaign committees now play an important role in providing a wide array of services to state parties: cash grants, professional advice, computer facilities, data processing, consulting on organizational development, fund-raising, campaigning, media relations, and redistricting. A major priority has been voter-list development and get-out-the-vote drives, which have been supported with money and professional personnel. By providing an array of services to their state and local affiliates, the national party organizations have gained unprecedented intraparty influence and leverage. These assistance programs operate in a manner similar to federal grants in aid to the states—that is, conditions are imposed by the national party on state parties receiving their aid, for example, requirements for hiring qualified consultants, developing an approved campaign plan, and cooperation with national party activities.

Integration and nationalization of the parties has occurred as a result of the national parties being able to generate vast sums of money and then to send some of it to the state parties. This pattern of national party committees distributing funds to the state parties has reversed the traditional state-party-to-national-party flow of intraparty money that existed in 1950 when the Report was published. Now the flow is in the opposite direction. With that shift, power has been increasingly centralized in the national parties, and the state parties have become more dependent on them for resources. Indeed, national party units now regularly become major players in state races, helping the state parties in their contests for control of legislative chambers and governorships (Bibby and Holbrook 1999, 84–85).

There has also been a major expansion in the aid provided to House and Senate candidates by the congressional and senatorial campaign committees as well as by the national committees. The Hill committees are now heavily involved in candidate recruitment while also providing such services as campaign management, issue and opposition research, polling, media assistance, money, and issue advertising (Herrnson 2000, 100–119). These rejuvenated congressional and senatorial campaign committees, which play active roles in setting campaign issue agendas and in recruiting and assisting candidates for Congress, would be welcomed by the authors of the Report.

Integration of State Parties Into the National Party Campaign Strategy

Because the national party committees can quite literally raise more money than they can legally spend in direct contributions to and in support of federal candidates, they have adopted a strategy of transferring millions of dollars to their state party affiliates for "party-building activities." Under 1979 amendments to the FECA, states may spend without limit on these party-building activities, for example, headquarters' overhead, voter lists, and election-day voter mobilization. A major component of these national-to-state-party fund transfers is soft money, raised outside the restrictions of the FECA.

In the 1999–2000 election cycle, the Federal Election Commission reported that these soft money transfers escalated to $145.2 million by the Democrats' national-level committees and to $129.4 by the Republicans'. Though the bulk of this money went to issue ads and candidate support, recent research has revealed that the state parties were able to use some of it for service programs, candidate recruitment, voter mobilization, larger staffing, and operating budgets, thereby modestly strengthening state-level party organization (La Raja 2001). This party-strengthening by-product of soft money transfers to state parties might have partially soothed the concern among authors of the Report about the surge in large soft-money donations.

As a result of these fund transfers, which the national parties make as a part of a strategy to influence the outcome of federal elections, the state parties have now become well integrated into national campaign structures and play a significant role in presidential, senatorial, and congressional elections. National party operatives are even inserted into state party headquarters to run state-level party campaign operations in states considered key to winning the presidency and other federal races. A notable development begun in the 1996 election and continued in 2000 was that of the national parties transferring funds to state parties, which then used these monies to purchase issue advertising developed by national party media-production companies (Marcus 1996; Abramson and Wayne 1997).

This heightened level of party integration and nationalization of campaign efforts constitutes a change of major proportions in the American party system. The observation of the authoritative parties scholar of the 1950s is now no longer true, that "no nationwide party organization exists. . . . Rather, each party consists of a working coalition of state and local parties" (Key 1964, 315). The post-

1950s trend toward more centralized and integrated parties would be greeted with approval by the authors of the Report, although they would find distasteful the heavy dependence of the national parties on corporations, unions, and individuals giving six-figure amounts in the form of soft money ($410 million in the 2000 election cycle). They would also be puzzled by the Supreme Court's decision in *Colorado Republican Federal Campaign Committee v. Federal Election Commission* (518 U.S. 604 [1996]), which authorized party committees to make independent expenditures to support their own candidates (expenditures made independently and without the collusion of their nominees), even though the *Colorado* decision did expand the party role in campaigns.

The soft money and independent expenditure loopholes in the regulation of campaign spending have enabled the national party organizations to counter in a limited way the general trend toward candidate-centered politics within the electoral process. The research of Magleby and his associates demonstrated that in targeted House and Senate races in 1998, candidates were frequently forced to compete with parties and their allied interest groups for control of the electoral agenda and the attention of voters (Magleby 1998, 19). In competitive nationally targeted races, the parties and their allied groups may actually outspend the candidates. The future of soft money, with its powerful impact on the parties and campaigns, is uncertain since the passage of the Bipartisan Campaign Reform Act of 2002 and pending court challenges. It is clear, however, that the national parties' ability to amass millions in soft money since the mid-1990s has thrust parties into the center of presidential and competitive senatorial and congressional campaigns and given parties a critical campaign role in helping to set the issue agenda of campaigns and in reinforcing the candidates' own campaign themes.

EXPANDING CANDIDATE-CENTERED POLITICS

Although the removal of barriers to voting, changes in the constitutional law of parties, and party rules and practices since 1950 have moved the parties closer to the model proposed in the Report, there has also been a strong countertrend toward more candidate-centered politics that shows no sign of abating. Evidence of this trend is found in nominations for state and federal offices, ballot forms, and legislation governing campaign finance.

The Direct Primary

The direct primary constitutes a nominating method that is distinctive to American politics. As Leon Epstein has observed, "In no nation apart from the United States are party nominees regularly selected by unorganized voters in legally mandated state-conducted elections" (1999, 44). The Report recognized that the direct primary had become "an established institution" of party nomination for state and congressional candidates and, therefore, pragmatically recommended that it be retained as a "useful weapon in the arsenal of democracy," even though it violated the reformers' belief in membership-based intraparty decision making. Hence, the Report gave the direct primary only grudging support and noted, "The primary election laws in many states badly need improvement" (Committee on Political Parties 1950a, 71).

The open primary was seen as undermining responsible parties because "it tends to destroy the concept of membership as a basis for organization"; in contrast, the closed primary was deemed "more readily compatible with the development of a responsible party system" because "it tends to support the concept of party as an association of like-minded people" (Committee on Political Parties 1950a, 71). Washington State's blanket primary and cross-filing (then practiced most notably in California) were viewed as particularly destructive of a responsible party system. Besides advocating the closed primary, the Report also called on state party organizations to engage in preprimary proposing and endorsements of candidates. Although the Supreme Court invalidated California's blanket primary system, the recommendations of the Report have been undermined significantly by changes in state laws and party rules and practices.

The states have not heeded the call for closing their primaries (Bibby 2000, 169–174; Maisel 1999, 194–200). Only sixteen states have completely closed primaries in which party registration is required for voter participation. An additional ten states have only semiclosed systems in that they permit voters to change their registration on election day.[3] California requires party-registered voters to vote in the party of their registration, but unaffiliated voters are able to choose the primary in which they will vote, provided party rules permit unaffiliated voters to participate. The balance of the states operate primaries with varying degrees of openness—eleven have semiopen primaries that permit all voters to participate but require them to publicly indicate in which party primary they wish to vote, and nine have completely open primaries in which voters decide in the secrecy of the polling booth in which party's primary they will vote.[4] In 1975, Louisiana adopted a so-called "nonpartisan" primary system that opens the primary to all registered voters. All candidates, regardless of party affiliation, are listed alphabetically in office blocs on the ballot. If a candidate receives a majority of the primary ballot, then that individual is declared elected; but if no candidate receives a majority, then a runoff election is held to determine the winner. The runoff may be a contest between two candidates of the same party or candidates of different parties.

The opening of primaries by allowing changes in party registration on election day; the enactment of Louisiana's nonpartisan primary; and the spread of the blanket primary from Washington, first to Alaska and then to California, were all indicators of a trend within the states toward more open primary systems, as was the Supreme Court's *Tashjian* decision permitting state parties to open their primaries even when state statutes mandated closed primaries. The one countertrend was the Supreme Court's decision declaring the California blanket primary unconstitutional in 2000 and thereby raising questions about the constitutionality of open primaries. Ironically, Justice Scalia suggested that an alternative system of opening primaries, the nonpartisan primary, could possibly pass constitutional muster.

Whatever form the direct primary takes, but especially in its open varieties, it lessens the incentives for formation of a dues-paying party membership, encourages a candidate-centered style of politics, requires candidates to build personal campaign organizations, and tends to "favor candidates who are media celebrities, wealthy, telegenic, or able to raise large amounts of money and willing to devote many months to soliciting votes" (Epstein 1999, 51; see also 49–50). The primary also diminishes the role of peer review of a candidate's governmental experience that was "supposed to have been a major factor in an organization's selection process" (Epstein 1999, 51). Clearly, the direct primary has profound consequences for the American party system, and it is so ingrained in the American political culture that there is no likelihood that it will be eliminated.

Declining Effectiveness of Preprimary Endorsements

Not only has there been a trend toward more open primaries, but preprimary endorsements by state party conventions have declined in effectiveness in the relatively small number of states where they are practiced, either through statutory mandates or party practice.[5] The research of Jewell and Morehouse has demonstrated that there has been an increase in contested gubernatorial primaries, particularly in states with informal rather than state-mandated endorsement procedures. They also found that although endorsed candidates in states with both legally mandated and informal preprimary endorsement procedures won contested primaries in at least 80 percent of the cases from 1960 to 1980, those winning percentages dropped to 53 percent between 1982 and 1998 (2000, 109–110). Even in states with traditionally strong party organizations, such as Connecticut, a party endorsement no longer is tantamount to winning the nomination. A candidate with substantial funds who runs an effective media campaign has become difficult to beat for an endorsee and the sponsoring party organization. Jewell and Morehouse conclude that most state parties that do not currently have endorsement procedures have shown little interest in adopting them, as was proposed in the Report. The Report's authors would probably have agreed with V. O. Key's observation that the nomination process remains a dilemma, since the introduction of the direct primary as a "means for popular control of party hierarchies also plants the seed for fission . . . of statewide party organization" (1956, 168).

Presidential Primaries and the Weakening of Party Organizations' Control of Nominations

It is hard to imagine a presidential nominating system further from that envisioned by the authors of the Report than the contemporary system. The notion that national nominating conventions should be decision-making bodies composed of party leaders elected by rank-and-file party members in recognition of their dedication to the party and its principles is totally alien to the body politic today.

To be sure, the system has been reformed, but the reforms have moved the system toward candidate-centered politics and away from dominance by party organizations. And this movement was intentional. The thrust for reform of the nominating process stemmed from the tumultuous 1968 Democratic National Convention in which Vice-President Hubert Humphrey was nominated, despite the fact that he did not win any presidential primaries. The McGovern-Fraser Commission Report analyzed the nominating system and deemed it unrepresentative of the constituencies within the Democratic Party and unresponsive to voter concerns. They called for a new system that was open, timely, and broadly representative of voters in the Democratic Party (Commission on Party Structure and Delegate Selection 1970).

Many state parties found that the easiest way for them to comply with the mandates of the McGovern-Fraser Commission, once they were adopted by the DNC, was to replace party caucus and convention delegate-selection methods, which had been dominated by party leaders, with selection by presidential primaries. These new primaries, created to conform to national Democratic Party rules, allocated delegates among the candidates for the nomination proportionally based on the candidates' votes in primaries, with the delegates themselves to be cleared by the candidates whom they had supported. Frequent changes in Democratic selection processes required alternations in state law. As a result, the Democratic reforms had a spillover effect on the Republicans as state legislatures passed delegate-selection statutes applicable to both parties that were consistent with Democratic Party national rules (Maisel 1999, 266–280; Bibby 2000, 222–229).

As a result of party rules and state statutory changes, whether states select their delegates through presidential primaries (which is the case in nearly forty states) or through party caucuses and conventions, the identity of the individual delegate is less important than that of the candidate he or she favors. Only in the New York Republican Party do voters cast ballots for individual delegates, the system envisioned by the 1950 Report. In the Democratic Party, delegates are allocated proportionally according to the vote in primaries or first-level caucuses. The Republicans use that system in some states and winner-take-all in others. However, in either case, the vote is for delegates supporting specific candidates and not, with the sole exception of New York Republicans, for the delegates themselves.

Some dissatisfaction was expressed among Democratic leaders after the first experiences with this system because formal party leaders and elected officials often failed to become convention delegates. To increase participation of party leaders and elected officials, Democratic rules were changed for the 1984 convention to create super or automatic delegate positions for these leaders. Having greater flexibility in their delegate selection procedures that enabled them to place party leaders on the states' national convention delegations, the Republicans resisted the creation of automatic delegates. Even with the Democrats' super delegates, no one can deny that the presidential nominating process is heavily centered on candidates for the nomination and their own campaigns. It is not the party-dominated process, which was envisioned by the authors of the Report.

One aspect of the evolving presidential nominating process that is enhancing the influence of party leaders is the trend toward "front-loading" of the presidential primary and caucus schedule into the first months of the delegate-selection season during January, February, and March. With the majority of delegates being chosen during this period in a series of primaries and caucuses across the country that follow in quick succession, it has become imperative that presidential aspirants have organizational support nationwide and especially in key states if they are to have any hope in winning their party's nomination. In 2000, national and state party leaders helped to provide this organizational support to George W. Bush and Al Gore and were an important factor in their defeating their party "outsider" rivals, Senator John McCain and former senator Bill Bradley.

The Report saw the national nominating conventions as a critical element in a responsible party system. However, the impact of the thirteen presidential nomination cycles since the publication of the Report has diminished the convention as a decision-making institution and the influence of the parties within the nominating process generally. With the presidential nominees known well in advance of the conventions (because of their having won the crucial primaries), the national conventions have become candidate-centered events controlled by the nominees' operatives and designed to showcase the nominees as they kick off their general election campaigns.

Campaign Finance Laws and Candidate-centered Campaigns

The Report saw accurately that the role of parties could be enhanced if campaign funds flowed through party coffers. To facilitate a financial link between parties and their candidates, the authors called for "a specified measure of government assistance to parties" (Committee on Political Parties 1950a, 75).

Here, too, the contemporary situation in regard to public money for parties rather than for candidates has diverged completely from that proposal.

The FECA and its various amendments follow a clear theme: campaign funds should be raised, spent, and accounted for by candidate committees. Disclosure of funding sources is deemed essential to a "clean campaign finance system." The role of parties in federal campaign finance law is specified in detail and limited. Knowledge of the details is not important to understanding the impact of the FECA. At the congressional and senatorial level, candidates' campaigns raise their own money and must disclose the sources of all funds. Party committees can give to and support their candidates' campaigns, but the amount of support is specified and limited. The FECA's limits on direct party contributions to House and Senate candidates and on party coordinated expenditures made on behalf of these candidates have been held by the Supreme Court to be constitutional (*Buckley v. Valeo,* 426 U.S. 1[1976]; *Federal Election Commission v. Colorado Republican Campaign Committee* [Colorado II] no. 191 [2001]). Nonetheless, the party committees have found ways to spend sums of money that vastly exceed the amount specified in the law through soft money and issue advertisements. The role of the parties in campaigns in which they invest in this manner is clearly substantial and growing, though not to the point of replacing candidate-centered organizations as the dominating element.

At the presidential level, the political parties play no role in financing the nominating process, even for incumbent presidents. The parties are given public money to pay for their national conventions. Once the nominee is chosen, however, the public funding provision of the FECA calls for money to go to the nominees, not to the parties. Perhaps the ultimate expression of this separation of the candidate from the party was the renegade Republican Pat Buchanan's 2000 takeover of Ross Perot's Reform Party in order to qualify for $12.5 million in federal funds that the party's nominee received as a result of Perot's garnering in excess of 5 percent of the vote in 1996.

While the FECA was intended to create a system of campaign finance with only a limited role for political parties, the soft money loophole in the law has enabled parties to play a critical role in presidential and targeted House and Senate contests. Party-developed issue ads, funded in part by soft money, mean that party messages now play a larger role in setting campaign agendas. However, the focus of party efforts is to service selected candidates whose nominations they do not control.

State campaign finance laws also encourage candidate-centered politics in many of the states. Among the states, the most common method of public funding of campaigns is to give funds directly to candidates. However, ten states do channel public funds through the state parties, and four give money both to parties and some candidates (Malbin and Gais 1998, 52–53). Recently enacted reform legislation in Maine gives public money directly to candidates in primaries and general elections rather than to parties or even party nominees. Independent candidates are treated the same as party nominees in terms of qualifying for public funds. Similarly, Vermont enables minor party candidates to qualify for public funds at levels comparable to major party nominees (Goldberg 2000). Minnesota's campaign finance reform legislation provided the 1998 Reform Party nominee for governor, Jesse Ventura, with four hundred thousand dollars in public funds that played a critical role in enabling him to defeat the two major party nominees (Jeter 1998). Thus, while reforms such as these are directed toward ridding the system of private money, they also threaten to undermine the two-party system.

Ballot Forms: From Party Column to Office Bloc

The party column ballot form, especially when combined with a provision for expedited straight-ticket voting by making a single mark, encourages straight-ticket voting. By contrast, the office bloc ballot form facilitates split-ticket voting (Bass 1999, 224, 260; Campbell, Converse, Miller, and Stokes 1960, 275–276, 285–286; Rusk 1970; Campbell and Miller 1957; Walker 1966; Weber 1980). However, as with the direct primary, the proliferation of presidential primaries, the demise of the national conventions as decision-making bodies, and changes in campaign finance regulation, the trend in the form that ballots take on election day has been to move away from encouraging partisanship.

At the time the Report was published, the party column was the predominant type of ballot, with thirty states using this form and eighteen using office bloc ballots (Bass 1999, 230–231, 237). However, by 1997 only a bare majority of states (twenty-six) continued the party column tradition; twenty-four did not. There was a similar move among the states away from providing voters with single-mark straight-ticket voting. Although twenty-seven states had provided for expedited straight-ticket voting in 1946, only eighteen did so in 2000 (Bass 1999, 232; Kimball and Owens 2000). Both of these developments hinder the expression of partisanship and encourage split-ticket voting. The impact of these changes in ballot form has been amplified by the weakening of partisan attachments among the electorate. As the authors of *The American Voter* noted, "Formal institutions have their greatest impact on political behavior when the attitudes relevant to that behavior are least intense" (Campbell, Converse, Miller, and Stokes 1960, 283).

The trend away from ballot forms that encourage straight-ticket voting has further undermined the reformers' vision of responsible parties capable of enacting their programs by increasing the likelihood that there will be divided party control of government at both the national and state levels (Bass 1999, 224). Indeed, divided government has become the norm in recent decades. Although ballot forms can hardly be considered the cause of split-ticket voting and divided government, they certainly facilitate it. Yet to the extent that voters continue or increase their tendency to split their tickets, changes in ballot forms are likely to accommodate them (Bass 1999, 263).

A STRONGER PARTY ROLE—CONTRADICTORY PATTERNS

Perhaps it is unfair to look to the Report as a basis for evaluating changes in the party system of the last half century, since many of the changes in the polity could not have been foreseen by its authors. At the beginning of a new millennium, we can only speculate on how the scholars serving on the committee would have viewed the parties of 2000. After all, the parties of the twenty-first century operate in a different milieu from those of 1950. In all likelihood, the call for responsible parties struck a responsive chord among the students of those who wrote the Report. Most students of today's political scientists would probably be appalled at the very thought of strong, disciplined, and responsible parties, if they thought about the status of political parties at all.

With that caveat, we can note that many of the recommendations of the Report have come to pass, not because of the suggestions of the Committee on Political Parties, but because of broader political and social changes, which have, among other things, altered electoral laws, court rulings, and party rules and practices. The result is a party system that has in important respects moved closer to that envisioned in the Report. Among the aspects of election laws, court decisions, and party rules and practices that are consistent with the goals of the Report are the removal of barriers to voting; strengthening the status of parties and the two-party system in constitutional law; campaign finance legislation that provides for limited public funding of presidential and some state campaigns; and party rules and practices that have resulted in stronger party organizations, heightened intraparty integration, and an increased party presence in campaigns. However, other changes in the legal and organizational milieu work against the Report's goal of party-centered politics. There has been a trend toward candidate-centered politics, which is reflected in a weakened party role in the nomination process at the presidential, congressional, and state levels; campaign finance reforms that channel public money to candidates rather than to parties; parties that act in service to their candidates; and state ballot laws that promote split-ticket voting. Moreover, the better-financed parties of the new century have become, contrary to the reformers' vision, highly dependent on individuals and groups that make large campaign contributions.

On balance it would appear that the legal and organizational environment for parties has moved in a direction that encourages more responsible parties, but this movement has been within the context of a trend toward candidate-centered politics. Based on what has transpired since the Report was issued in 1950, there is every reason to expect that the party system will continue to evolve in ways that are both consistent and at odds with the Report's objectives. Although the party system may not have changed in all the ways that the Committee on Political Parties advocated fifty years ago, American parties have shown remarkable adaptability and durability. The story of such developments, therefore, is not one of party leadership's responding to reform ideas put forth by political scientists; rather, it is one of adaptation to new challenges so as to guarantee a continued strong role for parties in the political process.

NOTES

1. Six States—Idaho, Minnesota, New Hampshire, North Dakota, Wisconsin, and Wyoming—are exempt from provisions of the NVRA because of their past performances in registering voters.

2. Though these commissions have had formal names, they have generally been referred to by the names of their chairs: the McGovern-Fraser Commission, which set rules for the 1972 delegate-selection process; the Mikulski Commission, which amended those rules for the 1976 process; the Winograd Commission, which made further changes for 1980; and the Hunt Commission, which altered the 1980 rules for 1984. After the 1984 election, the DNC appointed the Fairness Commission in response to complaints from Rev. Jesse Jackson, but that group made no major recommendations for change (see Maisel 1999, 266–280).

3. The closed primary states are Arizona, Connecticut, Delaware, Florida, Kentucky, Maryland, Nebraska, Nevada, New Mexico, New York, North Carolina, Oklahoma, Oregon, Pennsylvania, South Dakota, and West Virginia. Semiclosed primary states include Colorado, Iowa, Kansas, Maine, Massachusetts, New Hampshire, New Jersey, Ohio, Rhode Island, and Wyoming; California has a modified semiclosed primary that allows unaffiliated voters to vote in party primaries, if the party rules permit them to do so.

4. Semiopen states include Alabama, Arkansas, Georgia, Illinois, Indiana, Mississippi, Missouri, South Carolina, Tennessee, Texas, and Virginia. The open primary states are Hawaii, Idaho, Michigan, Minnesota, Montana, North Dakota, Utah, Vermont, and Wisconsin.

5. As of 2000, these state parties had a legal basis in state law for preprimary endorsements: Connecticut, Rhode Island, New York, North Dakota, Colorado, Utah, and New Mexico. Virginia law permits the parties to nominate by convention if they wish. There are also endorsements made by conventions under state party rules in a number of states, including Massachusetts, Minnesota, Delaware (Republicans), and California (Democrats) (see Jewell and Morehouse 2000, 106–118).

5

Power, Money, and Responsibility in the Major American Parties

Frank J. Sorauf

The title of the Report of the Committee on Political Parties of the American Political Science Association, "Toward a More Responsible Two-Party System" (1950a), sounds one of its two major themes: the search for greater party responsibility. It does not, however, announce the other one: the need for stronger political parties. Some fifty years later, the major parties have greatly fortified their political strength, largely by raising and spending cash in campaigns, but the search for effective mechanisms of responsibility goes on. Those chief concerns of the authors of the Report provide the central themes for this chapter.

Before and during World War II, most of the resources for running campaigns, apart from the modest efforts of the candidates and their supporters, came from the parties themselves. They provided volunteers for canvassing the neighborhoods, halls for rallies, casts of thousands for parades. What had to be purchased they bought with cash contributions from their candidates, patronage appointees, and assorted fat cats (Overacker 1932; Heard 1960).

Although the Report's authors apparently saw party control of campaign resources as essential for party strength, they feared control was compromised by the 1940 amendments to the Hatch Act (Corrado 1997, 30). Its $3 million limit on annual spending by a party committee and its limit of $5,000 on individual contributions to parties or candidates, they argued, promoted a "scattering of responsibility for the collecting of funds among a large number of independent and nonparty committees."[1] Thus, "Repeal of these restrictions would make it possible for a national body to assume more responsibility in the field of party finance." Greater responsibility would "happen" in consolidated and concentrated parties, but the Report never explained how to hold those powerful party committees responsible.

In retrospect, the hopes of the Report's authors to reestablish the old party hegemony in American electoral politics—including their earlier superiority in amassing campaign resources of all kinds—were doomed to failure. They tried to reestablish party-centered campaigning at the very moment it was beginning to disintegrate even further.

CANDIDATES AND THE NEW ELECTORAL POLITICS

Not long after the appearance of the Report and the debate it generated, the American parties confronted far more serious challenges than its authors wrote about. Neighborhood party organizations and voter loyalties to them began to fade after World War II. Television became the country's new source of political information; 9 percent of American households had TV sets in 1950, 85 percent in 1960, and 95 percent in 1970. Candidates increasingly ran their own campaigns, for which they largely raised and spent the necessary money. With the increased use of television, candidates replaced parties as the focus of most campaigning. Given the failure of parties to provide volunteer help, campaigns and candidates inevitably entered a primarily cash-driven economy.

In this great transitional period, from about 1950 to the passage of new reform legislation in 1974, campaigning also became increasingly expensive. Presidential-year spending on all campaigns, by all participants, rose from $200 million in 1964 to $425 million in 1972 (Alexander 1984, 11). Individual contributors to presidential candidates set new records of generosity. Clement Stone, a Chicago insurance executive, gave the record sum: $2.14 million to Richard Nixon's 1972 campaign. That campaign and its excesses, as well as its Watergate illegalities, led to the one comprehensive attempt in American history to reform campaign finance: the 1974 amendments to the Federal Election Campaign Act (Sorauf 1988, chap. 2).

By the time of the drafting of the FECA in the 1970s, the parties had largely lost control of campaigning, especially in national elections. When the Watergate scandals broke after the 1972 elections, it became clear that the perpetrators of the illegalities were from the Committee to Reelect the President (the so-called CREEP), a committee run by President Nixon and his White House staff. The Republican National Committee was hardly involved. Indeed, the organizational and fund-raising revival of the national party committees awaited the initiative and example that William Brock was to bring to the RNC in the mid-1970s.

The law that Congress wrote in 1974 clearly reflected the electoral politics of its time, especially its candidate-centered politics. The candidate was its singular focus, with limitations placed and disclosure forced on all money flowing into and out of the candidate's campaign. Not surprisingly, the Congress's goals in the FECA grew from the problems of the 1960s and 1970s. For example, only the single committee of the candidate was permitted to spend on the candidate's behalf, thus closing one of the largest loopholes of the 1925 Corrupt Practices Act, the law the FECA replaced (Corrado 1997, 29). It also met the problem of the wealthy fat cat contributor head on: individuals were limited to $1,000 per candidate per election and an annual limit of $25,000 in total contributions. Nonparty committees (the PACs of everyday usage) were limited in their contributions to $5,000 per candidate per election. And there were substantial limitations placed on candidates' use of their own resources on their own campaigns. The FECA's stance on the political parties, however, was far more complex.

Political party committees were limited to the same $5,000 per candidate that applied to the PACs. Contributions to a party committee, however, were not as limited as the contributions to the PACs or candidates. Individuals could give up to $20,000 per year to a national party committee and $5,000 to any other committee (chiefly the PACs), with a grand total limit of $25,000 a year. The PACs could give no more than $15,000 per year to a national party committee and $5,000 to any other committee—with no aggregate annual limit.

However, the national parties benefited from a special category of spending: coordinated ("on behalf of") spending, or party spending on a campaign with the candidate's knowledge. The limits for those expenditures were indexed to the Consumer Price Index and in the case of the Senate reflected comparative state populations. In 2000, they were $33,780 for a House campaign and for Senate campaigns ranged from $67,560 in the thirteen least populous states to California's $1,636,438.[2] Those limits apply twice, to all three national committees taken together and to all state and local committees taken together.

Despite the complexity of these provisions, the consequences for the parties are clear. As the FECA defines money—money raised under its limits and thus hard money—there is really no limit to the aggregate sums candidates can accept from all PACs and individual contributors so long as they can win the support of more and more of them. But national party committees are limited to three—the "national" committee and the party committees in the House and Senate—and each of them is limited to increases in coordinated spending at the rate of inflation. Worse, the limit on contributions to candidates is fixed at $5,000; inflation by 2000 had reduced the purchasing value of that sum to less than one-third of what it was in 1974.

If there was any overall philosophy governing the writing of the FECA, it was the hope that candidates would depend increasingly on small contributions from the folks back home—that the "giving constituency" would be a subset of the voting constituency. In that way, the FECA's drafters shared the hope of the Report that campaign funding would be returned to small individual contributions. But the FECA envisioned a citizen base, not a political party base, for campaign finance, and it accepted the assumption that candidates, rather than parties, would raise the funds. Perhaps the Report's authors sensed both the atrophy of the parties' grass roots and the loss of the parties' monopoly over electoral politics to the expanding involvement of interest groups in campaigns.

THE POLITICAL PARTIES UNDER THE FECA

Before the new FECA could be enforced in a single election campaign, the Supreme Court undermined its comprehensive structure (*Buckley v. Valeo*, 424 U.S. 1 [1976]). The Court upheld the FECA's limits on contributions, but it struck down the limits on candidate spending, on independent expenditures, and on candidates' use of their own funds in the campaign. The decision rested on the Court's ruling, for the first time, that the First Amendment protected the transactions of campaign finance and that the ill-fated spending sections of the FECA denied protected rights while the limits on contributions did not. Thus, what had been a regulatory system placing limits on all transactions in a campaign became one resting only on limits on contributions. The main impediments to escalating campaign costs had fallen.

Curiously, in *Buckley* the Supreme Court did not rule on the constitutionality of the FECA's limits on the parties' coordinated spending. For whatever reasons, none of the plaintiffs raised the issue, nor did the national parties press it until the late 1990s. In the mid-1970s and even the 1980s they were passive and, in truth, little constrained anyway by the limits to their spending on candidates. Rebuilding themselves, not legal challenges, preoccupied them.

William Brock and the national Republicans began that rebuilding after the 1972 elections. To provide the cash for reviving the party's national organization, Republicans greatly expanded the direct-mail solicitation of millions of their supporters and began the preservation of computerized lists of contributors. So armed, they increased party receipts from $8.9 million in 1975 to $17 million in 1979 and to $37 million in 1980.[3] In the last years of the 1970s, 75 percent of these receipts came from mail appeals (Kayden and Mahe 1985, 73–74).

The Democrats, weighed down with debts dating back to the 1968 campaign, did not begin their national rebuilding until the 1980s. Belatedly, they adopted the Brock model, which improved their fund-raising materially, though never to the level of the Republicans. In 1980, for instance, the DNC raised $15.5 million against the $77.8 million of the RNC. By 1987–1988, however, the DNC had raised $52.3 million, the RNC $90.1 million. By the end of the 1988 election cycle, party parity still eluded the Democrats. The three national Democratic committees in 1988 raised $81.1 million; the Republican committees took in $191.5 million.[4]

While the parties struggled for the organizational strength with which to recapture their old electoral dominance, the surviving parts of the FECA went into effect in the 1976 elections. Those campaigns and the ones that followed in 1978 and 1980 featured experimentation by all of the players in campaign finance. Especially, contributors of all kinds—PACs, individuals, and parties—tested the proposition that they could defeat unfriendly officeholders by financing their challengers. In the best-known case, the National Conservative PAC (NCPAC or "nick-pac") claimed credit for unseating four Democratic senators in 1980 and became the icon of triumphant "PACdom" and the new power of money (Sorauf 1999, 12–26).

The fear and loathing of PACs faded quickly. Indeed, very few incumbent members of Congress were defeated by PAC money or any other kind. Drawing on all the advantages of incumbency and on vigorous fund-raising of their own, incumbents rode out the first aggressive assaults under the FECA. Once again, more than 90 percent of incumbents running for reelection were successful; in the elections of 1984, 1986, and 1988 only an average of twelve House incumbents were defeated. The PACs and affluent individual contributors learned their lesson, abandoned the electoral strategy, and fell back increasingly on a pragmatic legislative strategy of supporting powerful incumbents, especially those of the majority party. Incumbents had quietly established their dominance in campaign finance.

Increasingly through the 1980s, congressional campaign finance slipped into stability. The number of PACs, which had grown from 608 to 4,009 from 1974 to 1984, stayed on or near the 4,000 plateau for the 1980s and 1990s.[5] More tellingly, their collective contributions to congressional candidates increased at a rate slower than the rate of inflation; they gave $132.7 million to congressional candidates in 1986 and $147.8 million in 1988. Spending by all congressional candidates edged up at a comparable rate, from $401.0 million in 1986 to only $411.4 million in 1990 as two-party competitiveness fell. The era of Ronald Reagan enabled Republicans to dominate presidential politics; in congressional politics, dominated by the majority Democrats, the two parties cultivated their safe seats and starved their challengers. The percentage of House elections won with 60 percent or more of the major party vote rose from 68.9 in 1982 to 88.5 in 1988 (Ornstein, Mann, and Malbin 1996).

The 1980s were also a time of consolidation for the parties. Democratic and Republican spending for all congressional candidates—contributions and coordinated spending by national, state, and local party committees—reached $23.8 million in 1982, and after moving to a high of $29.0 million in 1988, settled back to $23.7 million in 1990.

Within this overall stability, however, great changes began in the 1980s to transform the fund-raising of the parties:

- The fixed limits on contributions to candidates made it inevitable that the parties would spend larger and larger shares of their money in the coordinated spending that also permitted a more intrusive party role in campaigns.
- Democrats slowly closed the gap between their expenditures and those of the Republicans. Republican spending enjoyed a 4-to-1 margin over Democrats in 1982, but only a 1.4-to-1.0 edge in 1990.
- The 1980s also saw the beginning of major soft money raising by the parties.

Above all, the 1980s were the years in which legislative campaign committees (LCCs) matured. The party committees in the Congress had been around for years,[6] but they attracted notice again in the 1980s when Congressman Tony Coelho reinvigorated the Democratic Congressional Campaign Committee (DCCC) to compete with the more effective National Republican Congressional Committee (NRCC) (Jackson 1988). At the same time Willy Brown, the Democratic speaker of the state assembly, and his fellow California Democrats raised the unprecedented sum of $4.4 million for the state's 1984 legislative campaigns. Scholars also documented the role of LCCs in Illinois and New York.[7] Legislative party campaigning—whether operating through leaders, caucuses, or special campaign committees—had come of age as a potent factor in campaign finance.

The consequences of the new LCCs' strength were momentous. Legislative parties became increasingly independent from the rest of the party and its controls. Moreover, LCC activity eliminated any buffering party committee in the troubling relationship between raising money and making public policy. And by increasing their campaign role, the LCCs increased their opportunity to recruit candidates and influence campaign strategy. Local party committees were the hapless losers.

THE PARTIES BECOME DOMINANT

The 1980s interlude of stability in campaign finance was possible only because of the brief drying up of competition between the two major parties. That drought, however, ended in the 1990s. Public disenchantment with deadlock and careless ethics in Congress and state legislatures led to term-limit movements. Congressional unpopularity and drastic postcensus redistricting in many states led unprecedented numbers of members of Congress not to seek reelection. Sixty Democrats and Republicans contested open seats in the 1990 elections, but in 1992 that number rose to 144. Moreover, Republicans, seeing an opportunity to recapture the House, began to fund their challengers more generously. Ultimately, the Republican push for control of the House succeeded in 1994, but their small margin of control ensured competitive House elections into the new millennium. And in the 1990s, the Democrats recaptured the presidency.

Competition transformed the system of campaign finance. Aggregate spending by all congressional candidates rose from $446.3 million in 1990 to $1,005.6 million in 2000. In 1994 only 64.5 percent of House general elections were won with 60 percent or more of the major party vote, the lowest percentage since 1964 (Ornstein, Mann, and Malbin 1996). Thanks to a return to electoral strategies by some contributors, the PACs primarily, the impoverished challengers, who had spent just 16.1 percent of the total spent by all House candidates in 1990, raised that percentage to 23.7 in 1996.

Prepared by the rebuilding of the 1970s and 1980s, the parties responded quickly to the new competition. Party contributions to candidates and their coordinated spending in congressional campaigns rose so much that for the first time the FECA limits began to constrain them. They spent $23.8 million on candidates in 1990 (57 percent by Republicans); $59.5 million in 1996 (58 percent by Republicans); and in 2000, $58.0 million (56 percent Republican).[8] Just between 1992 and 2000 the national parties' total hard money receipts under the FECA—by all of their national, state, and local committees—rose from $445.0 million to $741.0 million. Republican committees raised 60 percent of the total in 1992 and 63 percent in 2000.

Behind the growth of the national parties' role in funding congressional campaigns was an almost invisible practice: agency agreements. Those agreements permit state party committees to transfer their spending quotas to the national party committees by making them their agents. In the early 1990s, about two-thirds of each party's state committees signed away their spending authority. The effect was twofold; it increased national committee spending, despite the constraints of FECA, and it ratified the increasing weakness of the state parties. The use of agency agreements declined in the second half of the 1990s as national–state party cooperation increasingly involved hard and soft money transfers to the state parties.

So far this examination of campaign funding in the 1990s has dealt only with the regime of the FECA—that is, with the candidate-centered getting and spending for the campaign that the FECA regulates. In the 1990s, however, the parties led a radical breaking out from the boundaries the FECA had defined. They did so by raising money outside the limits of the FECA (soft money), by spending money on the campaign "outside of the campaign" (issue ads), and by spending in ways the FECA's authors surely never intended (independent expenditures). Each of those assaults on the 1974 FECA's regulatory structure merits further explanation.

Soft Money

By the time the Federal Election Commission ordered the parties in 1991 to account for the soft money they raised, it was hardly a new phenomenon. Estimates in the press put the two parties' soft money revenues for 1988 at more than $40 million. The first official reports documented a total of $86.0 million raised in 1992; by 1996 the total had almost tripled to $262.1 million. In the 2000 cycle, the total was $495.1 million.

However, because it was raised outside the FECA's limits, soft money could not be used in campaigns for federal office.[9] Thus the two national parties at first spent the soft money on themselves: on staff, buildings, and equipment as well as on generic party advertisements on behalf of the party qua party. Soon, however, the parties, ever inventive, began to send substantial amounts of money to the state parties, sums that became even more substantial in the 1990s. The three national Democratic committees sent $149.8 million in soft money to state parties in 1999 and 2000; the Republican total at the same time was $129.9 million. The total of $279.7 million in soft money transfers far outstripped the $135.4 million in hard money transferred in the same cycle.

Much of the transferred soft money shored up state and local party organizations and supported registration and get-out-the-vote campaigns. Some also enabled state parties to finance state and local campaigns,[10] often in the hope that the support cultivated would rub off on the congressional and presidential candidates on the ticket. The House and Senate campaign committees began to use it to support promising state legislative candidates, either directly or in transfers, for two reasons: to influence congressional reapportionment by state legislatures and to promote candidates who might eventually run for Congress.

Unable to spend soft money directly on campaigns for federal office, the national party committees increasingly also transfer it in ways that indirectly support key candidates or key state parties. Money for voter registration or get-out-the-vote drives often goes disproportionately to states where a senatorial or presidential race is close. Soft money to key states may also permit them to save more of their hard money for presidential or congressional campaigns. And then there are the issue ads it will buy.

Issue Ads

Buried deep in the Supreme Court's lengthy opinion in *Buckley* was a brief passage interpreting a section of the FECA that limited campaign communications by individuals "relative to a clearly identified candidate." In order to hold those words constitutional, the Court ruled, they "must be construed to apply only to expenditures for communications that in express terms advocate the election or defeat of a clearly identified candidate for federal office."[11] Through that loophole the parties drove a herd of media brokers. Beginning primarily in the 1990s, radio and TV ads, ostensibly issue ads, supported or attacked candidates, even on the eve of an election, but maintained their status as non-campaigning ads by avoiding the crucial words "vote for" or "vote against" or some approximation of them.

Since pseudocampaigning by issue ads is not campaigning in the eyes of federal courts, there is no reporting of the practice to the FEC. A private organization, the Annenberg Public Policy Center of the University of Pennsylvania, reported a 1998 total of between $275 million and $340 million in total issue-ad expenditures, a range just about double its estimates for 1996. Those totals, unhappily for these purposes, include spending in national, state, and local campaigns by all political organizations.[12] In their study of TV advertising in the top seventy-five media markets in the 1998 congressional elections, Krasno and Seltz (2000) report a total of $20.5 million in political party spending on TV issue ads and $10.4 million by groups. Their definition of issue ads eliminated candidate spending, as well as party coordinated spending and party independent spending, and ads that appeared in smaller media markets. Moreover, the Krasno and Seltz data on cost covers only the actual purchase of airtime; much of the reporting to Annenberg apparently included administrative and production costs.[13]

For the parties, it is easy to integrate spending on issue ads into a total finance strategy. The House or Senate campaign committee of a party may not have the hard money with which to support a member in a tight race for reelection, or it may have spent hard money to the legal limit in that race already. Soft money then keeps it in the campaign by paying for issue ads attacking the opponent of its candidate.

Independent Spending

In mid-1996, the Supreme Court unexpectedly held that political parties may make independent expenditures in campaigns, providing they do not confer or plan with their own candidates (*Colorado Republican Federal Campaign Committee v. FEC,* 518 U.S. 604 [1996]). Immediately, two national party committees, one in each party, leaped into action, spending $11.5 million in the remaining months of the campaign. By the 2000 campaigns, independent spending by national party committees dropped dramatically to $3.9 million, probably because of the availability of a better alternative: spending on issue ads. Since it is outside the campaign, as independent spending is not, the issue ad can be paid for with soft money. Furthermore, the FECA mandated that independent spending be reported to the FEC, and no such requirement burdens the issue advertisers.

In sum, the mastery the national party committees now enjoy in campaign finance springs from a variety of sources:

- First, the national committees enjoy the same advantages they bring to any task in electoral politics: long-term, enduring commitments, full-time life as political organizations, and well-honed political expertise.
- They benefit, too, from their centrality to the business of nominating and electing candidates. Dominance of campaign finance is an extension of their long-held role in electing candidates.
- Their federated organization and their centralized fund-raising enable them to spend campaign funds at national, state, and local levels with

new efficiency and with coordinated strategies for presidential and congressional elections.

• Finally, of all the actors recognized by the FECA, the parties alone can use all of FECA's fund-raising and spending options—including independent expenditures—as well as the new extralegal options of soft money and issue ads.

The more complex campaign finance becomes and the more arcane its legal and political niceties, the more readily the parties dominate the regime. Small wonder that in less than two decades they have replaced PACs as the icons of American campaign finance. To some extent, especially in the higher-stakes campaigns, they have even wrested control of campaigns from candidates.

WHAT FINANCIAL POWER HAS WROUGHT

The political parties' role as funders of electoral politics has clearly changed in less than twenty-five years. Less clear but equally important is the effect that the new role of master financier has had on the parties themselves. To illustrate that point, consider the nationalization and centralization of the parties. Nationalization was under way with the Brock revitalization in the 1970s and the Manatt-led Democratic catching-up in the 1980s. Direct-mail solicitations of computer-based donor lists were managed nationally and were, therefore, a success for centralization. Success also gave the national committees a powerful cash tool for asserting their influence throughout the entire party hierarchies.

At the same time, the already weak state and local party organizations lost more and more power. Dependent on the charity of national committees, having surrendered their license to spend in congressional elections, and having acquiesced in the local initiatives of the LCCs, state and local committees lost their core electoral responsibilities. Moreover, they lost volunteer activists, even party elites, as cash from higher committees enabled them to contract for the phone banks and mailings once the province of volunteers. What issues or programs they supported were increasingly defined by powerful nonparty organizations within them (for example, labor unions within the Democrats, conservative Christians among the Republicans) and by candidates armed with poll results and demographic data.

At the same time, needing and having more money to spend on campaigns inevitably makes the parties—especially the legislative parties—even more exclusively electoral parties. Often to the displeasure of ideologues within the parties, they are more than ever obsessed with winning elections. Very rarely does party spending for candidates reward loyalty to party platforms or issue positions or even the legislative party itself. The goal in supporting legislative candidates is almost exclusively the maximization of the party cohort in the legislative chambers. Mavericks can count on the party's support if they have good electoral prospects.

The growth in number and power of legislative campaign committees further supported the turn to electoral pragmatism. Their ability to raise increasing sums of money in the Congress and in many state legislatures freed them from any dependence on, or control by, the national or state committees. Those latter committees now work chiefly in executive politics, thus establishing a party division of labor that mirrors the separation of powers. An integrated campaign on behalf of the entire party in a state or the nation becomes less and less possible.

No recent document or event better illustrates the new, fragmented electoral politics than Newt Gingrich's Contract with America. Heavily funded by the NRCC and almost entirely the work of the House Republicans, it was generated, tested, and vetted by extensive polling and focus group research. It had no attachment at the grass roots, and apparently, consultation about it with the RNC was quite limited (Kolodny 1998a). It was, moreover, a platform that largely avoided major policy issues in favor of issues with an immediate favorable response from voters. As a platform it served a limited instrumental purpose far removed from the central role in a mass participatory party that the 1950 Report envisioned.

In short, we see a greater functional fragmentation of parties that had for much of American history been fragmented regionally. Their different parts have different constituencies and different electoral goals and interests. In this separation of function by party committees, the whole is lost. As much as parties may talk about party interests or party principles, there are few authoritative voices to speak on behalf of, or to campaign for, the party as a party. We are, in short, further than ever from the 1950 committee's vision of integrated, responsible major parties.

Even if one "elevates" the analysis to the less precise categories of role or function, the party-as-funder does not measure up as well as it did fifty years ago. As hard as it is to measure matters of role or function, they are central to the pervasive belief—at least among scholars of parties—that the parties enjoy a special status and importance as political organizations. From function and role we derive "contribution" to the larger polity, and, thereby, we argue the importance of the parties in enabling the processes of mass representative democracy. More specifically:

- If we look to the parties to fund competition and thus inform the electorate about the candidates, party targeting (i.e., limiting) the races they will support—with the resulting abandonment of unpromising races for office—undercuts that ability.
- By looking for candidates to support who will raise ample sums of money, the parties limit the recruitment of new candidates into public life by disqualifying the less adept money raisers.

- By diminishing the importance of local party organization, the powerful national parties diminish their ability to foster direct, grassroots political activity and, thus, the political education of local citizens.

Thus, the intended consequences of party power are increasingly focused, and the unintended, systemwide consequences do not happen as often or as serendipitously. The case for party exceptionalism, and the consequent case for protected legal status, is thereby diminished.

Power, and in this case financial power, inevitably raises the central issue of the Report: responsibility. In the simple marketplace of campaign finance, the parties clearly are responsible to their donors, who may withdraw their money if they are not happy with its use. And yet it is apparent that, despite public grumbling, many of them do not. Periodic movements in corporate circles to boycott the major parties' raising of soft money have not greatly stanched the flow of soft donations. Fear of losing political access and favor blocks the show of resistance.

Alternative systems of responsibility have also failed or simply are not available. The option of grassroots, intraparty democracy, or even of representative governance by party elites, never achieved much; and by now, with the atrophy of the grass roots, it is a moot issue. Responsibility to voters is not an option either, since the question at most elections is the performance or commitments of candidates, not the political parties. The entire "responsibility to the voters" argument had greater credibility in 1900 or even 1950 when party-ticket voting and voter loyalty to a party were far more common. Moreover, there is really no longer a single "party." Each party committee and each organized group of party officeholders increasingly stands by itself, is funded by itself, and is largely responsible to itself.

Nor does the pluralist solution work with the two parties. The individual member of Congress may accept PAC contributions from any set drawn from the more than three thousand PACs active in an election, many of them representing differing interests in one policy issue or another. Countervailing and offsetting contributions are very possible. In the duopoly of the party system, any member of Congress represents only one political party, and the Madisonian rule of large numbers does not apply.

Thus by the fiftieth anniversary of the Report, the parties have been vastly strengthened, although not in the manner it advocated. Their nationalization and their abilities in massive fund-raising have enabled them to recapture a major place in American electoral politics. However, the search for mechanisms of responsibility through which to hold their power accountable remains as futile as ever.

Do any viable options remain? For at least the last one hundred years, when market, competitive, or intraorganizational means of accountability have failed, we have often accepted the option of responsibility to the American public through legislated regulation. As the attempts to regulate national campaign finance since 1906 so vividly illustrate, the regulatory solution has not always succeeded. One reason in the particular case of the FECA of 1974 is common. The regulated have been free to evade and innovate, but the regulators have lacked the political support for repairs to the regulatory regime. Reformist zeal tends to be intense but short-lived. "Re-reform" becomes a recurring necessity but an ever more distant possibility.

RESPONSIBILITY AND REGULATION

Ironically, support for new regulation of the party role in campaign finance grows at a time when existing regulations are under mounting attack. The parties—chiefly the Republican Party and its allies—argue in the federal courts that any regulation beyond disclosure of their getting and spending infringes their constitutional rights of political speech, association, and activity under the First Amendment. Not only are the sections of the FECA on the parties under attack, but so too are those in several state statutes.

The immediate reform agenda, then, especially for political scientists, centers not on more regulation of party transactions but on the question of whether any regulation can be justified and supported. Since the forum for answering that question is judicial, it takes a constitutional form. Under what circumstances may a legislature curtail the First Amendment right to get or spend campaign money?

The Issue of Corruption

In *Buckley v. Valeo* the Court permitted limitation of First Amendment rights only in circumstances of "corruption or the appearance of corruption."[14] In the early years post-*Buckley*, the Court interpreted the word "corruption" as an explicit quid pro quo, literally as bribery. More recently it has moved closer to the broader meaning implicit in Lord Acton's great dictum that "power tends to corrupt; absolute power corrupts absolutely."[15]

On the regulation of parties, neither the justices nor political scientists are in agreement.[16] The differences have been on display in a series of cases in which the FEC has accused the Colorado Republican Party of violating the FECA's limitations on party coordinated spending in the 1986 senatorial campaign in that state (*Colorado Republican Federal Campaign Committee v. FEC*, 518 U.S. 604 [1996]). In the initial appearance of the case before the Supreme Court, the Court surprised virtually everyone by holding that political parties could make independent expenditures supporting their own candidates. On the central issue, however, the constitutionality of limits on parties' coordinated spending, only four of the justices voted to invalidate the limits and permit unlimited party spending.

The position challenging the right of Congress to regulate parties on the "corruption" issue received a classic statement in a brief supporting the defendant Republicans filed by political scientists in the first *Colorado* case.[17] Party money spent in campaigns, they argued, is "probably" the "cleanest money in politics"; and extending the metaphor, it is so because a party follows a principle of sanitary engineering: "The solution to pollution is dilution."[18] Within the political party, in other words, there is some mechanism that dilutes the identity and interests of the donor from the money it receives and then permits the party to spend or give it with only the identity and interests of the party attached. It cannot therefore corrupt the recipient candidates or policymakers.

Jonathan Krasno and I have rebutted that argument several times.[19] Our position begins with a conviction that large contributions in support of an explicit policy interest potentially "corrupt" public officials by creating extra avenues of influence and representation, a heightened "access," in this representative democracy. As we wrote for the FEC in the *Colorado* case:

> The main issue remains the availability of the extra opportunities to persuade. Such opportunities resulting from campaign contributions corrupt the central relationship of mass, democratic representative government by permitting some citizens to acquire a preferred representational avenue, to be listened to more promptly or more intently or more often. While it is inevitable in a large popular democracy that influence will not be evenly distributed, it is not inevitable that the avenues of representation or opportunities to influence—the very heart of the representative processes—will be skewed by campaign contributions.[20]

Moreover, party money is not cleansed either of the donor's name or the donor's interests. The identity of the substantial donor, especially, is maintained by the special honors, meetings, briefings, and clubs the parties create to assure donors that they will not slip into anonymity.

Nowhere are those realities clearer than in the case of fund-raising by legislative campaign committees. With them there is no intermediary "party" that might soften or prevent the identification of donors; the same people raise and disperse the money. Moreover, they are also the leaders who will define the party's legislative program and who will mobilize party votes in the legislature. In short, LCCs sit precisely at the nexus of money and legislating that most directly raises the possibility of corrupting the representational processes.

Indeed, a case can be made that party money is, in instances such as these, the most "interested" and the "least clean" money. The politically sophisticated donor must surely realize that giving ten thousand dollars to an LCC can earn the gratitude of a whole legislative party and its leadership while two thousand dollars to five candidates can at most win the gratitude of five legislators.

The Issue of Party Exceptionalism

The claim that political parties, because of their importance in a representative democracy, must be given greater deference and greater freedom than other political organizations undergirds the case in public policy against regulating political parties. One of the principal authors of the Report, E. E. Schattschneider, gave the claim its enduring justification: "The parties, in fact, have played a major role as *makers* of governments, more especially they have been the makers of democratic government. . . . Democracy is unthinkable save in terms of the parties" (Schattschneider 1942, 1). Almost sixty years later those sentiments are alive and very well in political science.

The Supreme Court has yet to address the issue of party exceptionalism, but it has moved in a direction that suggests it is unwilling to grant blanket First Amendment protection from regulation. In a recent Supreme Court case upholding Missouri's limits on individual contributions to candidates, the majority, speaking through Justice Souter, set a standard of impact or consequence for such claims. The Court required "a showing of a system of suppressed political advocacy" as an indication of harm to the regulated parties and, more broadly, to the political system. In this particular case, Justice Souter propounded a specific test of "whether the contribution limitation was so radical in effect as to render political association ineffective, drive the sound of a candidate's voice below the level of notice, and render contributions pointless."[21]

No political scientist, I presume, would deny the importance of political parties and their contributions to mass, representative democracies. Certainly I do not. Democracy may be imaginable without the parties—*pace* Schattschneider—but the price of their absence, even their wounding, would be high. Yet with their rebirth as campaign funders comes a price, too, if we reject reform and regulation. Lord Acton made no exceptions to his dictum on the potentiality of power to corrupt, and neither should we.

Much of the resistance of political scientists to the regulation of the parties reflects a protective stance no longer necessary. The parties were indeed subjected to punitive regulation, largely in the states, and in the last century it often contributed to their inactivity and ineffectiveness. By the turn of the millennium, however, the worst of that legislation has been repealed or invalidated, and just as important, parties have found a path not only to new power but to a massive disconnect of old avenues of accountability. The end-of-year fundraising totals that the major parties reported to the FEC amply illustrate that new strength: $508 million in 1992 and $1.2 billion in 2000. The solutions offered by the Report for the problem of responsibility are unquestionably obsolete, although the problem itself is not. The search for a more responsible two-party system goes on.

NOTES

1. See the Report (Committee on Political Parties 1950a, 75). All subsequent quotations from the Report are also on 75, the only page in it concerned with party funding of campaigns.

2. The one exception to the uniform limit for all House districts is that the limit is doubled in states with only one congressional district. All the figures here are a sum of the limit applying to the party's state committee and the identical limit applying to the parties' three national committees taken together. If a state committee deeds its permitted sum to the party's national committees in an agency agreement, those national committees may then spend the entire sum.

3. These data come from the reports of the Federal Election Commission; all subsequent data will be drawn from the same sources unless otherwise noted.

4. In 1988 the two Republican campaign committees in Congress led their Democratic counterparts by almost four to one, $100.5 million to $28.7 million.

5. The FEC reported 3,835 active and registered PACs on January 1, 2000.

6. They are the Democratic Congressional Campaign Committee (DCCC), Democratic Senatorial Campaign Committee (DSCC), National Republican Congressional Committee (NRCC), and the National Republican Senatorial Committee (NRSC).

7. On Illinois, see Redfield (1995); on New York, see Shea (1995).

8. The data here include national, state, and local party committees' spending on congressional candidates because the FEC aggregates the data in that way.

9. There are two ways in which soft money is raised most commonly outside of the FECA: it comes from a prohibited source (e.g., a corporate treasury) or in prohibited amounts (e.g., an individual contribution of more than $20,000).

10. In 1997 and 1998 the soft money sums for this purpose were not great: $3.8 million for the Democrats and $11.1 million for the Republicans. They rose modestly to $6.1 million and $12.8 million in 1999 and 2000.

11. *Buckley v. Valeo*, 424 U.S. 1 (1976), at 44. The section of the FECA in question is 608(e)(1).

12. The Annenberg data may also include ads paid for with hard money and even some ads that candidates purchased.

13. See Krasno and Seltz (2000, 34). Their analysis reviewed a commercial archive of media trackings in the largest media markets; the yield was twenty-one hundred separate commercials that aired more than three hundred thousand total times.

14. *Buckley v. Valeo*, at 25.

15. Letter to Bishop Mandell Creighton, 1887, cited in John Bartlett, *Familiar Quotations*, 13th ed. (Boston: Little, Brown, 1955), 663.

16. The nine justices are known; the political scientists are those who have signed or written affidavits, memorandums, or briefs of amicus curiae in recent campaign finance cases.

17. Brief of amicus curiae for the Committee for Party Renewal in support of the defendants in *FEC v. Colorado Republican Party Federal Campaign Committee*, 41 F. Supp. 2d 1197 (D. Colorado 1999).

18. Ibid.

19. See Sorauf and Krasno's memorandums for the FEC in *Colorado Republican Party* and in support of the state of Missouri in *Missouri Republican Party v. Lamb*, 100 F. Supp. 2d 990 (E.D. Mo. 2000).

20. Sorauf and Krasno's memorandum for the FEC in *Colorado Republican Party*.

21. *Nixon v. Shrink Missouri Government PAC*, 120 S.Ct. 897 (2000). Justice Souter offered the formulation as a restatement of a passage in the Court's opinion in *Buckley v. Valeo*.

6

Campaign Consultants and Responsible Party Government

David B. Magleby, Kelly D. Patterson,
and James A. Thurber

The 1950 Report of the American Political Science Association's Committee on Political Parties concluded that "the expanding responsibilities of modern government have brought about so extensive an interlacing of governmental action with the country's economic and social life that the need for coordinated and coherent programs has become paramount" (1950a, 31). However, the Report also noted that both major American political parties were "ill-equipped to organize their members in the legislative and executive branches into a government held together and guided by the party program." Its authors then outlined a broad reform program that they hoped would make parties more "responsible, democratic, and effective" (v, 17).

Cultural changes, legal and institutional reforms, and technological developments have significantly altered the structures and activities of American political parties since 1950. Though scholars debate whether these developments have resulted in party decline or regeneration, most would agree that today's parties differ from those evaluated by the Report. The rise of political campaign consultants has arguably been one of the most significant developments in the party system. Has this development moved parties closer to realizing the goals envisioned in the Report? Here we take a fresh look at the aims of the Report by considering the impact of political consultants on the party system.

First, we briefly evaluate the recommendations in the Report and identify the critical actors in the party system. Next, we describe the rise of political consultants and their relationship to the political parties. Then we review principal-agent theory and use it to evaluate relationships among the various components of the current party system, including political consultants. Finally, we use survey data collected from professional campaign consultants to assess the extent to which their presence changes the predicted relationship between the parties and their candidates and how this relationship may affect the connections between citizens and their representatives deemed crucial to the responsible party model. We conclude that political consultants are very unlikely to help parties become more responsible.

RESPONSIBLE AND EFFECTIVE PARTIES IN GOVERNMENT

The central feature of representative government is a mediating assembly of legislators that stands between the citizenry and decisions on public policy (Brennan and Hamlin 1999). Such an assembly presents a serious challenge to democratic accountability. Since no single legislator can make policy decisions unilaterally, voters cannot reasonably hold any one legislator responsible for overall policy outcomes (Committee on Political Parties 1950a, v). One way to meet this challenge is with responsible party government. Here political parties serve as collective agents of the electorate by designing alternative policy agendas and implementing them, once in power. If successful, the parties can offer voters clear options and accomplishments as guides at election time. Following this logic, elections should be contests between two competing policy programs, not just a choice between two separate candidates. This situation allows voters a workable means of holding representative government accountable. As the Report states, "For the great many of Americans, the most valuable opportunity to influence the course of public affairs is the choice they are able to make between the parties in the principal elections" (15).

A prerequisite for responsible, effective, and democratic parties is that party organizations must have control over resources to develop, advertise, and implement their agendas. Among other things, this means controlling the means of communicating their policy goals to the electorate, emphasizing the contrasts between the parties. If necessary, parties must be able to use campaign resources as an incentive to induce their candidates to stick to the party's agenda. The rise of political consultants raises questions about the ability of parties to meet these criteria.

THE RISE OF CAMPAIGN CONSULTANTS

Although many of the institutions and relationships the Report analyzed in 1950 continue, technological developments and institutional reforms have changed the manner in which campaigns are conducted and the role of parties in these contests. It seems that the very ability of parties to enforce loyalty among their candidates through campaigns has eroded even further in the decades since the report was published. Though there is some debate about the extent of these effects (Patterson 1996), the party system clearly must cope with the increasingly candidate-centered nature of campaigns and the growing prominence of professional political consultants (Wattenberg 1984, 1996; Desart 1995; Polsby 1983; Nie, Verba, and Petrocik 1979; Thurber 1995). American political parties have been unable to perform the campaign tasks needed by candidates in the candidate-centered system, including designing campaign strategy and facilitating fund-raising (Kolodny 1998b). Their failure provided a niche for a new cadre of professionals. Candidates have long had personal staffs, but the last half century has seen an explosion in the number of professionals specializing in campaign tasks. Individual entrepreneurs now perform many of the tasks once undertaken by parties.

Consulting began as a side business of public relations firms who provided advice to individual candidates or to the political parties (Thurber and Nelson 2000; Johnson 1998; Luntz 1988). In 1933, the team of Whitaker and Baker became the first full-time campaign-only consultants. They designed a negative campaign to defeat California gubernatorial candidate Upton Sinclair and participated in several other high-profile campaigns (Johnson 1998; Mitchell 1992). However, it was not until the 1960s that the campaign consulting industry really began to professionalize. During this period, consultants became experts not only in communications and technology but also in resource allocation, or "the art of campaigning" (Nimmo 1970). Today there are more than seven thousand consultants (Johnson 1998, 3). Although they represent a small fraction of the public relations industry, their size and professionalism is growing. In 1992, 63.7 percent of all candidates for the House of Representatives reported hiring at least one consultant. The percentage rose to 76.8 percent in the 1998 races. Incumbent and open-seat candidates are the most likely to hire professional consultants (Medvic and Lenart 1997; Hernnson 2000).

The consulting industry has specialized to the point where professional consultants now provide a wide variety of services: polling, organizing and producing direct mail, managing press relations, developing and purchasing media ads, mobilizing volunteers, and crafting opposition research (for a more detailed breakdown of the consulting industry, see Johnson 2000; Thurber, Nelson, and Dulio 2000b). Congressional campaigns, particularly those of incumbents, prefer to hire pollsters, media consultants, and fund-raisers (Hernnson 2000; Medvic and Lenart 1997). Presidential campaigns normally hire the full range of consultants.

Scholarship on the consulting industry has focused on describing the activities typically carried out by consultants to accomplish their goals (see Thurber 2000 for a summary of this literature). Less attention has been paid to the effects of consultants on the political process. For example, what effect does the campaign consulting industry have on the relationship between candidates, parties, and the electorate? Do consultants promote responsible party government? Scholarship on the subject is limited in scope and narrow in depth. In part this lacuna is a reflection of the general lack of attention given the subject of political consultants by election scholars.

There are two general treatments of the relationship between consultants and political parties in scholarly literature, the "adversarial" and the "allied" views (Kolodny and Logan 1998; Kolodny 1998b). The adversarial view emphasizes the origin of consultants in public relations and advertising rather than in politics. Central to this argument is that consultants value winning elections more than achieving policy outcomes. Political consultants are entrepreneurs, and their goals are to produce results for their clients on election day and to gain a reputation as effective campaigners. Without such a reputation, business quickly dries up. Accordingly, consultants are motivated by economic gain and a desire to build a reputation for achieving success (Kolodny and Logan 1998, 155; Dulio 2001). Individual consultants assess the political climate and recommend policy positions and campaign strategies that increase the probability of an electoral victory, focusing on building short-term rather than long-term coalitions. The case study has generally been the methodological approach chosen to advance this claim (Thurber 2000).

The allied view suggests that consultants provide technical services that are beyond political parties' institutional capacity to deliver (Thurber 1999). As the role of consultants grew under the FECA restrictions, parties had the option of marginalizing the consultants or joining them. Parties then "positioned themselves as brokers between candidates and the private campaign industry" (Kolodny 1998a, 1–2). Parties provide "transactional services" (Herrnson 1988) by matching candidates to consultants while consultants raise funds, shape issues, perform opposition and demographic research, and carry out individualized services for all the party's candidates. This view generally rejects the party decline thesis, concluding instead that "the campaign techniques consultants provide have not destroyed the parties but have strengthened them" (Luntz 1988, 144).

The literature in this area suggests several reasons why parties and consultants both benefit from this symbiotic relationship. First, consultants are to some extent agents of the parties. Prior to each election cycle, to help candidates choose a consultant, the congressional campaign committees prepare a list of those who have previously demonstrated skill and loyalty. Hiring a consultant from this list can be a prerequisite for receiving party funding (Kolodny and Logan 1998, 156). Parties also hire consultants to work between election cycles if they have demonstrated loyalty in previous elections (Thurber, Nelson, and Dulio 2000c; Kolodny 2000; Kolodny and Logan 1998; Johnson 2000). This view suggests that a competitive consultant market makes these two activities vital for consultant firms to remain in business, which subsequently makes them beholden to the parties. Though some scholars make this argument, they also report data that indicate some consultants might also be fairly independent of the parties. Among the general consultant population, 47 percent responded that the parties were not helpful in securing clients; only 36 percent say that the parties were very helpful in recruiting clients (Kolodny and Logan 1998, 157). The data do not indicate if there are differences between large, established firms and new firms, each of which has different risk assumptions and hence may have different relationships with the parties.

This argument also raises the question of how consultants balance their responsibilities to the party with their responsibilities to the candidate. The key to continued party employment clearly is success in getting candidates elected. Indeed, both the consultants and the parties share the goal of wanting their candidate to win office. However, consultants face the dilemma of wanting to adjust the party message for short-term success while minimizing such tinkering for long-term party employment. Solutions to this dilemma would be for the consultant either to water down the message in order to focus on voter mobilization strategies or to develop negative campaigns.

A second theory advanced by the allied view involves the socialization of consultants. Recent research reports that over 50 percent of consultants have worked for political parties in some capacity (Thurber 1999; Kolodny 2000). This explanation does not ignore the adversarial view's observation that political consultants originated as a subfield of public relations. It does, however, argue that the initial experiences of the consultants shape their conduct and attitudes toward the political parties. Seeking party employment presupposes similar ideologies and goals. Working with party officials and local organizations reinforces their worldview and makes them personalize party programs. Further, consultants learn the tools of the trade through these initial experiences, which might limit their propensity to undermine party goals directly (Thurber 1999).

If this socialization theory explains the positive relationships between parties and consultants, then consultants who previously worked for the parties should use different campaign techniques and have different views from those with no previous party experience. Consultants with party experience are significantly more likely to coordinate their campaign strategy with party organizations. Interestingly, this shift in consultants' backgrounds coincides with a possible resurgence of political parties (DeSart 1995; Herrnson 1986). However, the research in this area still needs to assess whether these consultants have different views of parties or prefer to use techniques different from those who had never worked for parties. This theory also needs to explain how almost half the consultants with no previous party employment would relate to the parties. Further, any socialization thesis would have to explain why consultants choose to leave party service. If this explanation for the movement of individuals from party employment to professional consulting states that they "craved more freedom" or "sought more significant monetary rewards," then the limits on the extent to which consultants would seek to achieve party goals need to be acknowledged.

THEORIZING ABOUT PARTIES AND CONSULTANTS

This discussion of the impact of consultants on the parties assumes that an ideal party system exists that can be either undermined or strengthened. The very terms "adversarial" and "allied" assume a standard of democracy against which the work of consultants can be measured. For our purposes, the Report provides a framework for such an evaluation, offering a definition of democracy that delineates appropriate relationships among parties, candidates, and voters. Armed with this standard, we can assess the way in which consultants may or may not affect these relationships and thus the ideal of responsible party government. Clearly, individual theorists can and do differ about the desirability of responsibility in the system. However, some normative standard is needed to conduct a debate productively over the extent to which the presence of consultants may affect responsible party government (Patterson 1996; Pomper 1992; Geer 1998).

We believe that looking at the vast amounts of anecdotal, descriptive, and survey research in the field through the lens of principal-agent theory provides a good method for understanding the interactions between consultants and the more familiar political actors described in the responsible party model. Principal-agent theory models how a system of incentives and restraints in a hierarchical relationship determines outcomes by looking at these interactions in terms of a contract. Agency problems involve at least two players: a principal, who holds authority to take certain actions, and an agent, to whom the principal delegates authority. The principal enters into a contract with an agent with the expectation that the agent will work for the principal's benefit. By delegating responsibilities, the principal can overcome inefficiency as long as tasks are assigned to the agent with a comparative advantage in performing them (Kiewiet and McCubbins 1991).

Principal-agent theory's central assumptions are that individuals are rationally self-interested and that information is a commodity (for a general discussion of this literature and its assumptions, see Moe 1984; Bohren 1998; Eisenhardt 1989). Individuals in this paradigm have no moral aversion to misrepresenting their abilities or activities unless they are compelled to do otherwise. Once the principal hires an agent, he cannot completely monitor the agent's activities or perfectly measure their effect without investing in information systems. This contractual relation is potentially troublesome for several reasons. First, only the agent has complete knowledge about his skills and work ethic. Second, only the agent has complete information about the outcomes of his labor. Third, and most important, the principal and the agent each have different goals and attitudes toward risk. These forces may encourage agents to use the powers granted them to pursue interests that are not those of the principal.

Let us examine this third reason, that the principal and agent have different goals, more closely. In a business relationship the principal desires the long-term outcome at a minimal cost, but the agent desires the maximum remuneration for the minimum effort (Bohren 1998). This difference is not universal; similar backgrounds, self-selection, and the anticipation of a future relationship can reduce the variance between the two parties' goals. Similarly, if a competitive market or other economic circumstances make the agent risk averse, he is less likely to shirk his responsibilities and more likely to invest in building trust and a long-term relationship.

In this situation, the agent "is induced to pursue the principal's objectives only to the extent that the incentive structure imposed in their contract renders such behavior advantageous" (Moe 1984, 756). The principal's challenge, in this scenario, is to design a contract that will best induce positive behavior in his agent (Eisenhardt 1989). If the principal and agent have similar goals, their contract will emphasize the tasks that the agent will pursue to accomplish these goals. In this contractual relationship, the principal assumes that the agent will faithfully do these tasks and that he will focus his efforts on fulfilling the principal's goals. Principals also use this kind of contract when they are willing and able to monitor the agent's activities. When the two parties' goals are different, the principal will try to bring the agent in line with his goals by offering him a stake in their outcome. These outcome-based contracts are more expensive for the principal, but they are required to prevent the agent from shirking.[1]

Principal-agent theory has been widely applied in explaining economic interactions. Political scientists have also recently recognized its value in explaining interactions within hierarchical relationships. Although political scientists most commonly apply the theory to explain the relationship between elected officials and the bureaucracy (Moe 1984), it also helps to explain how the Supreme Court affects appellate court decisions (Songer, Segal, and Cameron 1994), the behavior of congressional committees (Maltzman 1995), and party leadership (Rhode and Shepsle 1987; Vega and Peters 1996; Sinclair 1999). Michelle Taylor uses principal-agent theory to show how political parties in Costa Rica use incentives to control legislators (1992).

We argue that the key relationships in the responsible party model are of a principal-agent variety and that the Report's description of the ideal party unknowingly applies the theory's contract logic to make parties more effective, democratic, and responsible. For example, the responsible party model implies that parties are agents of the voters at large, and further, that candidates are the agents of parties (Fig. 6.1). However, it is also the case that candidates are agents of the voters who are their constituents. The authors of the Report recognized the potential for goal conflicts among these various principals and the agents. Legislators have reelection and other personal benefits as their goal; they legislate in order to advance these goals (Sinclair 1999, 423). Constituents desire effective policies from Congress, but they also desire services from their local representatives and party officials. Parties want to be in power so that they can implement their policy agenda, and their need to service a national constitu-

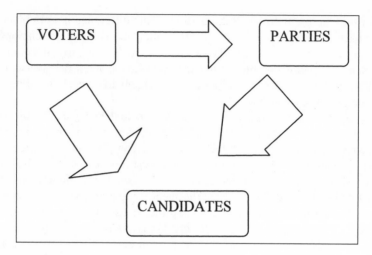

Figure 6.1. Possible principal-agent relations in the responsible party model

ency also forces them to rely on policymaking rather than on pork barreling. However, candidates desiring reelection will focus on constituent service instead of on policymaking (Mayhew 1974). They will also reject the responsible party's issue-based campaign for either personality-based or negative campaigns if doing so would increase their chances of reelection. All these conflicting goals help create the deficiencies in the American two-party system cited by the Committee on Political Parties.

The responsible party model explains how parties can enter into contractual arrangements to prevent its agents from shirking. Parties, in this model, should provide electoral services (money, polling, advertising, endorsements) to those candidates who work to implement their policies and promote their messages and can deny these benefits or even work against (by not renominating) those officials who do not. If the parties have a monopoly on the resources candidates need to get elected, candidates will not risk losing party favor. This contractual relationship will prevent shirking as long as parties have information on legislator and candidate activities (which they get by running the campaigns) and if the agents are risk averse (dependent on parties for the services needed to be reelected).

Parties do not have this ability in a candidate-centered system. Professional consultants add another dimension to the relationships between candidates and parties, making it even more difficult for the principals (parties) to enforce contracts with their agents (candidates) because consultants provide the services that parties used to—and perhaps should—control (Fig. 6.2). The potential exists for consultants to help candidates pursue goals different from those of the party

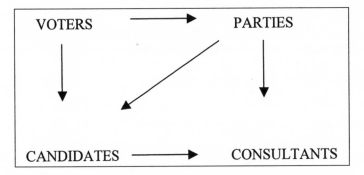

Figure 6.2. Possible principal-agent relations in the candidate-centered model

(Thurber, Nelson, and Dulio 2000b).[2] Such a difficulty evaporates if consultants share party goals, a position suggested by the allied view of consultants, especially the socialization theory. Yet the matching of party and consultant goals does not seem tenable if we assume that consultants are exclusively agents of the candidates.

We have outlined how several forces undermined the ability of parties to hold a monopoly over election services. This inability potentially changes the party's capacity to contract with the consultants because the consultants need not be as risk averse. However, the literature on consultants recognizes that they have relationships with both candidates and the parties. In this case the consultants are agents to multiple principals (Fig. 6.2). How do consultants respond to these multiple principals? To answer this question, we first must determine what motivates consultants: partisanship? money? influence? Or is it something else? And, what attitude do consultants have toward risk? Do they perceive party employment or earning notoriety for winning campaigns as being more important to gain employment? For example, principal-agent theory hypothesizes that if consultants are risk averse and reliant on parties for further employment, then they are less likely to shirk and more likely to invest in building trust (Eisenhardt 1989; Bohren 1988). Further, what type of relationship, if any, do consultants have with parties: does the party hire them for results, or does it direct them to perform specific activities? In asking these questions, we revisit several arguments made in the adversarial-allied debate. Although previous theories have hinted at what motivates consultants and how parties exercise control over them, we think that the principal-agent framework allows us systematically to investigate these theories' claims.

To evaluate the effect of consultants on the responsible party model, we must also examine how consultants affect the activities of candidates. If consultants really do substitute for political parties, do they change the type of message the candidates present, or do they at least see the need to coordinate messages with the party? Do they cause candidates, either through tacit encouragement or by providing them independence from the party, to abandon or neglect the party agenda once in office? Have they enhanced or decreased the role of interest groups in deciding campaigns?

CONSULTANTS' MOTIVATIONS AND GOALS

The framework provided by principal-agent theory points toward the motivations of political consultants and the possible differences in goals that may exist between the parties and the consultants. Consultants begin these particular careers for a variety of reasons; some of these goals coincide with those of a political party, but others do not. The most overwhelming reason consultants cite for entering the business of political consulting is their "political beliefs or ideology" (Table 6.1). A significant majority of consultants carried strong beliefs and ideologies that they wanted to see instituted by working for particular campaigns. No more than 20 percent of those consultants polled cite any other reason as their main motivation. Most interesting for the realization of a responsible party model is the 7 percent who claimed that they wished to help their party to become the majority party in government. The "thrill of competition" and "money" were cited more often than the party motivation.

Table 6.1. Main Motivations for Becoming and Being a Professional Consultant

	BECOMING		BEING	
	N	%	N	%
Your political beliefs or ideology	264	52.3	212	42.0
The thrill of the competition	92	18.2	80	15.8
The money you could earn	55	10.9	123	24.4
To help your party be the majority in government	37	7.3	38	7.5
The political power and influence that personally comes with the job	22	4.4	21	4.2
Other	35	6.9	31	6.1
Total Respondents	505		505	

Source: James A. Thurber, *National Survey of Professional Campaign Consultants: Who Are They and What Do They Believe?* Washington, D.C.: Center for Congressional and Presidential Studies, 1999.

Study Methodology: Yankelovich partners conducted 505 half-hour interviews of professional campaign consultants between April 5 and May 14, 1999. Respondents either were currently working as a political campaign consultant or had done so in the past year. Those who worked exclusively in media production or for a telephone bank were excluded. The study was conducted under a grant provided by the Pew Charitable Trusts. The margin of error for the total sample is +/- 4.4 percent.

Consultants can pursue their careers for reasons different from those they held when they began them. Although the motivations for becoming a political consultant may be compatible with goals of the party, reasons for remaining a consultant may not. When asked what their main motivation is for currently being a professional consultant, a significant plurality still mentioned their political beliefs or ideology (Table 6.1). However, money becomes more important as a motivation for continuing as a consultant than it was for beginning as a consultant. Almost one-quarter cite the money they could earn as their reason. The other motivations show little or no change. The goal of making a particular party a majority does not provide the motivation to most political consultants currently working in the field. These initial observations about motivations are important in the application of the principal-agent theory. Consultants clearly have goals different from those of the party.

This leads us to whether or not their experience with a party may change their motivations. If individuals have spent time working with the party, they may be better disposed to helping parties achieve particular goals (Kolodny 2000). Many consultants have experience with political parties, with almost 45 percent reporting having worked for a national, state, or local political party or party committee. However, there are only slight differences in the motivations for becoming a political consultant between those who have worked for the party and those who have not: neither group of individuals is much more likely to cite a desire to help the party become a majority as a reason for becoming a political consultant (Table 6.2). A majority of those who have worked and those who have not worked for a party both state that they became political consultants to pursue their beliefs and ideology.

When consultants are asked why they currently pursue their career, a slightly different story surfaces. Once again, there is only a small difference between those who worked for the party and those who did not work for the party, when the motivation is helping their party to become a majority (Table 6.3). Individuals who once worked for the party are only slightly more likely to cite achieving majority status as a motivation; they are more motivated by their political beliefs and ideology. Furthermore, individuals who did not work for the party are more inclined to list the thrill of competition as a reason for being a consultant. This second finding perpetuates the popular image of political consultants as hired guns, but such motivations are more likely to be cited by individuals who did not work for the party.

These data do not present a very clear picture, however. Although a desire to achieve majority status does not motivate consultants, beliefs and ideology do. Consultants do not practice their trade to help parties attain the holy grail: majority status.[3] Such a finding means that consultants and parties differ substantially over interests, a difference that creates friction in the principal-agent relationship. Yet both beliefs and ideology motivate consultants, and the prominence of these motivations can and does serve the interest of the party. Con-

Table 6.2. Main Motivations for Becoming Professional Consultants by Whether or Not They Ever Worked for a Political Party

	WORKED FOR A POLITICAL PARTY		DID NOT WORK FOR A POLITICAL PARTY		DK/NA		TOTAL	
	No.	(%)	No.	(%)	No.	(%)	No.	(%)
Your political beliefs or ideology	124	(54.9)	140	(50.5)			264	(52.3)
The thrill of the competition	43	(19.0)	48	(17.3)	1	(50)	92	(18.2)
The money you could earn	15	(6.6)	40	(14.4)			55	(10.9)
To help your party become majority	20	(8.8)	17	(6.1)			37	(7.3)
Political power and Influence	10	(4.4)	12	(4.3)			22	(4.4)
Other	8	(3.5)	14	(5.1)	1	(50)	23	(4.6)
DK/refused	6	(2.7)	6	(2.2)			12	(2.4)
Total	226	(100)	277	(100)	2	(100)	505	(100)

Source: James A. Thurber, *National Survey of Professional Campaign Consultants: Who Are They and What Do They Believe?* Washington, D.C.: Center for Congressional and Presidential Studies, 1999.

Pearson chi-square = 9.474 (signF = .092). DK/refused and DK/NA removed to compute chi-square.

Table 6.3. Main Motivations for Being Professional Consultants by Whether or Not They Ever Worked for a Political Party

	WORKED FOR A POLITICAL PARTY		DID NOT WORK FOR A POLITICAL PARTY		DK/NA		TOTAL	
	No.	(%)	No.	(%)	No.	(%)	No.	(%)
Your political beliefs or ideology	105	(46.5)	107	(38.6)			212	(42.0)
The thrill of the competition	26	(11.5)	53	(19.1)	1	(50)	80	(15.8)
The money you could earn	54	(23.9)	68	(24.5)	1	(50)	123	(24.4)
To help your party become majority	21	(9.3)	17	(6.1)			38	(7.5)
Power and influence	8	(3.5)	16	(5.81)			24	(4.8)
DK/refused	3	(1.3)	4	(1.4)			7	(1.4)
Total	226	(100)	277	(100)	2	(100)	505	(100)

Source: James A. Thurber, National Survey of Professional Campaign Consultants: Who Are They and What Do They Believe? Washington, D.C.: Center for Congressional and Presidential Studies, 1999.

Pearson chi-square = 9.425 (signF = .093). DK/refused and DK/NA removed to compute chi-square.

sultants tend to work for either one party or the other. Almost 40 percent of those polled report their firms worked only for Democrats, and almost 30 percent said their firms worked only for Republicans. Almost 30 percent said their firms worked for both parties, but here some firms have consultants who work exclusively for both parties, so the question probably understates the extent to which consultants align themselves with one of the two parties. This affiliation with one of the two parties does suggest that consultants probably view parties as vehicles for helping them to elect candidates who share their beliefs and ideology. To the extent that parties and consultants share roughly similar beliefs and ideology, then some integration of goals and methods does become possible.

A complication arises when parties and candidates have essentially different messages or when a candidate believes that a message different from that of the party is necessary for victory. Responsible parties must communicate a clear message to voters, one containing enough policy content for voters to make distinctions between them. Candidates should adhere to this message so that voters can hold candidates and the parties accountable for the achievement of the goals. Consultants believe that they are much better suited to perform all the activities pertaining to message development than are the parties. Thus, a conflict arises between the parties' need to communicate a coherent partywide message to voters and the consultants' belief that they need the freedom to pursue a strategy that maximizes the candidate's chances to secure victory, even if this strategy downplays or contradicts the party message.

The possible conflict between the parties and the consultants surfaces when consultants reveal the extent to which they believe they provide services that parties are incapable of providing. Fifty-five percent of consultants strongly agree and another 34 percent somewhat agree with the statement that they provide services that parties cannot (Table 6.4). Only a total of 10 percent somewhat disagree or strongly disagree. Interestingly, there is little or no difference

Table 6.4. Percentage of Political Consultants Who Agree Consultants Provide Services Political Parties Cannot

	No.	(%)
Strongly agree	279	(55.2)
Somewhat agree	170	(33.7)
Somewhat disagree	36	(7.1)
Strongly disagree	15	(3.0)
DK/refused	5	(1.0)
Total	505	(100)

Source: James A. Thurber, *National Survey of Professional Campaign Consultants: Who Are They and What Do They Believe?* Washington, D.C.: Center for Congressional and Presidential Studies, 1999.

between those who have worked for the party and those who have not. Both groups of individuals overwhelmingly agree that they provide services that parties are incapable of providing (Table 6.5).

The bulk of the services consultants believe the parties cannot provide relates to message development and dissemination. A significant majority of consultants strongly agree or somewhat agree with the statement that they replace political parties when it comes to providing management or strategic advice and when dealing with the media or campaign advertising (Table 6.6). In both cases over 85 percent of the consultants agree that they replace the political parties. More than 80 percent believe they replace parties with regard to polling and direct mail. Therefore, in all those areas where a particular institution crafts and disseminates messages to voters, an overwhelming majority of the consultants believe they have replaced the political parties.[4]

Just because consultants believe that parties are incapable of providing particular services does not mean that they do not see the parties as helpful. When the consultants were asked to rate how helpful the parties could be, a majority of them said that all the services they provided, except management or strategy advice, were very or somewhat helpful (Table 6.7). Once again, however, they differentiated among the various services. Consultants were more likely to say that parties were more helpful in areas not traditionally associated with the creation and dissemination of messages, such as campaign fund-raising, opposition research, and polling. Only 56 percent said the parties were very helpful or somewhat helpful with their coordinated advertisements. Surprisingly, get-out-the-vote operations were rated behind polling but just ahead of direct mailings.

Consultants' low opinion of the helpfulness of some party-provided services does not bode well for the future of political parties. Most political consultants believe the role of political parties at the national, state, and local levels has decreased very much or somewhat (Table 6.8). Concurrently, political consultants agree overwhelmingly that their role at the national, state, and local levels has increased very much or somewhat. The data suggest that consultants think that some of the activities performed by the parties are helpful but that the consultants themselves perform most of the important activities. They also do not believe that the role of parties has increased. Consultants clearly perceive a void in the services needed to conduct a campaign, a void that they see themselves as filling.

How do we interpret these data in light of the principal-agent theory? First, the findings suggest that consultants do not share similar goals with the party. A party is motivated by a desire to maximize the number of individuals who hold office—a necessary condition to control the policy apparatus—but consultants appear to be motivated by individual beliefs and ideology. The parties and consultants may share similar beliefs and ideology, but in the cases where there is divergence, the consultants have reasons to push for the election of the individual candidate. Second, the responsible party model envisions a contract

Table 6.5. Percentage of Political Consultants Who Agree Consultants Provide Services that Political Parties Cannot, by Whether or Not They Ever Worked for a Political Party

	WORKED FOR A POLITICAL PARTY		DID NOT WORK FOR A POLITICAL PARTY		DK/NA		TOTAL	
	No.	(%)	No.	(%)	No.	(%)	No.	(%)
Strongly agree	128	(56.6)	151	(54.5)	1		279	(55.2)
Somewhat agree	70	(31.0)	99	(35.7)	1	(50)	170	(33.7)
Somewhat disagree	17	(7.5)	18	(35.7)		(50)	36	(7.1)
Strongly disagree	9	(4.0)	6	(2.2)			15	(3.0)
DK/refused	2	(.9)	3	(1.1)			5	(1.0)
Total	226	(100)	277	(100)	2	(100)	505	(100)

Source: James A. Thurber, *National Survey of Professional Campaign Consultants: Who Are They and What Do They Believe?* Washington, D.C.: Center for Congressional and Presidential Studies, 1999.

Pearson chi-square = 2.506 (signF = .474). DK/refused and DK/NA removed to compute chi-square.

Table 6.6. Percentage of Political Consultants Who Strongly Agree or Somewhat Agree Consultants Replace Parties in Certain Services

	Frequency	(%)
Management or strategic advice	443	(87.7)
Media or campaign advertising	431	(85.3)
Polling	426	(84.4)
Direct mail	412	(81.6)
Opposition research	373	(73.9)
Campaign finance or fund-raising	352	(69.7)
Get-out-the-vote or field operations	278	(55)
Total respondents	505	

Source: James A. Thurber, *National Survey of Professional Campaign Consultants: Who Are They and What Do They Believe?* Washington, D.C.: Center for Congressional and Presidential Studies, 1999.

Table 6.7. Percentage of Political Consultants Who Say Services of Parties in Certain Areas Are Either Very Helpful or Somewhat Helpful

	Frequency	(%)
Campaign funds	355	(86.6)
Opposition research	324	(79.0)
Polling	294	(71.7)
Get-out-the-vote operations	296	(65.6)
Direct mailings	258	(62.9)
Coordinated advertisements	233	(56.8)
Management or strategy advice	152	(37.1)
Total respondents	410	

Source: James A. Thurber, *National Survey of Professional Campaign Consultants: Who Are They and What Do They Believe?* Washington, D.C.: Center for Congressional and Presidential Studies, 1999.

Table 6.8. Percentage of Political Consultants Who Say the Role of Political Parties or the Role of Consultants Has Increased Very Much or Somewhat

	POLITICAL PARTIES		CONSULTANTS	
	No.	(%)	No.	(%)
At the national level	157	(31.1)	402	(79.6)
At the state level	148	(29.3)	444	(87.9)
At the local level	100	(19.8)	436	(86.3)
Total respondents	505		505	

Source: James A. Thurber, *National Survey of Professional Campaign Consultants: Who Are They and What Do They Believe?* Washington, D.C.: Center for Congressional and Presidential Studies, 1999.

between voters and parties when it comes to message development and unity, but in the current candidate-centered system, the real relationship is between candidates and voters. Consultants control the functions where they and the candidates have the greatest incentive to shirk for the party: campaign strategy and message articulation. Little exists to bind the consultants who advise the candidates to the parties' message. Indeed, consultants work for the candidates, and the contract is really between those two entities. Hence, consultants who are referred by parties still have incentive to shirk. Ultimately, the consultant will be evaluated by the final result of the individual campaign.

Principal-agent theory can help to explain how consultants welcome co-operation with the parties in some facets of the campaign but not in others. Because consultants want to secure employment from the parties yet also want to be successful in campaigns, they welcome party help positively in such activities as mobilizing voters but discourage or resent party intrusion in such activities as message development and advertising.

Consultants attach importance to message development and dissemination in both candidate and initiative campaigns. Consultants who work in the latter cite the freedom to develop and advertise campaign themes in these efforts (Magleby and Patterson 1998). They compare and contrast the autonomy in initiative campaigns with the constraints they believe they face in candidate campaigns. Generally, consultants clearly perceive themselves as profession-als who should be allowed to apply their craft with few constraints in order to achieve their goal: victory for a particular candidate or an initiative. Party goals may receive some consideration, but they do not provide motivation for what the consultants do. Ultimately, the motivation to pursue party goals wanes in the face of the overwhelming need to secure victory for the individual candi-date. In the wake of these conflicting goals and motivations, it is very unlikely that consultants will help parties become more responsible.

CONCLUSION

Our actual claims for the argument in this chapter are relatively modest. There are compelling reasons to conclude that the type of integration envisioned by the responsible party model is not possible in a candidate-centered environment where consultants play an increasingly important role. This conclusion is not novel; party scholars have argued this point for three decades. Yet significantly, little evidence exists to conclude that the presence of political consultants fur-thers the aims of the responsible party model, as some theories seem to indi-cate. In the responsible party model, contracts between the voters and the parties assume primary importance. In today's campaign environment, contracts be-tween the consultants and the candidates become the focus of attention. Party goals of issue coordination and pursuit of majorities can and do receive some attention, but in the immediate pursuit to gain electoral success, the party is in no position to achieve such outcome-based contracts.

This conclusion need not be an indictment of political consultants and their growing presence in the campaign environment. Whether or not the rise of political consultants enhances democracy depends heavily on the assumptions made about democracy and its relationship to the party system (Dulio and Thurber 2000). Particular versions of democracy are actually possible without significant portions of the responsible party component. The current version of American democracy stresses a particular brand of responsiveness over the collective responsibility and accountability built into the responsibility party model (Pomper 1992). Consultants perform a variety of tasks that help the American party system to meet the norms of responsiveness and flexibility contained in other characterizations of democracy.

ACKNOWLEDGMENTS

The authors are grateful to the Pew Charitable Trust for their very generous grant that made this research possible. The Department of Political Science and the College of Family, Home, and Social Sciences at Brigham Young University also provided funds to support this research. We would like to thank Matthew Singer and Robert Floyd for their able research assistance on this project.

NOTES

1. The term "shirk" carries multiple meanings in the principal-agent literature. First, it implies an obligation that is being evaded. Second, it could mean the aversion of an obligation to deliberate. Third, it describes attempts by the agent to conceal his evasion of his responsibilities.

2. This dilemma is not entirely new. State and local party operatives often provided support and resources to candidates independent of the national party in order to focus the candidate on local priorities. One could argue that consultants have only stepped into the role of local party organizations and continued to frustrate the ability of national parties to coordinate their candidates. However, we assert that the difference in goals between parties and consultants is greater than the difference between national and local parties and that national parties are better able to monitor local parties than they are able to monitor and control consultants.

3. Although the responsible party model emphasizes the policymaking role of party organizations, majority status is a prerequisite to instituting policy. In the responsible party model, parties develop policy agendas as part of the dynamic of competition for control of the legislature. Policy agendas serve the purpose of differentiating one's self from one's competition and as a standard for evaluation and for mobilizing support.

4. See Dulio (2001) for a fuller discussion of how consultants perceive they have replaced parties and how they have impacted the political system.

7

The Dream Fulfilled?

Party Development in Congress, 1950–2000

Barbara Sinclair

In the 1950 Report of the American Political Science Association's Committee on Political Parties, "Toward a More Responsible Two-Party System," a group of eminent political scientists called for parties that "are able to bring forth programs to which they commit themselves and . . . that possess sufficient internal cohesion to carry out these programs" (Committee on Political Parties 1950a, 1). When they decried the state of affairs in which "either major party, when in power, is ill-equipped to organize its members in the legislative and executive branches into a government held together and guided by the party program" (v), the authors were certainly thinking of the congressional parties. Their recommendations for change make clear what specifically they saw as the primary problems internal to Congress. Arguing that "action within Congress can be of decisive significance" (7), they advocated strengthening the party organization in Congress, making committee leaders, then chosen solely on the basis of seniority, accountable to their party, and vesting control of legislative scheduling in the majority party. Nevertheless, E. E. Schattschneider and his colleagues on the committee were quite aware that "a higher degree of party responsibility cannot be provided merely by actions taken within Congress," for "the basis of party operations in Congress is laid in the electoral process" (7, 56).

By the beginning of the twenty-first century, congressional parties have changed enormously, compared to their counterparts at midcentury: they are more elaborately organized; their memberships are more cohesive; their leaders are stronger, especially in the House, and committee leaders are more accountable to their party colleagues; and the parties are more engaged in policy- and program-related endeavors, including efforts to set the agenda and to shape debate on the national stage. Has the dream of the Report's authors been fulfilled?

In this chapter, I trace the development of the congressional parties over the last half century. I then assess whether the changes in the congressional parties have contributed to producing the sort of democratic, responsible, and effective party system the Report advocated. I conclude—and believe the Report's authors would also—that the contemporary congressional parties are significant improvements over the parties of the 1950s. The current system is more transparent and certainly gives the public clearer choices than that of fifty years ago. Yet there is mounting evidence that the basic structure of the U.S. government prevents the full development of responsible and effective parties.

CONGRESSIONAL PARTIES IN THE 1950S

U.S. parties, it can be argued, had their origins in Congress (Aldrich 1995). Certainly since early in their history, the House of Representatives and the Senate have relied on parties and committees to provide the structure that enables them to get their work done. Parties organize the chambers and provide coordination; committees do most of the substantive work on legislation. The strength of the congressional parties and the extent to which they play a significant policy role, however, has varied over time. The strength of the congressional party, most scholars believe, is largely but not exclusively a function of the homogeneity of the party members' constituencies (Cooper and Brady 1981). Similar constituencies, it is argued, translate into similar legislative preferences among members.

At the time the Report was written, the Democratic Party, which was clearly the majority party in the country, was split along regional lines into a mostly conservative southern wing and a more liberal northern wing. Its presidential candidates were drawn from the North, and its congressional ranks were dominated by southern conservatives.

In the House of Representatives, majoritarian rules and the combining within the speakership of the positions of top party leader and presiding officer provide the potential for strong party leadership. However, in the aftermath of the revolt against Speaker Joseph Cannon earlier in the century, which was itself the product of a split within the then-dominant Republican Party, the speakership had been weakened. The Speaker was stripped of his powers to make committee assignments, to choose committee chairs, and to chair and control the Rules Committee. Seniority came to be the sole criterion for the designation of committee chairs, which automatically went to the majority party member with the most seniority on the committee. As a result, committee chairs were no longer dependent on their party for their positions and became independently powerful.

In the 1950s, conservative southern Democrats disproportionately held committee chairs. Coming from the one-party South, they could more easily amass the necessary seniority than could their northern colleagues. Lacking any mechanism for holding the committees and their chairs responsible to the party, party leaders coordinated and cajoled but played little policy role. The Rules Committee, which determines the flow of legislation to the floor, was also independent and in the hands of a bipartisan conservative coalition, so majority party leaders did not even have firm control over legislative floor scheduling.

The House parties were not elaborately organized, and Speaker Sam Rayburn made little use of what organization there was. The Democratic caucus met only at the beginning of each Congress, largely to ratify decisions made elsewhere. Rayburn did not want to provide a forum for the warring party factions to confront each other. He seldom used the whip system, which consisted of about eighteen regionally chosen whips, not all of whom could be counted on to support the leadership's or the party majority's position.

The Senate parties were even less elaborately organized, and the majority leader lacked even the powers that derive from being the chamber's presiding officer. The party caucuses had long existed as organizations, but the formally elected position of party leader dated only from the early twentieth century (Gamm and Smith 1999). As in the House, committee chairs were selected on the basis of seniority alone and were independently powerful. Committee chairs and other committee positions of influence were held disproportionately by conservative southern Democrats. With two successive Democratic leaders defeated at the polls, the position of party leader had sunk in prestige when a junior Lyndon Johnson assumed it. He was far more vigorous and influential than his predecessors (or his immediate successor), but he acted primarily as a broker and not as a policy leader. Like Rayburn, he avoided calling meetings of the Democratic caucus, and he largely deferred to the committee chairs.

In neither chamber did the majority party membership as an entity nor its leadership involve themselves in agenda-setting or in policy formulation. The committees performed these functions, largely independently of internal party direction. The president often set the agenda and attempted to shape legislation. But even if he was of the same party as the chamber majority, the committees were not bound to be responsive to his wishes.

FORCES FOR AND ROUTES OF CHANGE

Throughout the 1950s, liberal Democrats in both houses were discontented with this state of affairs (Bolling 1965). Liberals complained that no attempt was ever made to ascertain whether a party position could be reached on policy and that policymaking was left solely to the committees. They contended that senior committee leaders and the memberships of the most important committees were unrepresentatively conservative. They objected that even when liberal legislation was reported from a substantive committee in the House, it was likely to be blocked or watered down by the very conservative Rules Committee. Liberals, many of whom were junior, were also unhappy with the limited opportunities to participate meaningfully in the legislative process afforded to junior members. A lack of sufficient staff and a maldistribution of desirable committee positions were sources of discontent in both chambers. In the House, liberals also complained about autocratic committee chairs; in the Senate they chafed under Senate "folkways," which restricted their full participation (Matthews 1960; Foley 1980; Huitt 1961).

Until 1959, liberal Democrats lacked the numbers to do much more than complain. The 1958 elections, however, brought in significant reinforcements, with most of the new members being liberals from competitive northern states and districts. In the House, these new members swelled the ranks of the recently formed reform organization, the Democratic Study Group (DSG). In the Senate, the sheer size of the freshman class swept away the apprenticeship norm dictating limited participation by junior members; these senators from competitive states, many of whom had defeated incumbents, could not afford to wait to make their mark (Rohde, Ornstein, and Peabody 1985). In terms of policy outputs, however, the Eighty-sixth Congress (1959–1960) was a bitter disappointment to liberals. Despite the liberals' augmented numbers, the conservatives still managed to stymie the enactment of most of the legislation the liberals advocated (Sundquist 1968; Sinclair 1982).

The 1960 election of John Kennedy as president presented Democrats with a crisis. Given the distribution of influence in the House of Representatives, Democrats might well be incapable of even bringing much of the new president's program to the floor for a vote; it might be blocked by the Rules Committee in a chamber supposedly controlled by his own party. The DSG and the administration persuaded Rayburn that something had to be done. After a tough fight, the House agreed—by a 217 to 212 vote—to increase the size of the Rules Committee, enabling the majority party to add several usually loyal Democrats to the committee.

The regional and ideological split continued to create problems for Democrats at the national level, thwarting enactment of much of Kennedy's program during his three years in office. Lyndon Johnson's masterful use of public sentiment in the aftermath of the Kennedy assassination, then the huge Democratic majorities in the Eighty-ninth Congress (1965–1966), and the mandate these majorities conveyed, resulted in a burst of nonincremental policy change. Most of the liberal agenda developed during the late 1940s and the 1950s was enacted and much else besides. Yet even during the height of the Great Society, congressional Democrats often split along regional lines. After the 1966 elections reduced the size of the Democratic congressional majorities, the intraparty divisions again severely hindered policymaking.

Initial Changes in the Senate

The Senate, unlike the House, where no significant internal reforms were instituted during the 1960s, was beginning to change. Because a two-thirds vote is
needed to change Senate rules (that is, to cut off debate and bring a proposed
rules change to a vote), altering Senate rules is considerably harder than changing House rules, where only a simple majority is required. During the 1950s
and 1960s, Senate liberals made frequent attempts to change Rule 22, the cloture
rule, but always failed—stymied by the very rule they were trying to alter. Yet,
in the Senate, major change can occur without altering the rules. Senate rules
concerning floor debate and amendments are highly permissive, and the Senate
depended on informal norms to restrain its members from exploiting their prerogatives fully.

When a transformation in the political environment altered the costs and
benefits to senators of abiding by the norms, they changed their behavior and
thereby how their chamber operated. New issues, an enormous growth in the
number of interest groups active in Washington, and the greater role of the media
in politics resulted in senators being highly sought after as champions of groups'
causes and made the role of outward-looking policy entrepreneur available to
more senators. Successfully playing that role brought a senator a Washington
reputation as a player, media attention, and possibly even a shot at the presidency. Thus, an activist style based on a full exploitation of senatorial prerogatives became attractive to more and more senators (Sinclair 1989). To enable
themselves to take full advantage of these opportunities, senators expanded the
number of positions on good committees, the number of subcommittee leadership positions, and distributed both much more broadly. They increased staff
numbers and made more staff available to junior as well as to senior senators.

Senators were thereby able to involve themselves in a much broader range
of issues—and they did so. They became much more active on the Senate floor,
offering more amendments and to a wider range of bills. They exploited extended debate to a much greater extent, and the frequency of filibusters shot up
(Sinclair 1989, 2000b; Binder and Smith 1997). The media became an increasingly important arena for participation and a significant resource for senators
in the pursuit of their policy, power, and reelection goals.

Thus, in response to the new political environment, the Senate transformed
itself from an inward-looking, committee- and seniority-dominated institution,
in which influence and resources were quite unequally distributed, to an individualist, outward-looking institution with a much more equal distribution
of resources. In neither the old nor the new Senate did party play a major
role. Policy concerns had motivated liberal reformers but did not lead them to
strengthening party organs or the powers of the party leadership.

Eventually, the Senate and its parties did institute some reforms that
required rule changes. In 1975, it changed the cloture rule to reduce the vote

required to cut off debate from two-thirds of those present and voting to three-fifths of the total membership (usually sixty). The Senate parties made committee leaders more responsive to their party memberships by requiring member approval votes, not just seniority. However, senators did not give their party leaders significant new powers. Empowering their leaders to control the flow of legislation to and on the floor the way House majority party leaders do would mean significantly limiting their own prerogatives, and that senators have not been willing to do.

Initial Changes in the House

In the House the story was different, though at first it seemed that the result would not be. Like their Senate counterparts, House reformers were motivated by both policy and participation goals. Unlike in the Senate, rules changes were necessary in the House, but because they required only a majority vote, they were also considerably easier to bring about. Indeed, many of the issues reformers wanted to address were controlled by party rules and customs rather than by chamber rules and customs. Since the reformers made up a larger proportion of the Democratic caucus than of the full House membership, their chances of success were greater within the party structure.

In 1969, reformers won regular meetings of the House Democratic caucus and thereby established it as a forum for further reform efforts. Over the following six years, a spate of rules changes was instituted; some were changes in chamber rules, but many were alterations in the rules of the House Democratic Party.

The requirement that committee chairs and the chairs of appropriations subcommittees win majority approval in the Democratic caucus was intended to make the chairs responsive to the party majority, which by this time had a clear liberal majority. The provision for regular meetings of the Democratic caucus provided a forum where rank-and-file members could inform Democratic committee contingents of their views. When, in a few instances, the caucus formally instructed committees, they were put on notice that they had better listen to strongly held caucus sentiments.

Motives involving policy and responsiveness also underlay the shifting of the committee assignment function from the Ways and Means Committee Democrats to a new Steering and Policy Committee chaired by the Speaker. Ways and Means Committee Democrats were seen as too conservative and not accountable to the party. The Steering and Policy Committee was designed to be both representative and responsive. Its membership was a combination of members elected from regional groups, elected party leaders, and leadership appointees.

Granting the Speaker the right to nominate all Democratic members and the chair of the Rules Committee, subject only to ratification by the caucus, was a move clearly intended to give the leadership true control over the scheduling of legislation for the floor. By making Rules Committee Democrats dependent on the Speaker for their position on the committee, reformers made it an arm of the leadership.

A series of rules changes, some principally aimed at expanding participation opportunities, others also motivated by policy concerns, had the effect of increasing opportunities and incentives for participation in committee and on the floor. In an effort to spread positions of influence, members were limited to chairing no more than one subcommittee each. The subcommittee "bill of rights" removed from committee chairs the power to appoint subcommittee chairs and gave it to the Democratic caucus of the committee. It also guaranteed subcommittees automatic referral of legislation and adequate budget and staff.

The supply of resources available to the House and its members, most importantly staff, was expanded and distributed much more broadly among members. The institution of the recorded teller vote in the Committee of the Whole changed the dynamics of the floor stage, increasing the incentives for offering amendments and often for opposing the committee's position. Sunshine reforms opened up most committee markups and conference committee meetings to the media and the public, encouraging members to use those forums for grandstanding as well as for policy entrepreneurship.

The same alterations in the political environment that led to the individualist Senate also made a free-lance entrepreneurial style popular with House members. However, the payoffs of the style were less for members of the House; they were less able to establish a national reputation beyond the Washington policy community and certainly less likely to be perceived as possible presidential nominees. Furthermore, the costs were greater. House reformers had believed that their participation and policy goals were compatible, that the changes they instituted would produce better policy and provide greater participation opportunities for the rank and file. But by the mid-1970s, increased participation by rank-and-file members and large numbers of inexperienced subcommittee chairs had multiplied the number of significant actors and radically increased uncertainty. Floor sessions stretched on interminably, compromises worked out in the more representative committees were picked apart on the floor, and Democrats were forced to go on the record on politically touchy amendments over and over again. To further their goals within this environment, Democratic committee contingents, Democratic committee leaders, and the Democratic membership needed help and looked to the party leadership to provide it. In response to the demands of members, the party leaders began to make greater use of the tools and resources the reforms had given them.

A Hostile Political Climate as a Force for Change

The hostile political climate of the 1980s made it still more difficult for Democrats to advance their policy goals and threatened their reelection goal as well. Members increasingly demanded that their leaders aggressively employ the tools at their command to facilitate passing the legislation members wanted. The leadership responded, and by the late 1980s, the political party had become much more central to the policy process in the House (Sinclair 1995; Rohde 1991). The majority party leadership involved itself actively in all phases of the legislative process. Furthermore, as members came to believe that success in the policy and electoral struggle depends on effective participation in national discourse, leaders took an increasingly active part in setting the agenda and disseminating a party message.

The House Democratic Party's increasing ideological homogeneity made these developments possible. The change in southern politics that the Civil Rights movement and the Voting Rights Act set off had resulted by the early 1980s in a less conservative southern Democratic House contingent. As African Americans became able to vote and as more conservative whites increasingly voted Republican, the supportive electoral coalitions of southern Democrats began to resemble those of their northern party colleagues. As a result, the legislative preferences of northern and southern Democrats became less disparate.

The Republican Party also changed, becoming more aggressively conservative in the 1980s. Not only were fewer moderates being elected to the House, but more hard-edged, ideological conservatives were entering the chamber. The increasing proportion of House Republicans elected from the South accounted for some, but far from all, of this change in the party's ideological cast.

House voting polarized along party lines. In the 1970s, only 37 percent of all roll calls pitted a majority of Democrats against a majority of Republicans; 50 percent of roll calls were such party votes in the 1980s and 58 percent in the 1990s. With the parties increasingly ideologically polarized and an activist Democratic majority party leadership leading a relatively homogeneous membership, the minority Republicans were increasingly relegated to the sidelines, especially on high-profile issues. Their irrelevance rankled Republicans, and a bitter partisanship became the norm on the House floor (Cheney 1989; Connelly and Pitney 1994).

During the 1980s and early 1990s, House Republicans had in many instances imitated House Democrats by adopting rules that decreased the autonomy of their committee leaders and strengthened their party leadership. Committee leaders were made subject to a secret-ballot ratification vote in the Republican conference, the organization of all House Republicans; the Republican Party leader was given the power to nominate Republican members of Rules and more say on the party committee that makes committee assignments. Thus, while they were still in the minority, Republicans had augmented the tools available to their party leadership.

When Republicans won control of the House and Newt Gingrich became Speaker, political parties in the House were a far cry from the loosely organized and weakly led parties of the 1950s. Extraordinary political circumstances allowed Gingrich and the Republican Party to play an unusually aggressive policy role in the 104th Congress, but this represented an accentuation of an already well-developed trend (Sinclair 1995, 1999).

The same changes in the political context that altered the character of the political parties in the House affected the Senate as well and resulted in the Senate Democratic Party becoming more homogeneously moderate to liberal and the Republican Party more conservative. With the increase in intraparty ideological homogeneity and interparty polarization, senators elaborated their party organizations and became more willing to work with and through their party. By the late 1980s, these changes were translating into greater party voting cohesion in the Senate; 58 percent of Senate roll calls were party votes in the 1990s, up from 42 percent in the 1970s and 44 percent in the 1980s.

CONGRESSIONAL PARTIES AT THE BEGINNING OF THE TWENTY-FIRST CENTURY

Congressional parties at the beginning of the twenty-first century are very different from the parties the Report critiqued in 1950. They are more cohesive, more elaborately organized, and much more engaged in policy and program-related endeavors.

Congressional Party Cohesion

In both House and Senate, voting now falls heavily along party lines. The difference between how Democrats and how Republicans vote on recorded floor votes is considerably greater now than at any time in the last half century (Fig. 7.1).[1] This partisan polarization is evident at the committee stage as well; committee deliberations on major legislation are less likely to be bipartisan and more likely to be sharply partisan than they used to be (Sinclair 2000a).

Congressional Party Organization

Both parties in both chambers are now more elaborately organized and much more active than their counterparts of fifty years ago. The various party organs as well as the leaders' offices are professionally and quite generously staffed. Yet the congressional parties and their leaderships are not rigidly hierarchical or highly directive; they are, rather, inclusive and participatory. Members can now pursue both their policy and their participation goals—House members often most effectively—through the party and with the help of its leadership; as a result, the congressional party has become more central to members' congressional lives.

In the House, the Democratic caucus and the Republican conference are now active organizations that meet at least weekly. Each party elects a number

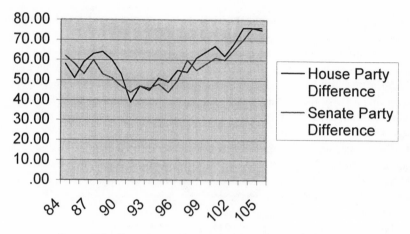

Figure 7.1. Congressional party polarization, 1950s–1990s

of leaders—a Speaker designate, a floor leader, a chief whip, a caucus (or conference) chair and vice-chair—and appoints a number more—various sorts of deputy and assistant whips, the chairs of some party committees. Party committees are charged with a variety of tasks. Both parties, of course, have a committee on committees that assigns members to legislative committees; on both sides of the aisle, party leaders chair and play an influential role in the assignment process. Both have policy committees charged with the discussion and dissemination of party policy positions. Both have active and professional campaign committees (Kolodny 1998a).

The contemporary party whip systems in the House number in the scores. In the 106th Congress (1999–2000), the Republican whip system consisted of fifteen deputy whips and forty-four assistant whips; the Democratic whip system consisted of thirteen deputy whips, forty-one at-large whips, and twenty regional whips. The whip systems are charged with ascertaining the voting intentions of the party's members on important legislation and, when necessary, with persuading members to vote for the party position. Each meets weekly, and subgroups meet as vote-mobilization efforts dictate. Both House parties also use ad hoc task forces or working groups to perform a variety of tasks that range from whipping to policy development to outreach beyond Congress.

Although the Senate parties are considerably smaller, they too have elaborated and activated their organization in recent years. Democrats and Republicans each meet in closed session for lunch on Tuesday under the aegis of their policy committees. Democrats who traditionally concentrated the chairmanships of their various party organs in their leader have devolved some of these positions, and more senators hold party leadership positions. The Democratic and Republican whip systems have increased in size and become more active. The campaign committees have become highly professionalized. Like their House counterparts, the Senate parties sometimes designate ad hoc task forces of members to develop policy or to publicize party positions.

More elaborate organization and staffing make the congressional parties capable of engaging in the broad range of activities that are now the norm. Moreover, the form that the organization and activity take promotes the communication and participation that are essential to party maintenance in the contemporary Congress. In neither chamber are members willing to be simple followers in a hierarchically structured party. The contemporary parties offer multiple opportunities for members to communicate with their leaders. Conference and caucus meetings and whip meetings, for example, allow members to convey their views and concerns directly to their leaders and provide a forum in which members can hold their leaders accountable.

In addition to expecting their leaders to consult them and keep them informed, members want opportunities to participate meaningfully in the legislative process. In the House, the freelance entrepreneurship characteristic of the 1970s became much less feasible for members as the majority leadership strengthened its control. Party-based activities provided new avenues for member participation, ones that help rather than hurt the party effort.

Partisan polarization also made participation through their parties more attractive to senators than it was when the parties were more heterogeneous and the ideological distance between them less. Recent Senate party leaders have sought to provide more channels for members to participate in and through the party. Still, individual senators exercise a great deal more discretion about when and under what conditions to participate on the party team than House members do and have available attractive alternative channels for participation.

Legislative Coordination and the Mobilization of Floor Majorities

Majority party leaders have long been charged with legislative coordination, especially through the scheduling of legislation for floor consideration, and with the mobilization of majorities for major legislation at the floor stage. Contemporary House leaders are more capable of carrying out these and attendant tasks effectively than their predecessors because they command greater resources. Even more important, their members' expectations support an activist leadership role. The Senate's nonmajoritarian rules continue to hinder Senate majority party leaders, despite some change in their members' expectations.

The House majority party leadership has controlled the floor schedule since the Speaker was given the power to name the majority party members of the Rules Committee. During the 1980s, the leadership developed special rules from the Rules Committee into powerful and flexible tools for managing floor time, focusing debate, and sometimes advantaging one outcome over others. The House majority party, whether Democratic or Republican, routinely brings major legislation to the floor under rules that restrict amendments. From 1993 to 1998, an average 61 percent of all rules and 79 percent of rules for major legislation were restrictive (Sinclair 2000b).

The parties' large, well-staffed whip systems make vote-mobilization efforts on a nearly continual basis possible. Given the number of whips, not all need be involved in every effort. For refining the initial whip count and for persuasion, Democrats rely on a volunteer subset of whips, which, of course, consists of those most interested in the legislation at issue. On both sides of the aisle, less senior members tend to be more active as whips. They have fewer demands on their time, and participation in whip efforts gives them a welcome opportunity to be in the thick of the action. They are backed up by experienced professional staffs and by the veteran top echelons of the whip system itself. Both parties work with allied interest groups in their vote-mobilization efforts.

Party leaders are in the business of facilitating the passage of legislation that furthers their members' policy and reelection goals and that now often requires early involvement in the legislative process. When committees are unable to put together major legislation that can both pass on the House floor and is satisfactory to most majority party members, leaders often craft necessary compromises either in committee or after legislation is reported out. When a committee is insufficiently responsive to the party majority, it falls to the leaders to pressure committee members to become so. Occasionally the leadership uses special task forces to draft legislative language on an issue. In 1999, for example, the relevant committees were unable to report out a managed-care reform bill satisfactory to most Republicans. The Speaker entrusted the job to a task force. Leaders can play such an assertive policy role because they do so as agents of a relatively homogeneous party membership. When the party leadership represents the membership, committee leaders know they must be responsive. The strong support of his membership made Speaker Gingrich's highly directive role vis-à-vis the committees in 1995 possible (Owens 1998).

Senate leaders also involve themselves in the policy process as agents of their members; they spend a great deal of their time attempting to work out differences among senators through direct negotiation or by facilitating negotiations. Senate committee leaders too are aware that they must be responsive to the members of their party. Thus, as the new chair of the Health, Education, Labor and Pensions Committee in the 106th Congress, moderate Jim Jeffords was extremely solicitous of the much more conservative Republican Senate membership. On the patient's bill of rights issue, for example, Jeffords participated in a leadership-appointed all-Republican task force to draft legislation and then passed that out of his committee unchanged (Sinclair 2000b, chap. 8). Jeffords's realization that, with a Republican president, expectation for such responsiveness would ratchet up even further probably contributed to his decision to leave the Republican Party in 2001.

The Senate majority leader lacks the control over the flow of legislation to and on the floor that the House Speaker possesses. Extended debate and the Senate's permissive amending rules mean that the Senate majority leader cannot keep off the floor issues his members would rather avoid or pass legislation they want with a simple majority. Thus the most basic precondition to party government—control over the legislative schedule—is thwarted by the chamber's rules.

Setting the Agenda and Promoting a Party Message

Setting the agenda and disseminating a party message are now central functions of congressional parties and their leaders. Members believe success in the policy and electoral struggle depends on effective participation in national discourse. Given his advantages of visibility, media access, and stature, the president will shape the debate to his advantage and dominate agenda-setting unless confronted by an organized opposition effort. During the 1980s, President Reagan taught Democrats that defining issues and party images to one's benefit was both possible and important and that competing as individuals with a media-savvy president was a losing strategy. Furthermore, partisan and ideological polarization, the suffusion of the political arena by news media with a negative bias, and a voracious appetite for conflict lead to more confrontational politics. This style of politics is played out much more on the public stage, with audience reactions often determining winners and losers. Within such an environment, political actors adept at using the media to push their issues to the center of the agenda and to frame the debate to favor their position are greatly advantaged; yielding the public forum to one's opponents is a recipe for policy and electoral defeat.

The congressional parties now generate agendas intended to serve both policy and electoral ends. They work systematically to disseminate party messages and to attempt to frame debate to their advantage. To that end, they have developed sophisticated structures and procedures. In both chambers and parties, the effort is highly inclusive and predicated on broad participation by members.

Speaker Newt Gingrich's Contract with America is the best-known instance of congressional party agenda-setting and one that conforms closely to the responsible party model. Through a highly inclusive process involving both House incumbents and Republican candidates for the House, Gingrich put together a legislative agenda, made it the centerpiece of a nationalized congressional campaign in 1994, and then, when Republicans won majority control of the chamber, worked to pass all the elements in the first one hundred days of the session. As early as 1987, Speaker Jim Wright proposed and pushed to enactment a congressional Democratic agenda, though it was not set forth as an electoral document. Both parties in both chambers now generate and publicize party agendas in each Congress. In the 106th Congress, Speaker J. Dennis Hastert reserved the first ten House bill numbers for the top Republican legislative priorities, "The Republican Common Sense Agenda." Senate Republicans had a similar agenda, which they introduced as S1 to S5. Even in the 107th Congress, with a Republican president, Senate Republicans put together their own agenda, though it did mirror President Bush's agenda closely. In the latter 1990s, Senate and House Democrats and President Clinton coordinated their efforts and agreed on a joint agenda, "Families First." Congressional Democrats continue to promote an updated version of that agenda.

These agendas are intended to serve both legislative and electoral purposes. Projecting a positive image of the party that will help in the next election is always a central concern in putting an agenda together, but it is not the only concern. Most party members would very much like to pass the measures included. No member is bound to vote for the component measures, but the agendas are constructed to include only measures broadly supported by the party membership.

The parties have developed multifaceted and quite sophisticated means of promoting their agendas and disseminating their party message (see Sellers 1999; Lapinski 1999). Congressional Democrats and Republicans have long had message groups to develop a message of the day and promote it through floor speeches and other means. All four party groups have state-of-the art studios, satellite capabilities, and media-savvy staff to aid both leaders' and members' message efforts. To make up for their loss of the president's bully pulpit, Democrats in 2001 set up rapid response teams of expert members to respond quickly to presidential proposals. They also focused increasingly on getting members to spread the message through their local media and on actively booking members on cable TV talk shows. Both are strategies congressional Republicans developed during their years of trying to compete with a Democratic president. Democratic and Republican congressional campaign committees have financed TV ads extolling their party's proposals and accomplishments or criticizing those of the opposition. In mid-2001, for example, with an energy crisis looming and polls showing Americans concerned about the environmental impact of the Bush energy program, Democrats ran TV spots criticizing the Republicans' approach.[2]

Congressional majority parties can use their control over the floor agenda to promote their message, an important strategy for majorities. House rules give the minority little leverage, so their message activities perforce rely less on legislative maneuvers (but see Sinclair 2000b, chapter 8).

Senate rules, in contrast, give the minority a great deal of leverage, and in the 1990s, exploiting Senate prerogatives to attempt to seize agenda control from the majority party became a key minority party strategy. The lack of a germaneness requirement for amendments to most bills severely weakens the majority party's ability to control the floor agenda. If the majority leader refuses to bring a bill to the floor, its supporters can offer it as an amendment to most legislation the leader does bring to the floor. The leader can, of course, file a cloture petition and try to shut off debate, but he needs sixty votes to do so. In 1996, Senate Democrats used this strategy to enact a minimum wage increase, and in the next few years, they forced highly visible floor debate on tobacco regulation, campaign finance reform, gun control, and managed-care reform, all issues the majority party would have preferred to avoid. In 2001 Senate Democrats, before they took control of the chamber, managed with the aid of John McCain and some other defecting Republicans to force the majority Republicans to bring campaign finance to the floor and to pass a strong bill. These procedural strategies have been accompanied by sophisticated public relations campaigns so as to garner as much favorable publicity as possible.

IS THE DREAM FULFILLED?

How would Schattschneider and his colleagues who authored the Report assess the contemporary congressional parties? Would they see significant progress toward a dream fulfilled? Or would the dream now look more like a nightmare? A number of the Report's specific recommendations have been instituted. In both chambers, committee chairs are no longer independent centers of power; they are now accountable to the party members to whom they owe their positions. The parties are more elaborately organized and more active; the Report's call for more frequent meetings of party members has certainly been fulfilled. The contemporary congressional parties are stronger but also more participatory and inclusive, as the Report's authors seem to have hoped. In the House, the majority party leadership has gained secure control over legislative scheduling, as the Report advocated. In contrast, cloture in the Senate continues to require a supermajority, so the majority party leader lacks such control and depends on cooperation from the minority.

These specific recommendations were by and large seen as a means to an end, not an end in themselves. More broadly, the Report called for parties that "are able to bring forth programs to which they commit themselves and . . . [that] possess sufficient internal cohesion to carry out these programs" (Committee on Political Parties 1950a, 1). How do congressional parties fare on these criteria? The contemporary congressional parties are much more engaged in policy- and program-related endeavors than their 1950s predecessors. All four now regularly draft and publicize a party agenda and work to convey a coherent party message to the public. During the latter years of the Clinton administration, the president and the House and Senate parties all participated in putting together an agenda, to which all then subscribed.

Presidents or presidential candidates and their congressional parties, however, do not come up with a common agenda on which to fight the election. The platforms the party conventions approve are presidential, not congressional, platforms. To be sure, usually some members of Congress participate in the platform-writing process, and much in the resulting platforms reflects consensus positions within the party. Yet the platform-drafting process is by no means a joint enterprise between the party's presidential candidate and the party's candidates for Congress. Nor do members of Congress have any formal voice in the presidential campaign, from which much of the agenda and priorities of the winning candidate emerge.

The problem is that the party's candidates for president, House, and Senate face different sets of voters, who can and do pick and choose among candidates of different parties across offices. Given these different electorates, the best strategies for the candidates of a party may well differ. To be sure, the issue appeals of a party's House candidates, Senate candidates, and presidential candidate will mostly be quite similar. With the demise of the one-party South, congressional candidates in one area are unlikely to espouse a set of positions directly at odds with their party's presidential candidate or with the party's congressional candidates elsewhere. Nevertheless, many congressional candidates face electorates very different from that of their party's presidential candidate, and they cannot depend on him to sweep them to victory; the fates of candidates for the different offices are simply not that closely linked.

The agenda of the winning presidential candidate will include much that the party's members of Congress strongly support; if the candidate is not an incumbent, he is likely to have picked up ideas from his party's congressional contingent. The agenda is unlikely to include much that badly splits the party, though completely avoiding such issues may be impossible. Thus, Democratic presidential candidates must take a position on trade. But even if divisive issues are avoided, the new president's agenda came out of his campaign and was designed to serve his electoral needs, not those of his party's members of Congress. Since they had limited input, their commitment is likely to be limited as well.

Do the congressional parties of today "possess sufficient internal cohesion to carry out these programs?" Data on voting in committee and on the floor indicate that contemporary congressional parties act quite cohesively. To be sure, neither party is an ideological monolith; within each there are strains between more centrist and more ideologically extreme members, and the differences tend to have a constituency basis. Yet compared to fifty years ago, contemporary congressional parties are much more cohesive, and that cohesion is, in good part, a function of more homogeneous electoral coalitions within each of the parties.

Party leaders in the House of Representatives command much greater tools for engineering passage of legislation—true control over the floor schedule, powerful and flexible special rules, a large and active whip system. Leaders in both chambers provide their members with greater reelection-related help, especially funding and fund-raising help, than their predecessors did. Yet party leaders, inside or outside Congress, do not control the reelection of their members and thus cannot coerce them once elected. Furthermore, congressional party leaders have absolutely no interest in pressuring a member to vote in a way that will result in his or her losing the seat to a member of the other party.

The 103d Congress, the only recent extended period of fully unified government, illustrates the extent of and limitations on a party's ability to enact its program into law. Although only peripherally and indirectly involved in shaping the Clinton agenda, the House and Senate Democratic Parties and their leaders largely embraced it. In committee and on the floor, congressional Democrats supported Clinton's positions, which most of the time coincided with their own, at very high levels (Sinclair 2000a). The one issue that badly split congressional Democrats and divided a majority of them from their party's president was the North American Free Trade Agreement (NAFTA). The demise of health care reform, certainly the Democrats' biggest failure, was not the result of ideological splits within the party but of opponents' success in the battle for public opinion. Opponents' intensive campaign through the airwaves and at the grass roots raised a host of doubts about Clinton's plan; it was the altered views of their constituents that made it impossible for Democrats to put together majorities for any significant health care bill. Members feared being blamed at election time for their failure to produce, but they feared voting for an unpopular plan even more. Senate rules also took their toll on legislative productivity in the 103d; Republicans made good use of minority power in that chamber to extract concessions on or to kill outright legislation with majority support. Their ability to do so, however, depended on their winning the public relations war—as they did on Clinton's economic stimulus package, for example. When Democrats came out on top in the fight for public opinion, as they did on the Brady gun control bill, Republicans could not maintain their filibuster.

The lesson that the 103d Congress teaches is that, in attempting to enact a program of any ambitiousness, even parties that are quite ideologically homogeneous and that act quite cohesively are likely to run up against barriers stemming from the structure of the U.S. government. Senate rules pose a problem, but the more basic obstacle is an electoral system that disconnects the fates of the party's elected officials. The division over NAFTA provides an example of the familiar circumstance of different constituencies with different stable interests leading Democrats to divergent positions and behavior. Democratic members of Congress representing rust-belt districts saw NAFTA as a threat to their constituents' jobs; the president, representing a national constituency, and Democratic members of Congress from more affluent, "new economy" districts saw it as an economic opportunity for their constituents. Seven years later, a similar alignment appeared on permanent normal trade relations with China because the interests invoked were similar. The Clinton health plan case is more interesting because it did not founder on a divergence in stable constituency interests among Democrats. Rather, a party coalition was disrupted by a successful public relations campaign that altered public opinion. When their constituents began to express deep concern about the Clinton plan, congressional

Democrats up for reelection in a few months' time could not rely on the leader of their party to ensure their reelection. He did not even have to face the voters with them. Beyond raising funds, neither the president nor their chamber party leaders could do very much to help them win reelection. Thus it was no wonder that the party's problems in Washington and with public opinion set off an everyone-for-himself reaction.

The structure of the U.S. government makes divided control possible; during the second half of the twentieth century, the president was of one party when the other party controlled at least one house of the Congress almost two-thirds of the time (thirty-two of fifty years). The twenty-first century began with unified government, if barely, but unified Republican control lasted less than six months, when Senator Jim Jeffords's leaving the Republican Party switched control of the Senate to the Democrats. (That neither the new president nor Republican congressional party leaders could prevent Jeffords's move shows again the limits of party power in a system where parties do not control candidate selection or election.)

When control of the government is divided, partisan differences in policy views and electoral interests act as barriers to either party's enacting its program. Furthermore, the president and his own party's members of Congress are more likely to perceive their optimal strategies as conflicting because of their differences in status. Thus the president most likely will want legislative accomplishments, but the congressional party may well see them as burnishing the reputation of the opposition congressional majority and so as a barrier to regaining majority status.

What then would the Report's authors conclude? Almost certainly they would see the contemporary congressional parties as significant improvements over the highly "irresponsible" parties of the 1950s. Yet they would probably also be sobered by mounting evidence that the basic structure of our government prevents the full development of responsible parties. When the electoral constituencies of a party's elected officials are relatively homogeneous, parties can and do bridge the divide across the branches and chambers, but the electoral system ensures that bridge will often be rickety and unreliable.

In recent years, observers in the academic and Washington communities have concerned themselves more with questions about the potentially negative impact of high partisanship than with questions about party responsibility. Does high partisanship lead to ideological extremity? Does high partisanship result in lower legislative productivity because true policy differences make compromise harder and/or because partisan electoral advantage is valued above legislative output or because of both? Does high partisanship produce a shrill, nasty politics that turns off most voters? Although these questions cannot be fully explored, much less answered here, they do require some attention.

To argue that high partisanship leads to ideological extremity reverses the more plausible order of causation. Furthermore, at least when the margins of chamber control are narrow, as they have been in recent years, party leaders work to mitigate extremity to the extent that it hurts the party's electoral prospects. Candidate recruitment by House leaders in recent years provides a particularly interesting example. On both sides of the aisle, leaders have worked to recruit candidates that fit the district, even if that means candidates from outside of the mainstream of the party. Thus, Democratic House leaders have persuaded fairly conservative Democrats to run in southern districts and then supported them strongly; Republican leaders have promoted moderates in moderate districts. Of course, if member ideological extremity underlies high partisanship, members may oppose such expedient behavior. For example, when Speaker Newt Gingrich recruited moderate California assemblyman Brooks Firestone to run in the moderate Santa Barbara area, conservative California House Republicans rebelled and supported a conservative. The conservative won the party primary and lost the general election.

To the extent that true and deep policy differences underlie high partisanship, compromises will be harder to reach, and the result is likely to be lower legislative productivity. Again, however, it is the policy differences, not the high partisanship that derives therefrom, that seem to be the cause. Does high partisanship lead to partisan electoral advantage being valued above legislative output? Certainly the two are not always perceived as being at odds; for the party in control of a chamber or branch, legislative productivity is likely to be seen as providing electoral advantage—as was the case for congressional Republicans in 1996, for example. For the party in the minority, however, electoral advantage may well lie in having an issue, not a law; and, depending on chamber and chamber margins, the minority may be able to block action.

Partisan polarization does seem to have been accompanied by a nasty, ad hominem politics, by the "politics of personal destruction." One could argue that the same forces that lead to partisan polarization also create high-stakes politics. When the stakes are high, the barriers to action that the American governmental system imposes generate a high level of frustration. Combine that frustration with the more capable party organizations that partisan polarization fosters, and the result is parties willing and able to do whatever it takes to increase their chances of policy and electoral success. If the media select for conflict, sensationalism, and personal attack, the likely result is a politics that plays to what the media rewards with coverage.

So are we worse off than when the Report was published in 1950? Is the quest for responsible parties altogether wrongheaded? The congressional parties do present a clearer policy message than they did fifty years ago, and a party's candidates are much more likely to be conveying the same message. Partisan battles contain considerable issue content; the fights in Congress are policy fights over issues important to real people—managed-care reform and prescription drug coverage, energy and the environment, taxes—and a fair amount of the issue discussion does filter through to the attentive public. The congressional parties are fairly cohesive and tend to act in concert within their chamber. This may not be enough to enable the majority party to enact its program. The barriers the system erects are formidable. Yet the current system is more transparent and certainly gives the public clearer choices than that of fifty years ago.

NOTES

1. *Congressional Quarterly* party unity scores adjusted for absences are the measure used. The formula for party difference is Dem score – (100-Rep score).

2. *Congressional Quarterly Weekly,* April 14, 2000, 818–820; *Washington Times,* May 26, 2001; *Roll Call,* March 1, 2001, July 26, 2001.

8

Presidential Leadership in a Government of Parties

An Unrealized Perspective

Charles O. Jones

In 1950, the Committee on Political Parties of the American Political Science Association published its Report: "Toward a More Responsible Two-Party System" (1950a). In his critical review of the Report at twenty years, Evron M. Kirkpatrick, then executive director of the APSA, wrote: "The Report is probably the most publicized document ever published by a committee of the Association" (1971, 965). I expect that statement remains true today. Few, if any, scholarly treatments of American political parties fail to acknowledge the Report; some even engage the issues involved.[1]

Given this notoriety over time, one might expect continuous high praise for the Report. Not so, however. I know of no essay exalting the Committee on Political Parties and its Report, though some scholars, like Gerald M. Pomper, judged that conditions two decades later made the proposals "more useful and feasible" (1971, 917). Yet lack of praise for the Report should not be interpreted as weak support for its quest. One of the leading advocates of responsible party government, James L. Sundquist, properly identifies those several political scientists and journalists who prefer single-party government as enhancing responsibility (Sundquist 1988, 616–624, 1992, chap. 4). And so the subject of the Report is of continuing interest, even devotion among some, but the document itself has few enthusiasts. Still, the APSA imprimatur serves to legitimate it as a symbol, a sort of talisman for reformers.

In comments on the Report, William G. Mayer recently observed that it "has come to be fashionable of late to impugn the analysis and recommendations of [the APSA] committee" (1998, 214). That comment implies that it was not fashionable earlier to so fault the committee's work. Again, not so. As Kirkpatrick noted in 1971: "In the two decades since its publication it has more often served as a foil than as a model" (968). His own critique was from the perspective of political and policy science, and he found the Report wanting.[2]

The shortcomings of the APSA Committee Report, and the failure of the discipline and profession to clarify more effectively their roles in the public policy field derive from at least four inadequacies: (1) poor handling of value analysis, that is, inadequacies in goal thinking and derivational thinking; (2) failure to explore the interaction of the decisional system and the distribution of values, that is, of policy outcomes; (3) lack of sufficient attention to kinds of thinking peripheral to scientific thinking: goal thinking and derivational thinking (item 1), trend thinking, and developmental analysis; and (4) insufficient empirical theory and inadequate data (1971, 986).

Some of these criticisms were sounded immediately after the Report's publication. Julius Turner presented data to demonstrate that "the Committee has underestimated present party responsibility" (1951a, 143). In this "dissent from the floor," he also worried that certain of the reforms would accentuate the present defects.

Austin Ranney followed Turner's dissent with an extensive critical review. He raised fundamental questions about core concepts in the Report: what is party? what is responsibility? The Report stressed party as a member-based organization, which is somewhat odd, given the variation among states in party registration, types of primaries, and political participation by eligible voters. Responsibility was judged to be external to the electorate at large and internal to the party membership. Ranney properly asked, "What persons should be considered 'party members'?" and "how may this 'accountability' be institutionalized and made effective?" (1951, 489; see also Ranney 1954). He found the Report lacking in both respects. He criticized it for failing to undertake what is necessary to achieve majority-rule democracy, citing the views of the public to which the Report recommended accountability: "The point is that the same popular beliefs about government which sustain our present anti-majoritarian constitutional system will continue to sustain . . . our anti-majoritarian party system. Only when the American people have fully accepted the doctrine of majority-rule democracy can the doctrine of responsible party government expect to receive the popular acclaim which . . . it has so far been denied" (1951, 499). Put otherwise, it is difficult to make over a political system by fiddling with the dependent variable.[3]

Many other critical reviews followed these first evaluations. Kirkpatrick identified several such works, concluding that "collectively, these criticisms amount to an indictment of the Report's analysis and recommendations as ill-conceived, ill-formulated, and, most often, simply mistaken about parties, about people and about political systems" (1971, 968–969). He stated further: "I know of no major work that undertakes a defense of the Report but there are distinguished political scientists who support responsible party government and argue the case much more cogently than the Committee" (1971, 969 n. 5).

Why should it be that a Report so disparaged survives to be commemorated? Perhaps because, as Kirkpatrick observed, there remains a strong preference for party government among many political scientists. In reflecting on the durability of the Report, Epstein (1986) observed that "virtually all students of American politics agreed at least that effective parties of some kind were necessary, and many may well have preferred the committee's kind of effective parties, although they did not always share the committee's belief that they could be established in the United States" (34).

One of the leading advocates of party government, James L. Sundquist, wrote a much-cited paper in 1988 in which he worried about the state of theory for understanding the role of political parties. He explained that although the Report was criticized in several commentaries, support for party government itself was not an issue among political scientists: "The debate was joined on whether party government should or could be made *more* responsible, not whether it should exist at all. Nobody argued that the parties as they existed in 1950 were too tightly disciplined, and that the need was that they be made *less* responsible. Nobody argued that the ideal system was the one that was to be ushered in a few years later: coalition government in which *no* party is or can be held responsible" (619; emphasis in original).

Some observers argue that Democrats had strong reasons to favor responsible party government. Liberal Democrats were frustrated in their effort to gain more support for their agenda, from 1938 to 1950 (Epstein 1986, chap. 11). Those frustrations increased markedly, subsequent to the publication of the Report. Democrats remained the larger of the two parties as measured by party self-identification in surveys, and yet they regularly lost the White House. Between 1952 and 2002, Democrats won just five of the thirteen presidential elections while retaining House majorities in twenty of the twenty-five Congresses and Senate majorities in seventeen of twenty-five. Having to live with split-party government for thirty-two of fifty years is hardly sustaining for those devoted to the party responsibility model. Voters continually failed to satisfy the conditions necessary to produce party government, even neglecting to produce single-party government in many of the states (see Fiorina 1996, chapter 3). Yet, as Sundquist observed, "This established theory [of party government] presupposed one essential condition: there would in fact be a majority party in control of both branches of government" (1988, 625).

So the question remains: why does the theory (if it is that) survive? Self-identification by voters shows that there is no majority party in the electorate—rather, two minority parties and a huge number of Independents. Neither party has consistently won Congress and the presidency since the New Deal era. The Eighty-ninth Congress and Lyndon B. Johnson aside, it is a stretch to state that the Democrats "controlled" the two branches, even when they won both (as with Truman, 1949–1953; Kennedy, 1961–1963; Carter, 1977–1981; or Clinton, 1993–1995).

Perhaps the answer is that it just makes sense to want "a more responsible two-party system," especially for Democrats unable to win the White House very often. This response did not satisfy Sundquist. He explained that the conditions for party government were frequently met in this century prior to the publication of the Report. He comments on the "casual ease" with which the Report spoke of the "party in power." Divided government was barely mentioned—"confined . . . to one subordinate clause of eight words" (1988, 625). But "divided government invalidates the entire theory of party government and presidential leadership, both elements of it" (626). Accordingly, many scholars decried these split results as preventing the proper unifying function of government. Sundquist agreed. He offered evidence of stalemate, concluding that "it is the system that is at fault" (631).

Still, the matter of two-directional results clearly troubled Sundquist. The system permits split-party control, which, in turn, encourages "coalition government" (Sundquist's term). And so "there is a disjunction between theory and practice, between the long-accepted and not-yet-abandoned ideas about how the government of the United States should work and the way in which it is now compelled to try to work" (631). Thus, he called for serious intellectual discourse on the dilemma posed by the theory of party government and the practice of divided government. Those who think the party responsibility model was wrong "have an obligation to provide a new body of theory" (634), and those who are its advocates "must come to grips with the question of how our election system . . . should be altered to restore unified government" (635).

This chapter is a partial response to Sundquist's request. I am moved to modify his characterization of the theory and practice, however. He refers to "party government" and "coalition government." I see the distinction as that between "party government" and a "government of parties." The practice has not been that of party coalitions in the usual sense or as associated with multiparty parliamentary systems. Rather, it has been one of bi-, co-, and crosspartisan patterns, supplementing an occasional straight partisanship in the classic mold (see Jones 1994, chapter 1).[4]

The search for the alternative theory Sundquist asks for begins sensibly with a reconsideration of the nature and purposes of the separated system. For it is the separation of elections and institutions that produces a government of parties and the creative tension characteristic of our lawmaking process. A "government of parties" concept itself is derivative of this structure: a federalized separation of powers as institutionalized in the separation of elections, bicameralism (save Nebraska), differential constituencies, and staggered terms. The consequence is that each of the two parties organizes independently in the multiple institutional settings fostered by this arrangement. Thus, for example, the Republicans are organized as such in the House, the Senate, nationally, and within state governments, with no one of these establishments in control of the other. Party here, party there, all Republican, all Democrat, no one in charge, everyone navigating and dickering, with third parties or Independent candidates along the edges searching for an opening.

THE REPORT AND PRESIDENTIAL LEADERSHIP

Sundquist directly, and other scholars by implication, asserts that presidential leadership is a, perhaps the, key to party government. That working assumption is not apparent in the Report, however. It stresses the weakness of party organization in vesting "leadership of the party as a whole in either a single person or a committee" (Committee on Political Parties 1950a, 3). But the Report even warns that one of the dangers of inaction in meeting the need for party reform may well be an overextended presidency. Lacking an effective party program, the president may well act on his own, then reaching "directly for the support of a majority of the voters" (94).

Where then should party leadership be centered, if not in the president? The answer is revealing of this basic premise of the Report: American political parties can organize alongside working governments in a manner as to form and integrate policy programs. The parties can do so within the present constitutional arrangements—no amendments are necessary. The consequence of reform will be an effective two-party system that achieves integration, programmatic coherence, leadership responsibility to membership, broad participation, cohesion, effective opposition, clear choice for the voters, and resistance to pressure. By this conception, elected leaders, including the president and those in Congress, will be effective advocates and implementers of party programs. Party, therefore, will emerge as a self-standing structure layered into the separated and federalized system.

Numerous proposals were offered as contributing to this goal. Several were gratuitous, others were hortatory. But one in particular is revealing of the conceptual basis for the Report and for comprehending the role of the president in its version of party government. Having concluded that neither the national convention nor the national committee was effective in remedying the problems of the two-party system, the Report recommended formation of a "Party Council." The idea for such a coordinating council derived from a proposal by Charles E. Merriam some thirty years earlier. Troubled by the number of party units and the lack of integration among them, Merriam suggested a council of some six hundred to seven hundred members drawn from the national executive, Congress, statehouses, national party committee members and state chairs, and other prominent party leaders. The out-party would include defeated nominees for president and governor.

The Report's authors favored this concept but judged that the size proposed by Merriam made it unwieldy. "What is now most needed is a body that can meet frequently, consult easily with other party agencies, deal with current party problems, and become a source of continuing advice to the president or, in the case of the minority party, to some other recognized party leader" (Committee on Political Parties 1950a, 42). A body of fifty members was proposed, representing five groups: the national committee, the congressional party organization, the state committees, the party's governors, and other party groups (Young Republicans and Young Democrats) and the party at large (members to be chosen by the national convention). What about the president? He and the vice-president (or nominees for these offices), national party officials, and "perhaps" cabinet officials appointed by the president "ought to be considered ex-officio members and fully entitled to participate" (43).

The Party Council was clearly intended to be competitive with, perhaps even controlling of, the White House in regard to party, political, and policy matters. As envisioned in the Report, the Party Council would "settle the larger problems of party management"; propose a draft of the party platform; "interpret the platform in relation to current problems"; choose party leaders outside the party organizations; make recommendations "in respect to congressional candidates"; and make recommendations regarding "departures from general party decisions by state or local party organizations." Further, in presidential years the Party Council would be a place for discussing, perhaps even screening, presidential candidacies. In addition, it might select a "party cabinet" of its members to advise the president.

As has been pointed out by most critics, the Report has many flaws and ambiguities. And indeed, the section of the Report on sources of support and leadership for reform was not very optimistic. It is recognized that the president could be influential "in attaining a better organized majority party" (Committee on Political Parties 1950a, 89). The Report stressed how beneficial it would be for a president to have the backing of a responsible party. Reference is even made to the president as "party head." But he must share, a goal presumably ensured by his relationship to the Party Council. The ambiguity of these arrangements is evident in the statement regarding the role of the president:

> It is clear that any President or candidate for the presidency who intends to work consistently and continuously in the direction of party responsibility may have to be prepared to share responsibility with other truly representative leaders of the party in the shaping of the party's program. He must also be prepared to use the party and its leaders in the process of policy-formulation.
>
> The President could gain much when party leaders in and out of the Congress are working together with him closely in matters concerning the party program. As party head, the President could then expect more widespread and more consistent support from the congressional leaders of his party.

These, in turn, could present a more united front. As a result, on issues where the party as a party could be expected to have a program, the program of the party, of the party leaders in each house of Congress, and of the President would be the same program, not four different programs (Committee on Political Parties 1950a, 89).

It is true enough that if everyone agreed, then everyone will have agreed. What is not clear is how that agreement is to come about or where. Nor is it certain who is in charge of what, or who is responsible to whom. And that is where I have to leave it as far as the Report is concerned. For the Report fails to clarify the precise role of a key power holder—the president. Indeed, it is even implied that he may be an impediment to the realization of the intraparty democracy judged to be critical for creating a coordinated program for which the party will ultimately be responsible.

BACK TO BASICS: THE PRACTICE ABOUT WHICH IT IS SAID THERE IS NO THEORY

The practice to which Sundquist refers is the ordinary workings of the separated and federalized system. The concepts upon which the system is based, that is, the separation of powers and federalism, do not lack for theory. These concepts have been a subject of interest to theorists for centuries. What is not well explicated and, indeed, seemingly resisted, is theoretical development of the role and function of political parties in such a system. Rather, scholarly attention has been directed to devising means by which a party might perform unifying and centralizing functions to overcome what are judged to be the deficiencies of the distributions of powers within and between governments. That effort is a curious expenditure of intellectual resources for particular reasons. Parties function to organize and exercise political power. A separated and federalized system intentionally distributes power horizontally and vertically. Accordingly, parties will, themselves, be separated and federalized. Just as there is no central, all-powerful governing unit, there will not be a single, unifying party structure. Therefore, reform impulses are more constructively directed to improving the effectiveness of parties in their several institutional and governmental locations. For if there is sound theoretical justification for distributing and preserving powers among institutions, then it follows that a constructive political party is one that contributes to the effectiveness of the institution within which it is operating. Contrariwise, a political party overcoming the advantages of the separation of powers and checks and balances is antithetical to the very purposes of the design. The threat is not great, however. An effective separated powers system resists most efforts at unification, including those devised by party government advocates (for example, a Party Council).

Again as suited to the theme here, I will concentrate on the presidency in further discussion of the practice for which we need a theory. One caveat: treatment of one branch of a separated system inevitably involves its intersection with other branches. One important feature of the separation is that the workings of one branch are enhanced by the effective operations of the others. As I have argued elsewhere, this feature fosters the speculative imagination, inviting, as it does, the understanding and absorption of alternative perspectives (Jones 1999a).

Consider what happens electorally during a two-term presidency: four House elections for all members, thus four distinct Congresses; four one-third-up elections in the Senate, producing both continuity and change among four Senates, with no senator ever running twice with the same president and several never running with the incumbent. The results are as planned: separation, independence, interdependence. Party naturally organizes throughout the institutions and their units, as oriented to the setting, to purposes, and to constitutional and political limitations. No one party structure will look exactly like another, either between the two parties or among the three elected institutions (White House, House, Senate) and the national organization. This is the government of parties at the national level.

Least clearly articulated is party organization in the White House. The president is said to be his party's leader. How so? What structure does he head? Granted, he has increasingly large legions of political advisers, consultants, and liaison personnel. He has substantial influence in who manages the national committee of his party but only limited leverage, if any at all, in the selection of congressional party leaders. Basic writings on the presidency have little to say about the president as party leader for the very good reason that there is not that much to say. Attention is directed to his political, policy, and administrative leadership, all of which have an effect on the party. But he is hardly in charge. Neither he nor his advisers are typically invited to the huge majority of party meetings in Washington. Indeed, a president meeting with a congressional party caucus makes news, often with reports that he was "surprisingly" well received.

Please bear in mind that none of this discussion is to suggest the president is unimportant. Rather, it is to direct attention to his role and function in regard to his political party. In relation to Congress, a large part of the president's job is to clarify his policy preferences, seek their approval, and see to the implementation of the laws that are passed. Seldom is this done by command, as was explained by Richard E. Neustadt (1960) forty years ago. Persuasion and negotiating skills are required, as suited to the variation of partisan conditions characterizing contemporary presidential-congressional relations. It hardly needs repeating that cross-partisan politics has been the norm since 1968. Republican and Democratic presidents have had to court opposite-party members of Congress in one house or both over 80 percent of the time. Among other effects of this pattern has been a realization among party and committee leaders that split control can be satisfying. As one senior Democrat explained, a president of your party tells you what *he* wants; a president of the other party asks what *you* want.

Here then are the basics: separation of elections, multiple party structures but no one in charge, high potential for split-party control, limited formal role of the president as party leader, and continual adjustment to shifting partisan alignments on issues. One major challenge for scholars is to specify more clearly (or at all) the connections among various party structures and between them and the president (for example at the national level: House party with Senate party, party in congressional committees with chamber party organization and leadership, House and Senate campaign committees and the national committees with each other and the other units, and the many interlacements with the White House). In the anniversary spirit of "a more responsible two-party system," we need an improved understanding of which parties we want to be more responsible to whom and why. However, that goal cannot be achieved without a better understanding of responsibility in a separated system.

RESPONSIBILITY IN A SEPARATED SYSTEM

My more serious consideration of the issue of responsibility in our form of government followed my lecture at Kyung Pook University, Taegu, Korea. Speaking of the role of the presidency in a separated system, I identified four partisan strategies: straight-, bi-, co-, and cross-partisanship. I stressed the problems of exporting a separationist system, pointing out that "the separated system is not well understood primarily because most analysts prefer a presidency-centered responsible party system and are therefore not moved to accept a separationist perspective seen by them to be flawed" (Jones 1999b, 33). In the question period, a student asked how such a system as ours could foster responsibility at all. I weakly responded that responsibility as commonly understood was simply sacrificed. I resolved then to improve my understanding of that important feature of our politics—a serious challenge. For few concepts are as complex in a separated system. But the issues involved must be engaged if we are to evaluate the Report at its half century or if we are to undertake reforms designed to provide more responsibility.[5]

"Party responsibility means the responsibility of both parties to the general public, as enforced in elections" (Committee on Political Parties 1950a, 2). A fascinating circularity is envisioned by which parties design programs at the grass roots, put these programs into effect, then check with the grass roots in elections to judge whether they still approve what they supported earlier. This appears to be the essence of the intraparty democracy of which Ranney was so skeptical. Of relevance, however, is the Report's apparent misgivings about party leaders. One gets the impression in reading the Report that any slippage that occurs between program design and accountability is because of a failure of leadership responsibility. And so corrections are needed, notably an overarching Party Council to represent and preserve intraparty democracy. Alas, as Sundquist acknowledged, any such solution falters under conditions of split-party government.[6]

To be responsible, by ordinary dictionary definition, is to be "liable to be called on to answer, liable to be called to account as the primary cause, motive, or agent." By this standard, is there responsibility in the separated system? Surely the answer is yes. Arguably, the two most influential books on Congress in the postwar era, *Congress: The Electoral Connection* by David R. Mayhew (1974) and *Home Style* by Richard F. Fenno Jr. (1978), teach us about responsibility. Seeking reelection is making oneself "liable to be called on to answer." Designing a "home style" involves the definition of constituency and the determination of responsiveness and responsibility. Agency is at the core of responsibility. Mayhew, Fenno, and the legions of scholars following in their wake have shown us how it works in the House of Representatives (with Fenno directing attention as well to the Senate in recent years).

What is portrayed by these scholars is individual, not collective, accountability. As Fenno has shown, a style is developed to suit the representative's definition and understanding of "home." Seldom does this exercise extend to accounting for the national party.[7] If anything, conditions for senators are even more personally varied. Fenno explains why in his brief monograph comparing electoral and representational conditions in the two chambers (1982) and in his description and analysis of *Senators on the Campaign Trail: The Politics of Representation* (1996). This failure by congressional candidates to identify and support a party line does not preclude there being a common theme to their individual accountabilities or an effort by the national party apparatus to specify such a theme. Identifying the latter is simple enough to achieve: study the campaign literature, press releases, and public statements of the campaign committees and their spokespersons. Efforts at developing a common policy theme must be carefully constructed, however, so as not to interfere with individualized campaigns suited to a particular state or district.[8]

The first phenomenon—a common theme to individual accountabilities—is more difficult to identify and to interpret as party responsibility once spotted. Scholars have found that certain issues are commonly associated with the two parties. Relying on content analysis of local newspapers, Gregory Flemming (1999) confirmed this to be the case for House campaigns in 1992 and 1994. Many of the works on congressional elections refer to general differences between the two parties' candidates, typically as associated with who becomes a Republican and a Democrat in the first place, as well as the processes of recruiting (Jacobson 1992; Herrnson 1998). What is lacking is a fully developed comparative study of the two parties across the chambers to determine the extent to which the sum of individual candidate accountings can be interpreted as a composite party responsibility. If such a phenomenon exists, then we would have the beginnings of an understanding of party responsibility as it applies to a government of parties in a separated system. One can at least hypothesize naturally occurring bonds of issue positioning, adjusted to constituency differences and maintained by socialization. What is seen as lack of discipline by the standards of a party government model may be simply a zone of tolerance for diversity among states and districts in a government of parties.

Clearly, no one can imagine that an encompassing concept of party for identifying and analyzing congressional responsibility can be simple. Once again Fenno illustrates what is involved. In *Congress at the Grassroots* (2000) he explores the political life of a congressional district (the Georgia district represented at different times, and in different shapes, by Democrat Jack Flynt and Republican Mac Collins). Regarding party, he shows how it is that the representative manages at home and in the House (42–50, 141–146). He illustrates how it is that party in these two locations is given meaning by the working representative/lawmaker. Seldom have I read a more revealing portrait of the dual meanings of political party for elected officials. I doubt one needs to read anything more in judging whether a Party Council, as envisaged by the Report, can be effective. Flynt and Collins meant to command how party would work in the district and to extract from party in the House what suited their interests at home. At the very least, this work that seeks to connect Washington to states and districts as electoral units suggests that we have hardly scratched the surface in our understanding of party responsibility.

What then of responsibility of the president? For openers, if election is the principal time of accountability, then the Twenty-second Amendment (which was not yet ratified in 1950) limits that accounting to one reelection. An associated complication is that of the differences in term lengths. Responsibility as a composite of individual accountabilities is tested electorally every two years in Congress. Comparable presidential accountings take place every four years, though the incumbent may not be on the ballot. There are occasional midterm elections in which the president's record is said to have been a major issue, for example, 1946, 1974, 1982, and 1994. Even where evident, however, the presidential effect may vary substantially among electoral districts. More often the midterm elections are state- and district-oriented elections.

The record of postwar presidential elections displays their differences as accountability events (see Table 8.1). Of the fourteen elections from 1948 to 2000, six were straightforward direct accountability contests, in which the incumbent sought reelection. Four were reelected (all by Electoral College landslides) and two defeated. In five of the six elections, party accountability was ambiguous in that the president's party did not win House and Senate majorities. Even in the sixth (1992), though Bush lost, the Republicans had a net gain in House seats and held the Democrats to no gain in the Senate.[9] The four reelections were remarkably similar—an overwhelming win for the president and

Table 8.1. Variations on a Theme of Accountability in Presidential Elections, 1948–2000

Type of Result (No.)	Election Years (Party)	Split Party Control	One-Party Control
Direct Accountability			
President reelected (4)	1956 (R)	X	
	1972 (R)	X	
	1984 (R)	X	
	1996 (D)	X	
President defeated (2)	1980 (D→R)	X	
	1992 (R→D)		X
Associated accountability			
Successor elected (2)	1948 (D)		X
	1964 (D)		X
Successor defeated (1)	1976 (R→D)		X
Vice-president elected (1)	1988 (R)	X	
Vice-president defeated (3)	1960 (R→D)		X
	1968 (D→R)	X	
	2000 (D→R)		X
Party accountability (no incumbent or vice-president running)			
Incumbent party defeated (1)	1952 (D→R)		X

Notes: A former vice-president won in 1968 (Nixon), and one was defeated in 1984 (Mondale). Truman in 1948 and Johnson in 1968 were eligible to seek reelection but decided not to run.

a high incumbent return in Congress. Voters essentially returned the same split-party government, a result that could be interpreted as rewarding cross-party responsibility, hardly what the Report's authors had in mind.

Half of the fourteen elections involved associated accountability. These elections were of two types: successors seeking election (Truman, Johnson, and Ford) and vice-presidents seeking election at the end of a president's term (Nixon, Humphrey, Bush, and Gore).[10] In Truman's case, he had served nearly a full term following Roosevelt's death early in his fourth term. Truman was eligible to seek reelection in 1952 by special dispensation in the Twenty-second Amendment but decided against running. Therefore, in terms of time served, his election in 1948 might also be classified as "direct accountability." The Johnson and Ford cases are more clearly those of successors. Both were in the process of putting their stamp on the presidency, but their accountability was ineluctably tied to their predecessors. Johnson's win was accompanied by Democrats winning two-thirds majorities in the House and Senate, thus offering the purest conditions for party government in the postwar period, though one cannot imagine Johnson inviting advice or direction from a Party Council.

Until 1960 no vice-president in the twentieth century ran as his party's presidential candidate subsequent to his service in that capacity. Beginning in 1960 five have been candidates, Nixon twice. Perhaps the earlier reluctance was due to the fact that no such candidate had won since Martin Van Buren in 1836. Whatever the reason, vice-presidents are now accepted as potential presidential candidates upon the completion of their president's term. One of three vice-presidents won, Bush in 1988 (see Table 8.1). Seemingly, Bush gained from a strong economy and a relatively calm international scene. Some analysts interpreted the election as a third Reagan term, and indeed the election did have many of the features of the reelections in 1956, 1972, and 1984.

The other three elections with vice-presidents running were among the closest in history. Nixon in 1960 and Humphrey in 1968 were very narrowly defeated; Gore in 2000 actually won the popular vote and lost in the Electoral College only with the intervention of the U.S. Supreme Court. The 1968 contest was clearly an associated accountability election as Humphrey sought to manage the volatile Vietnam issue. In 1960, Nixon, too, had to account for an economic recession. The 2000 election was fascinating in accountability terms. Vice-President Gore sought to benefit from a robust economy while distancing himself from the Clinton scandals. He lost to the son of the president Clinton defeated in 1992. It was difficult to read the results as a referendum on the Clinton presidency, given Gore's effort to run "as his own man" and the president's own high job-approval ratings. Therefore, accountability was more disassociated than associated, in spite of Gore's partnership in the current administration. Curious indeed!

The associated (or disassociated) accountability elections have produced several more one-party governments than those for which there was direct accountability for the incumbent president. Four of the seven produced Democratic governments (1948, 1960, 1964, 1976), one a Republican government (2000). The latter is the ultimate display of the government of parties, with the Republicans and Democrats at nearly equal strength in both houses of Congress and the president having won by just four electoral votes. The extraordinary fifty-fifty split in the Senate even resulted in a historic power-sharing agreement between the two parties, later to be abrogated when Senator James Jeffords (R-Vt.) left his party for independent status and voted with the Democrats for organizational purposes.

That leaves just one election in the postwar period in which there was no incumbent, successor, or surrogate running directly or associatedly to account for the record in office—a party accountability election. In 1952, Truman was eligible to run but decided not to do so. His approval ratings were very low, an unpopular war was being waged, and scandals marred his full term, 1949–1953. Since neither the president nor his vice-president was running, his party had to be held accountable. Eisenhower won handily, and Republicans won House and Senate majorities for just the second time since 1928.

The potential for such outcomes as those presented in Table 8.1 was, no doubt, what encouraged the Committee on Political Parties to prepare its Report. Yet these patterns in accountability are wholly legitimate in a separated system. What is portrayed in Table 8.1 is not the lack of accountability but a mosaic of responsibility associated with the separation of elections and the variations in term lengths that sustain the separation of institutions sharing and competing for powers. The explicit implication is that a research orientation more suited to the workings of the separated system is needed, both for better understanding and for preparing recommendations designed to make improvements.

THE PARTY AND THE PRESIDENCY

I now turn more directly to the relationship of party to the presidency. Does the president lead his party? Most treatments presume that he does. And who leads the opposition party that is referred to in the Report? The notion that the defeated presidential candidate leads his party as titular head has long ago been abandoned, if it ever made sense. Perhaps the president leads both parties, especially in split-party governments.

Remarkably, some sophisticated treatments of political parties have little to say about the president as party leader, concentrating more on Congress.[11] Still, Sundquist (1992, 91) insists that the "doctrine of presidential leadership" is central to the theory of party government. By this view, a president leads through his party, which (consistent with the tenets of the party government model) will be a majority in Congress. The president sets the agenda, submits the bills, and meets with congressional party leaders, who will have had a role in planning the party program. As Sundquist concedes, the "era of divided government" changed all of that. Often the reformer's reaction is to restore what Sundquist believed was the central role of the president in party government, presumably as outlined in the Report.[12] But what the student needs is an understanding of how and whether presidents lead the parties in the contemporary version of the separated system, a version normally featuring split-party government.

Leon D. Epstein (1986), John H. Kessel (1984), and James W. Davis (1992) directly engage the matter of the role of the president in relationship to the party. All three strongly emphasize the influence of the separation of powers. As expected, given his work on comparative party systems, Epstein isolates the American presidency as a special case. He also stresses historical or founding principles as continuing to influence presidential status, as does Davis (chap. 1). Thus, for example, the office "was originally nonpartisan," and it "retained its nonpartisan attributes even after the emergence of partisan election and partisan leadership" (Epstein, 80). This ambiguity has continued, as there are ceremonial functions and certain issues (defense, foreign affairs) where the president is expected to be above partisanship, however much he may serve as party leader otherwise.

Epstein and Davis also contrast "presidential party" with "congressional party" in interesting and relevant ways. The first "is more nearly a figure of speech" than the latter (Epstein, 84). And yet it was the presidential election that "is primarily responsible for the existence of national parties," not congressional elections (83). As a concept separate from the national party organization, the presidential party is ordinarily quite personal, that is, as associated with a candidate and his win (see Davis, chapter 6). Kessel anchors this followership in issue advocacy and thus is comfortable with a concept of "presidential party" (323–326). He also has identified some continuity among activists from one president to the next, as has Davis. Epstein is somewhat more cautious in this regard. In any event, the presidential party as defined by election activists remains separate from the national party organization. Certainly the latter is supportive of a president, but it has party maintenance functions that extend beyond the personal needs of the incumbent. And the relationship of supporters with the losing candidate typically ends with his defeat, though, as Kessel shows, various activists, at that point, may begin their search for a new candidate.

Davis (1992) offers the most comprehensive survey of the president as party leader. His book with that title was written because "no full-length study of the American president as party leader has appeared in the twentieth century" (ix). As with Epstein and Kessel, Davis considers the presidential party. Additionally, he reviews the important effects of divided government and the associated impact of presidents "going public." He writes of a "scenario of a postparty president" (206–207) while acknowledging the importance of party for making the system work. Davis offers little comfort for party responsibility advocates in this account, a perspective that merits little treatment in his book (173–174). Most of the developments he describes encourage alternative visions of the role and functions of political parties in a separated system. As he concludes, "If presidents and lawmakers are disposed to cooperate, sufficient avenues for cooperation exist, and additional pathways are scarcely needed" (209). As argued here, that cooperation occurs within a government of parties and by various partisan interactions.

If anything, the historical ambiguity of a president's partisan role has been accentuated with reforms in the nominating process that have contributed to candidate-centered organizations (Ranney 1975; Polsby 1983). The consequences for governing are notable, possibly profound. A president enters with a loyalist coterie that may seek to govern as a substitute for party, a strategy that can be further rationalized in split-party government. Party remains available for use by presidents in seeking support. But there is no coherent structure suited to the demands of the party government model.

Another line of research identifies changes of note regarding presidents and parties. In *The President and the Parties* (1993), Sidney M. Milkis describes the impact of the New Deal on the political parties. He shows how it was that the Democratic Party became "the party of administration" by enacting programmatic entitlements. The result was "a more centralized and bureaucratic form of democracy that focused on the presidency and executive agencies for the formulation, the enactment, and the execution of public policy" (301). Traditional party politics was "diminished"; "*personal* responsibility of the president" was "exalted" (301). These arrangements make unlikely the kind of two-party competition called for in the Report unless an antiadministration party should develop (as appeared to be the purpose of Speaker of the House Newt Gingrich during the 104th Congress).[13]

What, then, can one say about the president as party leader? If anything, the changes identified by scholars appear to have created more ambiguity, not less. Presidents are left to fashion means by which they can have influence within their own party structures on Capitol Hill and elsewhere, and, given the frequency of split-party government, with the other party's structures as well. We appear to be far beyond a time when party renewal of the APSA Committee variety can be rationally devised or practically implemented. Reform, if it is to come, must accommodate the modern government of parties.

EFFECTIVE LEADERSHIP IN A GOVERNMENT OF PARTIES

I suggest altering the mission for reform-oriented political party scholars. A different question should direct their research and proposals for change. The primary question for the Committee on Political Parties was how to get more responsible and effective party government. I propose this alternative: how do we make a government of parties work more effectively? I understand that few, if any, scholars are admitted devotees of the Report. But here we are attributing significance to its leverage while often proclaiming that we do not take it seriously. Personally, I find Sundquist's position persuasive. He observes that the party government model continues to dominate the thinking of many, perhaps most, scholars and certainly of a huge majority of political analysts in the media. By this view, split-party government is bad for all the reasons cited in the Report. Single-party government is better, but according to the Report, it must be more fully integrated for purposes of achieving more responsibility. Sundquist himself agrees with those sentiments but is troubled by the persistence of political conditions antithetical to realizing "a more responsible two-party system." And so he asks the question, if not party government, what? In so doing he crosses an important threshold—from seeking to achieve unitarian, parliamentary-style outcomes in a separation of powers system to asking for an alternative model, one suited to a separationist rationale for governing.

Sundquist's challenge remains to be met, even as our experience in governing continues to defy the conditions necessary for party government. We understand and frequently deplore the shortcomings of the separated system, but what are the benefits? David R. Mayhew (1991) has shown that split-party government is not gridlocked to the point of low productivity but quite the reverse. The reaction to Mayhew's findings has often been, well, but how about this? Or, can he really be right? A crossing-the-threshold reaction might have been, what do you suppose explains those findings? Or, are there other partisan configurations?[14]

Mayhew himself questions why it was that the high productivity of major legislation by the Ninety-third Congress (1973–1974)—matching that of the Eighty-ninth Congress (1965–1966)—was overlooked. Part of the answer seems to be analysts' preoccupation at the time with Watergate rather than with the compensatory features of a separated system when the presidency is under siege. But the policy record of more recent split-party governments also invites the interest of party scholars. How was it that Reagan was successful in getting House Democratic support for his agenda-bending tax and budget cuts in 1981? What explains the productive One hundredth Congress with a lame-duck President Reagan and a revitalized congressional Democratic Party? What does the 1992 stalemate between a beleaguered President Bush and a scandalized Congress (notably the House banking scandal) tell us about conditions for cross-party conflict? How is it that the one-party Democratic government in 1993 and 1994 failed to enact major Clinton priorities and one of the most contentious split-party governments in decades produced a flood of legislation in 1996? Each of these cases is illustrative of the workings of a government of parties, as well as instructive as to differences among and within split-party and one-party arrangements.

The past fifty years have witnessed an extraordinary variety of political conditions for governing in the separated system. We now have a decent enough sample to prepare comparative analyses of these partisan variations. A first step is to embrace an altered perspective of the role and function of political parties in the American system, one that acknowledges the plurality of settings within which parties legitimately organize and participate in governing. Effectiveness is then judged by the extent to which the advantages of this arrangement are realized. Presidential leadership is often vital for achieving this goal. Seldom in recent decades could it have been fulfilled by reinforcing strictly partisan strategies.[15]

NOTES

1. For example, the more contemporary studies pulled from my shelves include Aldrich 1995, 10–12; Coleman 1996, 3–17; Cox and McCubbins 1993, 275–278; Epstein 1986, 33–37; Maisel 1990, chap. 15. Oddly, the Report is not included as an entry in the encyclopedia of political parties, though it is most likely cited more than any other source among individual entries (Maisel 1991).

158 CHARLES O. JONES

2. Kirkpatrick, then at the Department of State, was himself a member of the APSA Committee.

3. In his comments on this chapter, Leon D. Epstein makes the point that responsible party advocates treat party as an independent variable, and therein lies a major difference in perspective between unitarians and separationists. That difference is at the heart of the arguments made in Ranney and Kendall (1956, part 6).

4. In part the distinction between a multiparty coalition government and a government of parties is in the locus of agreements. In the former, they typically occur prior to legislative confirmation, that is, among the party leaders in the coalition; in the latter, they occur within the legislature itself and are, therefore, more public. The nearest analogue in our system would be the so-called Conservative Coalition of Republicans and southern Democrats as it operated on certain issues in the postwar period. It came closest to serving as a unified, if not exactly a one-party, government during the early years of the Reagan administration.

5. LeRoy Rieselbach (1994) and David T. Canon and Kenneth R. Mayer (1999), among others, make a distinction between responsibility and responsiveness. Canon and Mayer explain that the first has to do with collective decision making in a legislature, the latter with accurate reflection of constituent interests. This important difference is of the essence of separationism, which seeks to preserve, rather than to eliminate, what Canon and Mayer call "the collective dilemma" (103–105). As they state, "It is not possible to have it all" (103). A principal goal of a separated system is to prevent any one segment having it all.

6. Actually, one possible effect of such party councils in a split-party government might well be a hardening of policy positions, thus thwarting cross-party agreements that have been so characteristic of contemporary lawmaking. Jon Bond and Richard Fleisher (1999) illustrate the effects of increased ideological purity in congressional parties in recent years. As they observe, "The greater polarization of the parties also means that presidents are dealing with members in both parties who relish 'a fight to the bloody end' with those in the opposition party. . . . Some might yearn for the good old days of weak and undisciplined parties" (8).

7. One interesting possible exception occurred in 1994 with the Contract with America. Most Republican House candidates (incumbents and challengers) signed on as supporters of the contract in a highly publicized ceremony on Capitol Hill. Interestingly, many commentators at the time mocked the exercise. An exception was David Broder of the *Washington Post,* who recognized it as suiting conditions of classic party responsibility.

8. The *Washington Post* (Allen 2000, 1) reported that the National Republican Congressional Committee would "tailor their ads [in 2000] for each district, instead of promoting a generic national message." This reassurance was, in part, a reaction to criticism by candidates to generic ads by the campaign committee in 1998 attacking President Clinton on the Lewinsky affair.

9. Later the Republicans had a one-seat net gain when Kay Bailey Hutchinson won the Texas Senate seat vacated by Lloyd Bentsen, who became secretary of the treasury in the Clinton administration.

10. There are two other cases of vice-presidents running subsequent to the end of the administration in which they served: Nixon, 1968, and Mondale, 1984.

11. For example, Aldrich (1995) discusses political parties and governance with hardly a mention of the president as leader. Principal attention is directed to congressional voting. Neither "president" or "presidency" appears in the index. In a collection of essays on the American party system edited by L. Sandy Maisel, the single chapter on partisan presidential leadership concentrates on the president's appointments (1990, chap. 13). There are two chapters on Congress. A recent collection of fine essays, *Partisan Approaches to Postwar American Politics* (Shafer 1998), has an essay by Randall Strahan on partisan officeholders but not one specifically on the president. Likewise, the collection of papers, *The State of the Parties* (edited by Shea and Green 1994), lacks one on the president as leader (again neither "president" or "presidency" makes the index). I do not make this point to criticize these works but to note that the president as party leader is not typically judged to be a topic deserving of special treatment.

12. In fact, the Committee on Political Parties was wary of presidential leadership, per se. They proposed the Party Council as a coordinating unit and on which the president would serve ex officio.

13. John J. Coleman (1996) comes to similar conclusions as Milkis by emphasizing the emerging fiscal state. "By institutionalizing fiscal policy, introducing new components of policy making, and encouraging plebiscitary voting, this state set in place the long-term conditions for party decline and, I argue, the keys to party renewal"(3). Coleman concentrates his research on Congress.

14. A recent positive contribution to Mayhew's research is that by William Howell, Scott Adler, Charles Cameron, and Charles Riemann (2000). They examine all legislation enacted from 1945 to 1994 and identify four categories. They find that divided government depresses the production of "landmark" legislation, has no effect on passage of important legislation, and seemingly stimulates the passage of least significant legislation. They call for more research, including attention to "the theoretical foundations of legislative productivity" (302). A further refinement should be a more sophisticated treatment of the variations allowed by a government of parties. Not all "divided governments" are alike, nor are all "unified governments." Still to be accomplished is an analysis of legislative production associated with the variety of party splits that have been experienced in this period when both parties keep winning. Also worth nothing: Schattschneider (1942) contrasted total legislative production for divided and unified government (90).

15. I appreciate the comments and assistance of my colleagues David T. Canon and Leon D. Epstein.

9

The Party in the Electorate as
a Basis for More Responsible Parties

Herbert F. Weisberg

The party in the electorate is an important facet of the political party, though it was barely appreciated when the Committee on Political Parties of the American Political Science Association wrote its Report, "Toward a More Responsible Two-Party System" (1950a). Paradoxically, it could be argued that the party in the electorate has served as the basis for a greater degree of party responsibility since the Report was written. My purpose in this chapter is to examine how the party in the electorate contributes to creating more responsible parties.

The early work on political parties recognized parties foremost as organizations and secondly in terms of their operation in government. The recognition of their role in the electorate was tertiary, partly because appreciating that role required extensive attention to public opinion through sample surveys, which were not available until the 1950s. However, these different aspects of party cannot be seen as separate; each affects the other intimately. Analysis of how responsible a party system is or should be cannot skip over the party in the electorate, since the party as an organization and the party in government must both answer to the party in the electorate. Indeed one problem with the Report is its minimal recognition of the role of the latter

Even today, most of the summaries of research on political parties dealing with the state of the subfields (Epstein 1975, 1983; Crotty 1991, 151–154; Janda 1993) give minimal attention to the party in the electorate. In fact, Janda's review of the subfield (1993, 183) argues that a general theory of parties need not encompass voting behavior, accepting Schlesinger's argument (1991) that this flows from defining parties as organizations. Yet it is impossible to discuss party responsibility in a realistic manner without dealing with the role of the party in the electorate. An appropriate starting place is to consider the development of this concept.

THE HISTORICAL DEVELOPMENT OF THE CONCEPT OF THE PARTY IN THE ELECTORATE

Pre-1950 Views

The awareness of the party in the electorate was very limited until the 1950s, but it developed quickly thereafter. In the pre-1950 literature, scholars were aware of the idea of party loyalties. In particular, it was recognized that many citizens were loyal to one party or the other because of the Civil War, whether supporting the party of the Union or opposing the party of Reconstruction.

Some early discussions of party loyalty virtually foreshadowed the concept of party identification. For example, Walter Weyl wrote that "a man had to cling to something, and in America, where traditions were weak and where men, following their social instincts, became 'joiners,' the temptation to cling to party became resistless. . . . This party loyalty found expression in a traditional voting, which obscured contemporaneous issues" (1912, 60–61). Similarly, Graham Wallas described a party as "something which can be loved and trusted, and which can be recognized at successive elections as being the same thing that was loved and trusted before; and a party is such a thing" (1921, 103–104). Likewise, Pendleton Herring wrote that some "citizens align themselves with one party or another because they are attracted by the 'game of politics.' Party loyalties are frequently fixed at a very early age" (1940, 102).

Although the notion of party loyalty was thus clear by 1950, there was not consensus that this meant that parties should be seen as having a definitional base in the electorate (Ranney 1968, 153–154). There was disagreement among party researchers as to whether primary voters, supporters (including financial contributors), and identifiers should be included as part of the notion of party. Ranney cites early authors on each side of this debate. Bryce (1889, 10ff.), Merriam (1922, chap. 2), and McKean (1949) accepted the party in the electorate as part of the concept of party, but Brooks (1923, 14), Robinson (1924, 3–4), and Schattschneider (1942) rejected that view. In particular, Schattschneider argued, "Whatever else the parties may be, they are not associations of the voters who support the party candidates" (53). Before chairing the Committee on Political Parties, he was on record as asserting that "the concept of the parties as a mass association of partisans has no historical basis" (54).

The authors of the Report seem to have been aware of the idea of party loyalists, as when they referred to "those who identify themselves as Republicans or Democrats" (Committee on Political Parties 1950a, 69) and when they distinguished partisans from nonvoters and floating voters, though not in those terms (90). Yet they were not comfortable with the view of political parties as based in the electorate, which is not surprising, given Schattschneider's opposition to that perspective and his leading role in drafting the Report. Party membership was critical to the Report, since developing intraparty democracy requires that party members be able to participate in intraparty business, but the Report did not even define party membership (Ranney 1951, 489–492). It is not clear whether party members were meant to be the party in the electorate, or if they were seen as a more activist rung. In any event, within just a few years, the party's subfield gained a richer understanding of the party in the electorate.

The Concept in the 1951–1960 Literature

The decade from 1951 through 1960 was the period in which the political science discipline became more comfortable with the concept of the party in the electorate. By the end of this period the notion of the concept became firmly entrenched in the literature because of the sway of three books.

The first was V. O. Key Jr.'s influential parties textbook, which brought the phrase "the party in the electorate" to the attention of the discipline. The first two editions (1942, 1947) had not focused on the party in the electorate, but the last three editions (1952, 1958, 1964) did. The term itself had been coined by Ralph Goldman (1951, ch. 17) in his doctoral dissertation, as Key meticulously acknowledged (1958, 181 n. 1), but it was Key's *Politics, Parties, and Pressure Groups* that popularized the term. Key included the party in the electorate as part of his definition of parties and described it by stating that "within the body of voters as a whole, groups are formed of persons who regard themselves as party members" (1958, 181). He calls this an "amorphous group" but at the same time a "social reality." More generally, his inclusion of a discussion of the electorate and a realignment of it in a political parties text stood as evidence of the importance of the party in the electorate.

Another major book of this decade was *The American Voter* (Campbell et al. 1960), which turned the discipline's attention to party identification as the essence of the party in the electorate. This book was itself the culmination of a decade of research. It was just as the Report was being written that the book's authors began focusing on party identification as their key concept for understanding mass voting. The University of Michigan researchers first used the party identification concept in a report (Belknap and Campbell 1952) of a study that used just a vote-intention question to measure partisanship, recognizing explicitly that it was a crude measure. The now famous question, "Generally speaking, do you usually think of yourself as a Republican, a Democrat, an Independent, or what?" was first tried by Warren Miller in an Ann Arbor survey in 1951 (Kessel 1988, 301). The full question series was initially employed in the Michigan researchers' 1952 national survey, and the concept of party identification played an important part in their report on that election (Campbell, Gurin, and Miller 1954). But it was *The American Voter* that turned the discipline's attention to party identification as the essence of the party in the electorate. That volume developed a rich theory of voting, with party identification playing a central role as a long-term determinant of the vote decision. Party identification became the crucial concept for our study of the party in the electorate.

A third major book of this decade that should be crucial to our understanding of the relationship between the concepts of party responsibility and party in the electorate was Anthony Downs's *An Economic Theory of Democracy* (1957). The Report may have accepted the notion of party loyalty that underlies party identification, but it could not have anticipated Downs's work. He moved the argument to a different level, discussing party strategies for maximizing their vote share, given a series of assumptions about the electorate. His model yields two main derivations: that in a two-party system the parties should converge in policies and that this convergence should be to the position of the median voter in the distribution of voters. All of this depends on a series of assumptions that are thoroughly unrealistic (Stokes 1963), particularly a unidimensional policy space along with no abstention. Still, the Downs model is critical to consider since it so explicitly contradicts the possibility of party responsibility in a two-party system. Party convergence is just the opposite of what the Report called for, but Downs shows that under some assumptions the optimal policy position for parties is to converge. Even recognizing that the Downs results may not hold under different assumptions, minimally Downs showed that party responsibility is not necessarily an equilibrium position for the parties. Before his work, political scientists did not notice this tension between ideological parties and party divergence. The Downs model has been modified over the years, but Downs makes clear that any call for party responsibility must be explicit as to how it views the nature of ideological competition in the mass electorate.

Together these three books made scholars in the political parties field recognize the importance of the party in the electorate. Key made it relevant to our substantive theories, the Michigan authors made it central to our empirical theories, and Downs made it part of our formal theories. By enriching our theories of parties, these three works had the further effect of weakening the theoretical basis of the Report.

Party Divergence Under a Modified Version of the Downs Model

Empirical studies of the party in the electorate abounded after 1960, but there was also important formal theory work showing that two-party competition along an ideological dimension need not lead to convergence. Four factors are of particular importance.

First, multidimensional spatial competition would generally not lead to an equilibrium solution (McKelvey 1976), in which case convergence would not be expected. However, if we are dealing with Euclidean space, the effective competition dimension can be seen as the line connecting the two parties in the space, returning the model to basic unidimensionality. Enelow and Hinich (1984, chap. 4) similarly distinguish between issues and "predictive dimensions," such that multiple issues can be related to the same predictive dimension, in which case what matters is the median position on the predictive dimension.[1] Multidimensionality thus does not necessarily imply divergence.

A second factor to consider is the possibility of selective abstention. Ideological extremists can decide not to vote as a way of punishing their party if it moves too far from them. This logic pulls the parties slightly apart even in unidimensional competition, as each moves slightly away from center to mollify its ideological extreme (Garvey 1966). If either party moves too far away from the center because of its extreme wing, the other can win in a landslide, as happened in the 1964 and 1972 presidential elections. However, a slight shift away from the center by both parties is not enough to hurt either party's chances for victory and may be enough to keep ideological extremists from abstaining.

Third, the candidates may care about policy matters. Downs assumed that parties seek only to win elections, but Wittman (1983) showed that convergence would not occur if the candidates care about policy. Calvert (1985), however, proved that the divergence would be small because of the effect of the electorate pushing candidates toward the center.

The fourth and most important factor to consider is the nomination process. Candidates have to obtain their party's nomination, and Downsean logic implies that the optimal strategy for a candidate (at least once the race has settled down to two contenders) is to move to the median position of those who choose the party's nominee. Hypothetically, once the nomination is secured, the nominee can try to move quickly to the median position of the entire electorate, but that amount of movement is unlikely to appear authentic. It is more likely that the candidate will move back somewhat closer to the median voter position but not get there entirely. Thus a nomination process has the effect of leading to some divergence between the candidates even with unidimensional politics.[2]

Downs pointed out logical issues involving the relationship between the party in the electorate and responsible parties, but this subsequent work implies that some candidate divergence is to be expected under the mildest modifications of the Downs model. However, the amount of divergence to be expected is minimal, certainly less than the Report advocated. The modest amount of party divergence expected according to a modified Downsean model is of the order of magnitude that developed in the second half of the twentieth century.

THE PARTY IN THE ELECTORATE IN THE SECOND HALF OF THE TWENTIETH CENTURY

Empirical evidence about the party in the electorate before 1950 is, unfortunately, fragmentary at best, but the National Election Studies (NES) surveys provide considerable information about the concept since then. This evidence on party identification will be reviewed here since partisanship is at the core of the party in the electorate. Particular attention will be given to whether partisan change since the 1950s should be characterized as party dealignment, realignment, or a resurgence of partisanship, because there is evidence that can be interpreted in each of these ways (Niemi and Weisberg 2001, chap. 21).

Levels of Identification and Party Dealignment

To what extent does the electorate identify with parties? Is the party in the electorate a minor part of the total electorate, or does it encompass most citizens? And how has this changed over time—is the public dealigning, with fewer people identifying with parties, or are party ties becoming more prevalent? These questions are basic to understanding the role of the party in the electorate in contemporary politics.

It turns out that the public can relate to the party identification scale with ease. As *The American Voter* authors wrote, "The fact that nearly everyone in our sample could be placed on a unitary dimension of party identification . . . [is an] important finding . . . about the nature of party support within the electorate " (Campbell et al. 1960, 127). The conclusion that nearly all citizens can self-locate on the party identification scale remains true, though with some variation over the years since then. In the 1950s, about 90 percent of the public considered themselves closer to one party or the other, with only the slightest amount of prodding. The 1952 survey occurred at the high for this series, 92 percent, which was replicated only in 1964.[3] That value subsequently fell as low as 82 percent in 1974, but since 1988 it is back to the level of the 1950s and 1960s, with nearly 90 percent of the public considering themselves closer to one party or the other.

Three types of respondents do not consider themselves closer to either of the major parties. "Apoliticals" do not relate enough to politics to deal with terms like "Republican" or "Democrat." This is a small group, 3 to 4 percent through the early 1960s when southern blacks were not permitted to vote, but just 1 to 2 percent in most surveys since that time. A second small residual group consists of people who consider themselves members of other parties and do not describe themselves closer to one major party rather than the other. The largest group is Independents, and they have been the most important of these three types, particularly because of their relevance to debates as to whether politics has dealigned.

The proportion of the public who consider themselves Independents rather than Republicans or Democrats varied over the second half of the twentieth century. The 1950s were at a low point for political independence, whether defined narrowly (to include just pure Independents) or broadly (to include leaners also). There was a substantial increase in Independents during the late 1960s and early 1970s, if only the first party-identification question is used (so we include everyone who calls themselves Independents), but there was little change in the percentage of pure Independents. Independence peaked in the post-Watergate period (1974–1978). The total proportion of Independents hit a record 40 percent in 2000, but the proportion of pure Independents has steadied.

The increase in Independents is one aspect of a dealignment from parties and the growth of candidate-centered politics that many observers feel has occurred since the 1950s (e.g., Wattenberg 1996; Aldrich and Niemi 1996). There has been a corresponding decline in strength of partisanship, but it follows a mixed pattern. The proportion of strong identifiers has fallen since the 1950s, but the low for strong identification was between 1972 and 1980. The proportion of strong identifiers since 1982 has been at the 1966–1970 level, above the 1972–1980 lows but below the 1952–1964 highs. The trends are clearer and more linear for weak identifiers and for leaners. Weak identification declined after 1986, falling below 30 percent for the first time in 2000; the proportion of leaners has risen to a new high of 28 percent (Fig. 9.1).

Attitudes toward the parties have changed less. Feeling thermometer ratings of the political parties are available since 1978. The average rating of the two parties was a few degrees less favorable in the 1990s than previously, falling from the 58–60 range to the 55–56 range. This change is not large, but it shows less satisfaction with the parties. The ratings of Republicans hit lows in 1992, 1996, and especially 1998, and the Democratic low was in 1994. Yet the average rating for each party has at least been above 50 (except for the Republicans' exact 50 in 1998), not as low as might be expected during a party dealignment period. This suggests that the party in the electorate remains strong and therefore must be taken into account in discussions of party responsibility.

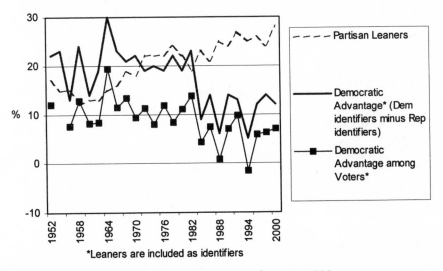

Figure 9.1. Partisanship trends, 1952–2000

The Party Balance and Party Realignment

Having described the extent of party identification in the electorate, we now examine to what extent one party has a majority over the other in partisanship. Along with that, there is the issue of whether there has been party realignment in recent years, with the partisan balance changing.

The first readings of party identification found that the majority of citizens identified with the Democratic Party in the 1950s, even as the country was electing a Republican as president. If Downs's logic implied parties of equal strength, then that condition was not satisfied. The Democratic Party has remained ahead in polling since then, but the size of its lead has diminished (Fig. 9.1). The Democratic advantage was at its high point in 1964, at the time of the Johnson landslide over Goldwater, but it fell during the Reagan years in the 1980s and hit its low in 1994, when the Republicans scored their surprise takeover of the House of Representatives.

The partisan-identification changes during this period were large enough in the South to speak of realignment there. The once solid Democratic South no longer has a large majority of Democratic identifiers. About three-quarters of southerners identified with the Democratic Party in the 1952 survey but only half in the 1992–2000 surveys. Correspondingly, the proportion identifying with the Republican Party has risen from 14 percent to the high 30 percent range. There is still a Democratic plurality in the states of the Confederate South, but even that plurality would be transformed to virtual parity if only the partisanship of white southerners were examined.

This diminished Democratic lead in partisanship is not as dramatic a realignment as the New Deal realignment of the 1930s. Yet it is more dramatic than it may seem at first in that Democratic identifiers tend to turn out to vote at elections at lower rates than Republican identifiers, by an average of about 7 percent. As a result, a slight Democratic lead among survey respondents can translate to a more even partisan balance among actual voters. Indeed, in the 1988 and 1994 elections, the difference between the proportions of Democrats and Republicans among actual voters was negligible (Fig. 9.1). The Democrats can no longer count on an automatic partisan advantage among voters. Downs's median voter now has a pivotal position in deciding election outcomes.

Several social groups modified their partisanship during this period (Stanley and Niemi 1999, 2001). Native southern whites became less Democratic and more Republican in their identification, and blacks became more Democratic. Catholics became less Democratic, and white Protestant fundamentalists became more Republican. The changes in group support have been so substantial that Stanley and Niemi (1995) have written of the demise of the New Deal coalition. Still, even if the Democratic advantage in partisanship has been considerably eroded, it has not been reversed. Yet the party in the electorate has changed enough to make party coalitions more cohesive, especially because of the changes in the South.

Partisan Loyalty and Partisan Resurgence

The level of identification and the party balance would matter little if partisanship were not related to the vote. Therefore, the next important step in describing the party in the electorate is to question the extent to which party identification is related to vote choice. Are partisans loyal to their party when they enter the voting booth? And is this changing over time? Are parties becoming irrelevant to voting, or is there evidence of party resurgence?

Even if *The American Voter* was recounting the election of Republican presidents during an era of a Democratic majority in mass partisanship, the usual account is that party identification was strongly related to the vote. Indeed, the common finding is that party identification has a higher relationship to the vote than any other attitudinal variable has. Yet the discipline began to think that party identification was less important when Nie, Verba, and Petrocik (1979) found that the relationship between partisanship and vote had decreased. For several years now, researchers have been reporting that that relationship has gone back up. This position has been argued most effectively by Bartels (2000), who shows that partisanship is again a strong predictor of presidential voting.

For the breakdown of the two-party vote by partisanship and the proportion of each party voting Democratic (with leaners counted as partisans), see Figure 9.2. Democrats were least likely to defect to the Republican candidate in the Clinton elections of the 1990s; they defected most from George McGovern

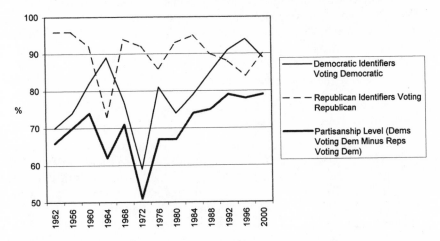

Figure 9.2. Partisan presidential voting loyalty rates, 1952–2000 (only major party voters)

in 1972. Republicans were least likely to defect to the Democratic candidate in the Eisenhower elections of the 1950s; they defected most from Barry Goldwater in 1964. The net result is that the difference between Democrats and Republicans in their voting has climbed back from its 1972 low to a high since 1992.

Bartels (2000) examines the importance of partisanship in voting more elegantly, using a probit analysis of major party voting regressed on strength of partisan identification. He finds that the relationship between partisanship and the vote diminished in 1964 when measured against the three prior presidential elections. Party voting went back up in 1968, setting the Wallace vote aside, but it plummeted in 1972. Bartels shows that party voting for the presidency has climbed steadily since that 1972 low, returning by 1984 to the levels of the 1950s. Setting aside the Perot vote, the level of partisan voting for president in the 1990s was the highest in this half century. A similar analysis for the congressional vote shows that partisan voting fell from the 1950s to lows in 1978 and 1980 but has climbed since, though it is still below the pre-1964 levels.

Certainly there have also been several important Independent candidacies for the presidencies since 1950: George Wallace in 1968, John Anderson in 1980, and H. Ross Perot in 1992 and 1996, as well as Ralph Nader and Pat Buchanan in 2000. Taking voting for minor party and Independent presidential candidates into account changes the preceding conclusions about partisan voting only slightly. The partisan loyalty rates in 1996 and 2000 were still fairly high compared to the 1964–1984 period (not shown).

Regardless of third-party efforts, it is clear that the two-party system remains very stable. Polls suggest that the public would be open to a third party, but that is in answer to hypothetical questions that bear little relationship to the choices that voters face when deciding whether to support a specific new party. Faced with real third-party choices for president, the public overwhelmingly goes back to the two major parties. The two-party system remains alive, if not always well. And the party in the electorate now has even more loyal partisans in the years since the Report was written.

A Decade by Decade Analysis

It is useful to step back to look at the several trends described here decade by decade. The 1950s were a high point for identification with the parties and a low point for political independence. The Democratic majority of that period peaked in 1964. The 1970s were a very different era. The change began with the least partisan of all presidential elections of this period, the 1972 Nixon-McGovern race. By the 1974 post-Watergate election, the proportion of the public considering themselves closer to one party or the other fell to its low while the level of political independence climbed. Nie, Verba, and Petrocik (1979) wrote *The Changing American Voter* to describe how the party in the electorate during this period differed from the 1950s as depicted in *The American Voter,* but later surveys show that the 1970s were also not typical.

The 1980s were a transitional period. The most important change was a decrease in the Democratic advantage in partisanship. The level of identification with parties climbed back up from its low while the proportion of Independents inched back from its high. The importance of partisanship in presidential voting went back up to the levels of the 1950s.

The 1990s and 2000 stand out as the most partisan of these periods. Putting aside the third-party vote, the relationship between partisanship and presidential voting was at its fifty-year high in the Clinton and Gore elections. The Democratic lead in partisanship hit its fifty-year low as the Republicans regained control of the House of Representatives in 1994, though it has gone back up some since. Meanwhile, the proportion of weak identifiers fell to a new low while the total proportion of Independents hit new highs.

These survey data show that changes did occur in the party in the electorate over the second half of the twentieth century, but the consideration of party responsibility requires an examination of one more piece of the puzzle: the differences between the parties as seen by the parties in the electorate.

THE IDEOLOGICAL POLARIZATION BETWEEN THE PARTIES

The authors of the Report sought greater ideological differences between the parties than existed at the time. Unfortunately, it is not possible to trace ideological polarization among the mass public back to the 1950s because ideology was not measured in the early Michigan election studies. *The American Voter's* authors concluded that the public is not ideological in its politics, and this result discouraged researchers from measuring ideology. Even without direct measures, though, it is useful to recall the general situation when the Report was written. The Democratic Party contained both northern liberals and southern conservatives, and the Republican Party contained both northeastern liberals and midwestern conservatives. As a result of these mixtures, both parties had more moderate ideological images than they do at the dawn of the twenty-first century. Meanwhile, the conservative coalition of southern Democrats and Republicans dominated Congress, blocking liberal legislation. Under these circumstances, it would be surprising if there was substantial ideological polarization between the parties at the mass level during that period.

Ideological polarization between the parties has increased since then. The usual account is that the change began as Democrats took the lead in passing and enforcing civil rights laws and other liberal legislation. Traditionally Democratic white southern conservatives began to vote for the Republican Party, electing many conservative Republicans to Congress. Newly enfranchised African Americans in the South voted for Democrats, so the remaining southern Democratic representatives had to appeal to those African-American voters to win reelection, and their voting records became more like those of northern Democrats. As a result, the Democrats in Congress have become more cohesive in their voting; conservative coalition votes in which the majority of southern Democrats vote with the majority of Republicans have become rare; and the Republican Party in Congress has become more conservative. Additionally, there is more party voting in Congress, with the majorities of the two parties more often voting in opposite directions. The empirical evidence to be reviewed here shows that ideological polarization of the mass electorate also increased during this period, in line with the moderate divergence of parties expected under the modified version of the Downs reasoning.

Self-Placement on Ideology

One way to examine polarization at the mass level is to look at the relationship between ideology and partisanship. The NES began direct measurement of ideology on a seven-point scale in 1972. It is important to recognize that the problems that the early researchers saw with ideology were real—many respondents do not attempt to answer the ideology question. The level of ideological awareness is much lower than the level of partisan awareness. If the Downsean dimension is seen as ideology, many people cannot locate themselves on the continuum. The proportions of Republicans who placed themselves on the scale over the years range from 73 to 86 percent, and the proportions for Democrats ran about ten points lower (62 to 76 percent). Independents are least relevant for the comparisons being made here, but their rates were even lower, from 40 to 67 percent.

The self-placement rates for both Republicans and Democrats were lowest at the beginning of the Reagan administration, in 1980 and 1982. The conventional wisdom is that the country became more ideological with the Reagan conservative revolution, but the data show that period to have been a low point in terms of ideological awareness. The highs occurred in 1994 for the Republicans and in 1998 for the Democrats. Ideological awareness was higher in the 1990s and 2000 than in the 1970s or 1980s.

One measure of ideological polarization is the difference between the proportions of Republicans and Democrats who consider themselves conservatives on the seven-point scale (see Figure 9.3). The low for this series was in 1972, with high points in 1994 and 1998 showing that there was now moderate ideological divergence of the parties in the electorate. Republicans were the source of this change (Fig. 9.3). Only about half of Republicans considered themselves conservatives in the 1970s and 1980s, but that proportion went up to the 60 percent level in the mid-1990s due to greater ideological awareness among them, along with fewer of them considering themselves liberals or middle of the road.

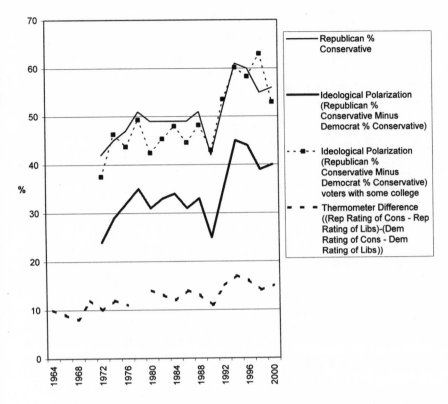

Figure 9.3. Ideological self-placement, 1972–2000

As to be expected, ideological polarization was more extreme among more sophisticated voters. For the trend in ideological polarization for voters who have at least some college education, see Figure 9.3. The degree of polarization for these voters is always higher than for the total set of respondents, and the increase over time is sharper than for the total sample. Their polarization level in 1972 was relatively low, but it was higher in the 1974–1990 period and then climbed to new highs since. There is substantial ideological polarization among the group for which it would be most expected.

The Report assumed that the public did not see the political parties as standing for different programs, but it was written before surveys were available to provide empirical evidence. The NES surveys ask people whether there are important differences between the two parties. There is a clear trend for presidential election years, with values of at most 55 percent through 1976 and values of at least 59 percent since 1984 (Fig. 9.4).[4] The public has become more certain that there are important differences between the parties, though one-third of the electorate still does not see such differences. Looking at only college-

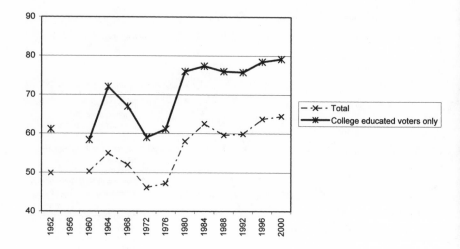

Figure 9.4. Citizens see important differences between parties, 1952–2000

educated voters, the proportion of the public who see differences between the parties is even higher, above 75 percent in presidential election years since the Reagan victory in 1980. Thus, the public now sees differences between the parties to a greater extent than when the Report was written.

Reactions to Liberals and Conservatives

Feeling thermometer ratings of liberals and conservatives can be used as another measure of ideology. These thermometers have been used in the NES surveys since 1964. The differences on this measure between Republicans and Democrats are limited. Republican identifiers always give a higher average to conservatives than to liberals, and Democratic identifiers are always slightly more positive to liberals than to conservatives. The Democrats gave more of an edge to liberals in later years, but the change is slight.

For a summary measure of party ideological polarization, we can take the difference in how much higher Republicans and Democrats rate conservatives over liberals. The low for this series was 8 in 1968 (Fig. 9.3). Our usual understanding is that the 1960s were an ideological period, but party polarization on ideology during that period was limited, probably because conservative southern Democrats diluted that party's ideological purity. The high for this series was 17 in 1994, with high readings also for the two Clinton and the Gore election years. The differences are not large, but party identifiers had become more polarized in their reactions to liberals and conservatives by the 1990s and 2000.

The change over time on the thermometer measure is much smaller than that on the ideological self-placement measure. This difference may be related to the lower level of missing data on the thermometer items. Many people who give "don't know" responses to the ideology self-placement question still rate liberals and conservatives on the thermometer scale, but their lack of ideological awareness may dampen the thermometer differences.

The thermometer evidence fits well with the data from the seven-point ideology scales. Party ideological polarization on the seven-point scales was lowest in 1972, the first year that the NES used seven-point scales. If the thermometer data were truncated to start at 1972, that also would be its low value. The implication is that, regardless of the measure used, ideological polarization of the parties was low in the 1960s, went up a little by 1972, increased further in the 1980s, and is at a high in the 1990s and 2000.[5] It is important to note that this increased ideological polarization occurred before the Clinton impeachment and before George W. Bush's campaign for the presidency as a "compassionate conservative," and there is no sign of these events further increasing polarization.

Party Divergence at the Level of the Attentive Public

While there certainly is not complete ideological polarization between Republican and Democratic identifiers, the data show that there are ideological differences and that these have grown, especially for the attentive public. The different degrees of divergence at different levels of the electorate provide another basis for party responsibility. The general public's ability to understand ideological competition is limited; some people view politics in this way, but others do not. This allows the parties and candidates to rely on ideology as a selective campaign appeal. Within limits, they can take ideological stands to impress the attentive public while knowing that most of the public will not notice those stands enough for nonconvergence positions to hurt them. Ideological stands can be used to mobilize supporters, without too much worry that those stands will lose support among the general public. In short, it may be possible for candidates to have their cake and eat it, too: they can diverge somewhat without paying the costs for that divergence.

The greater perceived divergence for the attentive public was evident in Figures 9.3 and 9.4 when one looks at ideological polarization among voters who have at least some college education. Similar results would be obtained if the attentive public were defined in other ways, such as focusing on people who are interested in politics, who follow the campaign in the media, or who have greater amounts of political knowledge. People who do not have these characteristics are less likely to be ideologically aware enough to punish their preferred party when it takes ideological stands.[6]

Financial contributors provide another basis for party divergence. By the 1990s, direct mailing to potential financial contributors became a widespread tactic of interest groups. Groups sent out mailings to potential contributors on a variety of topics, from the importance of passing a constitutional amendment making English the official language to both sides of the gun control debate. People who contribute to one of these groups end up on the mailing list of other groups of the same ideological persuasion. These groups generally had alliances with the parties, often by having Republican or Democratic members of Congress write the solicitation letters. Soliciting funds in this way has the effect of promoting party divergence. Since funds are being generated on the basis of these appeals, there is an incentive to bring the issues to floor votes in Congress so the members can show contributors that they are attempting to pass (or block) the legislation of interest. The parties vote differently in Congress on these issues, so the contributors who care about such issues notice party differences on them. Compromise legislation becomes more difficult to craft since each party has a financial incentive to maintain the issue; party convergence would not yield as much in financial contributions as divergence does.

Thus, the limited public awareness of ideology need not prevent parties from appealing to the attentive public on the basis of divergent ideology and programs. The existence of an attentive public provides a basis for party divergence. The divergence is not extreme, but the parties do stand for different programs, as the Report desired.

THE PARTY IN THE ELECTORATE AND RESPONSIBLE PARTIES

We can now look directly at the relationship between party in the electorate and party responsibility. The Report's call for more ideologically distinct parties was partially realized by 2000. The ideological differences between the parties that have become pronounced in Congress are echoed in the party in the electorate.[7] However, ideological polarization of the parties is far from complete. Even at their highs, all the series discussed here do not show strong ideological polarization. Ideology per se is of limited relevance to the public; thus many people do not respond in these terms.

Most important, though, is the coincidence of two trends we have reviewed. The 1992–2000 period was the high point both for partisan voting and for ideological polarization. The party in the electorate is voting more in accord with party responsibility notions, even if partisan voting is still more prevalent than ideological polarization.

The Report largely ignored the party in the electorate and in so doing missed an important basis for party responsibility. The party in the electorate was reinvigorated in the second half of the twentieth century, with the decline in party identification rates partially stemmed, the development of true two-party politics in the South, and a return to partisan polarization in voting. Meanwhile, polarization between the parties in Congress was accompanied by Republican and Democratic identifiers becoming somewhat more polarized ideologically and more people seeing differences between the parties. The limited amount of ideological polarization is to be expected, given a modified version of Downs's model of ideological voting. The existence of an attentive public permits party divergence. The parties can diverge enough to satisfy the people who care (the more educated with more political knowledge, those interested in politics who follow campaigns, and the people who participate in nominations and financial contributions) while not diverging enough to lose votes among the public at large.

In retrospect, the distortions produced by the one-party South were responsible for many of the problems that the authors of the Report saw with the party system of the time. The presence of that conservative bloc in the Democratic Party blurred its ideological image. When the Republican nominee in 1964 cast a vote against the Civil Rights Act of that year, a clear message was sent to southern whites as well as to blacks. The partisanship of southern white voters correspondingly changed, electing many conservative Republicans to Congress and causing many of the remaining southern Democrats in Congress to be more beholden to the liberals in their districts. The result was to make the Republican Party in Congress more conservative while leaving the congressional Democratic Party more liberal. The Reagan presidency tagged the Republican Party even more clearly as conservative, as did the Republican Congress of the 1990s. The half century preceding the writing of the Report was generally a period of unified government, and the half century following was a period of divided government that has made disputes between the parties more prominent. Party differences became clearer to the electorate, encouraging the parties to take different stands on more issues. Thus, realignment in the South had a snowballing effect, leading to movement toward the type of differences in party programs that the authors of the Report favored.

The question remains as to how this projects into the future. We have seen how trends can be temporary, as when the diminished partisan impact during the 1970s was largely reversed by the 1990s. Should we believe that the increased ideological polarization of the parties would be more permanent? There were more reasons for party differences when the economy was weak, when there were large government deficits, and when the nation was in the Cold War. Still, party differences on social issues remain, as well as differences on tax cuts and on instituting new government programs. As long as the parties duel in Congress and across branches of government on such issues, there is likely to be partisan ideological polarization among party activists, and the party in the electorate is likely to continue to perceive party differences. Yet it would be a mistake to view this as a permanent development. Ideological polarization could diminish if a Republican president or Congress pursues a more moderate agenda. The lesson of the latter half of the twentieth century is that party differences can emerge in our political system through the interaction of the party in government with the party in the electorate. This is no guarantee of party responsibility in the future, but it should be taken as an encouraging sign.

APPENDIX: OVER-TIME TRENDS (PEARSON'S R CORRELATIONS OF
SERIES WITH TIME, 1952–2000)

Partisan identification levels
    Consider self closer to one party than other   −.193
    Pure Independent   .450
    Independent, including leaners   .852
Strength of identification
    Strong identifiers   −.512
    Weak identifiers   −.790
    Partisan leaners   .900
Party thermometers
    Democratic Party thermometer average   −.625
    Republican Party thermometer average   −.501
    Average thermometer ratings of two parties   −.768
Democratic identification advantage
    Dem identifiers minus Rep identifiers, only strong and weak identifiers   −.719
    Dem identifiers minus Rep identifiers, including leaners as identifiers   −.629
    Dem identifiers minus Rep identifiers, South only (including leaners as
        identifiers)   −.906
Democratic advantage among voters only
    Dem turnout rate minus turnout rate   .430
    Dem electorate minus Rep electorate   −.543
    Dem electorate minus Rep electorate, South only   −.871
Partisan presidential voting loyalty rates, major party voters only
    Dem identifiers voting Democratic   .567
    Rep identifiers voting Republican   −.197
    Partisanship level: Dems voting Dem minus Reps voting Dem   .541
Partisan presidential voting loyalty rates, including third-party voters
    Dem identifiers voting Democratic   .428
    Rep identifiers voting Republican   −.372
    Partisanship level: Dems voting Dem minus Reps voting Dem   .412
    Partisanship level: Reps voting Rep minus Dems voting Rep   .328
Ideological awareness level
    Democrats   .350
    Independents   −.234
    Republicans   .578
Ideological self-placement
    Republican percent conservative   .733
    Ideological polarization: Republican percent conservative minus Democrat
        percent conservative   .704
    Ideological polarization, voters with at least some college education   .789
Important differences in what parties stand for, presidential election years only
    Democrats   .789
    Independents   .494
    Republicans   .785
    Total   .790
    Voters with at least some college education   .794

Thermometer ratings of liberals and conservatives
(Index = average score given to conservatives minus average score given
   to liberals plus 50)

Democrats	−.800
Independents	−.430
Republicans	.350
Party difference: Rep index minus Dem index	.826

Positive correlations show increasing values over time; negative correlations show
decreasing values.

NOTES

1. They also deal with multiple predictive dimensions, in which case there might
not be an equilibrium.

2. Aldrich (1995, 180–192) also shows that the existence of party activists leads to
equilibrium positions for candidates in which there will not be complete convergence
between the parties.

3. Data reported in this chapter are generally based on tables in the cumulative
National Election Studies dataset available at their web site: <*http://www.umich.edu/
~nes/nesguide/nesguide.htm*>; the results using statistical controls involve direct analysis of that cumulative file. Linear trends can be detected by correlating each time
series with a time variable; the appendix shows these correlations for several series.

4. This question has also been asked in several midterm election surveys. Since it
is necessarily affected by the campaign, though, its values for midterm elections are
discontinuous with presidential election years, with values 4 to 34 percent lower than
in the preceding presidential election year.

5. NES respondents are also asked to place the parties on seven-point ideology
scales, allowing analysts to compute the difference in locations ascribed to the parties, but this measure is susceptible to partisans pushing the party they dislike to an
ideological extreme.

6. The only cost that occurs for limited party divergence is when ideological terms
acquire negative connotations. The term "liberal" was more acceptable than the term
"conservative" in the 1950s, but that changed to the point that George Bush could attack Michael Dukakis in 1988 on the basis of the "L-word." The term "conservative"
is more acceptable now, and surveys consistently show that more people consider themselves conservatives. As a result, most liberal politicians prefer to be called moderate,
which has the effect of minimizing apparent ideological polarization.

7. For analyses of the causal direction of the mass and congressional changes, see
Hetherington (2001) and Mockabee (2001).

10

Toward a More Responsible Two-Party Voter

The Evolving Bases of Partisanship

Gerald M. Pomper and Marc D. Weiner

We report the discovery of a missing link. In its epochal advocacy of "a more responsible two-party system," the Report of the Committee on Political Parties of the American Political Science Association (1950a) dealt with political parties yet largely ignored the audience for those parties, the electorate. Perhaps in retribution, American voters ignored the Report. We now find evidence of a significant change in mass attitudes that may partially realize the Report's goals.[1]

VOTERS IN THE REPORT

The Report's silence about voters was evident in the basic goals of the original advocates of "responsible parties": "first, that the parties are able to bring forth programs to which they commit themselves and, second, that the parties possess sufficient internal cohesion to carry out these programs" (Committee on Political Parties 1950a, 1). Voters, they hoped, would respond appropriately to the changed parties, but they were portrayed as submissive. The electorate was regarded as reacting to party initiatives, the passive means to promote party accountability by choosing between programs adopted by coherent, hierarchical, and, therefore, now-responsible parties. To the extent the Report's authors considered ordinary citizens, they dealt with them almost entirely as members or potential members of the formal party organizations. The Committee on Political Parties paid attention to voters behaving as voters at only two places in the Report (Pomper 2001).

In the first mention, the emphasis was still on voters in their roles as party activists. The committee predicted—or better, hoped—that policy-oriented parties "would prompt those who identify themselves as Republicans or Democrats to think in terms of support of that program, rather than in term of personalities, patronage and local matters" (Committee on Political Parties 1950a, 69). This assertion can be applied to ordinary voters who "identify" with the parties with the casualness of an NES questionnaire.

The second, and more elaborate, discussion of voters came at the end of the Report, as the Committee (90–91) divided the electorate into three groups: nonvoters, standpatters or traditional voters, and party switchers. (See the similar categorization of Key 1966, and before him, Miller 1953.) These groups are claimed to be fertile ground for programmatic parties. Nonvoters might be mobilized if "a real choice is presented." Among traditional voters, "the rank and file in each party want their party so organized that the views of the party majority will be respected and carried out." Particularly important was the third group, party switchers, those "willing to make an electoral choice and [who want] a choice to make."

Critics of the Report were more cognizant of the importance of voters as independent actors. They understood that reform programs would be only theoretical exercises if they did not reflect the realities of electoral politics. A quarter century later, Ranney underlined the Report's irrelevance to real politics: "Regardless of how enthusiastic college professors might be about the report's prescriptions, party politicians and the man in the street showed no interest whatever, let alone the kind of fervor needed to make possible such sweeping changes" (1975, 43–44).

American political parties are not intellectual creations of political scientists, a reality long recognized by the most notable empirical theorists. "A political party is first of all an organized attempt to get power" (Schattschneider 1942, 35); it is "the creature of the politicians, the ambitious office seeker and officeholder" (Aldrich 1995, 4). Unless the voters cast ballots on the basis of party programs, parties will not focus on programmatic differences.

Now, after fifty years, we can bring voters back in. Based on analyses of partisanship spanning five decades, we find evidence that the hopes, even if not the prescriptions, of the Report's authors are becoming empirical realities. The missing link between mass attitudes and party responsibility is emerging. Voters are now prepared to pay attention to those programs to which the parties commit themselves and to respond to the efforts of parties to carry out these programs. We substantiate this development through four arguments: voters increasingly perceive policy differences between the major parties; these changed perceptions have increased the relative importance of the cognitive, compared to the affective, bases of partisanship; this changed relationship cannot be adequately explained by social or individual characteristics alone; and this changed relationship is due to the new character of American politics. We conclude with a discussion of the sources and likely impact of these changes on electoral behavior and American politics generally. We expect these new perceptions of the parties to move the nation closer to the Report's goal, "a more responsible two-party system."

PARTY DIFFERENCES

Conventional wisdom tells us that there are few significant differences between the parties. Even Thomas Jefferson, the first American party leader, minimized party differences, declaring, "We have called by different names brethren of the same principle. We are all Republicans, we are all Federalists." With far less elegance, George Wallace said, "There's not a dime's worth of difference" between the parties. Ralph Nader echoed this attitude in his derisive attacks on the two major parties during the election of 2000.

Scholars, however, are more likely to perceive differences. Tocqueville, with the insight of a foreign observer, found fundamental differences of political philosophy: "The domestic controversies of the Americans at first appear to be incomprehensible or puerile. . . . The deeper we penetrate into the inmost thought of these parties, the more we perceive that the object of the one is to limit and that of the other to extend the authority of the people" (1954, 1: 185–186).

Examination of party platforms also shows extensive policy differences. In a basic textbook, Wayne (2000, 167–168) details the contrasts between the Republican and Democratic 1996 platforms on such major issues as abortion, the budget, crime, education, foreign policy, and welfare. These party differences persisted in the 2000 election, as Republicans consistently favored private market solutions to problems of education, social security, and medical care, and Democrats consistently sought governmental remedies (Pomper 2000). The most systematic comparative study concludes "not only that the Democrats and Republicans are reasonably cohesive internally when compared with political parties in other systems, but also that their platforms are quite clearly differentiated from each other in an ideologically consistent fashion" (Klingemann, Hofferbert, and Budge 1994, 138).

We want to know what voters think, and so we examine a long-standing National Election Studies measure—voter perceptions of important party differences. Even as early as 1952, a majority of respondents believed that there were significant differences in what the parties stand for. Though politicians might disparage their alleged commonality, the electorate was quite capable of perceiving distinctions between the parties. This majority observation continues with virtually no change for a quarter century.

There is a notable, and persistent, change in these perceptions beginning at the time of the 1980 election. From that point on, close to two-thirds of the electorate perceives "important differences in what the parties stand for." The step change is clearly seen in Figure 10.1. This is a pattern of "dynamic evolution," closely resembling changes in public affect toward the parties and perceived "clarity" of their issue positions on race (Carmines and Stimson 1989, chap. 7 and Fig. 7.3).

Paralleling this change is another important trend that exists in the background of this analysis: the decline of party identification. The decline in party

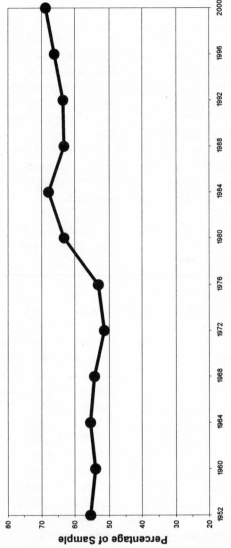

Figure 10.1. Perception of party differences (percentage of respondents who indicate a perception of important differences in what the parties stand for [1952–2000])

loyalty has been clear (Miller and Shanks 1996, chap. 7) and is explained most persuasively by intergenerational change (Mattei and Niemi 1991). Of particular note in this well-documented change is the location of this decline in the 1970s and the subsequent stabilization of the level of partisanship about the same time as the change in perceived party differences.

Despite common belittling of the parties, voters increasingly see differences between them. And despite the anguish of some commentators (Wattenberg 1984), party loyalty continues. For the political system, these altered sentiments carry implications that might well warm the hearts of the Committee on Political Parties.

THE BASIS OF PARTISANSHIP

Partisanship, or party identification, has long been recognized as the single most important influence on the individual vote. There is less consensus, however, on the sources of partisanship. For our purposes, we want to examine the relative effects of two sources of party loyalty, which we term "affective" and "cognitive" partisanship (see Mayer 1998).

When first developed, the concept of partisanship relied considerably on affective influences, particularly family tradition. According to the seminal work on electoral behavior, "We use the concept here to characterize the individual's affective orientation. . . . An orientation toward political affairs typically begins before the individual attains voting age and this orientation strongly reflects his immediate social milieu, in particular his family" (Campbell et al. 1960, 121, 146–147). It reports a "high degree of correspondence between the partisan preference of our respondents with that which they report for their parents."

We term this familial inheritance of basic political orientation "affective partisanship." For the moment, we are concerned only with the existence of partisan loyalty, not its Democratic or Republican direction. Following the argument of *The American Voter* and its progeny, we examine the likelihood that a respondent with parents who identify with a political party will also declare a partisan identification. For this purpose, we construct a measure of parental partisanship. (Unfortunately, we can track this measure only through 1992, after which the National Election Study ceased probing respondents about their parents' partisanship.)

The remembered partisanship of parents has not changed greatly over the course of the three decades from 1964 (Fig. 10.2). Though recall data do occasion some skepticism, previous research has validated remembered partisanship (Andersen 1976). Moreover, the reported changes in the recalled partisan direction of parents also seem to conform to gross changes in electoral loyalties in the earlier generation consistent with the electoral realignment of the New

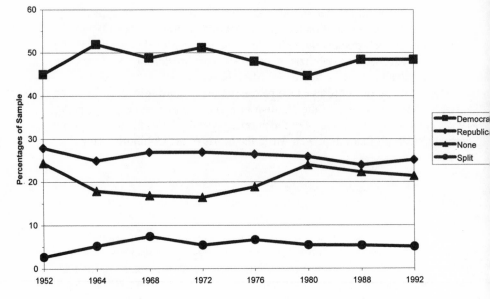

Figure 10.2. Parental partisanship, 1952–1992

Deal. For present purposes, we will trust that children do not systemically dis-
tort their parents' party loyalties.[2]

In contrast to affective partisanship, party loyalty might be based on a cognitive assessment of Democratic and Republican programs, in keeping with the
dictums of the Report. More recent literature in political science argues that such
rational calculations do explain partisan attachments (Fiorina 1981; Popkin
1991). Party identification is based on a kind of calculation by the voter, in which
he or she computes a "running tally" of party preference.

Focusing again on the existence rather than the direction of partisanship,
we have defined our measure of the voters' perception of important party differences to capture the component of cognitive partisanship. By comparing these
two sources of partisanship, affective and cognitive, we reach our central preliminary finding that the relative importance of cognitive partisanship has increased considerably.

To reach this conclusion, we estimated the odds in any given election year
that a potential voter will be a partisan. One can literally bet that this voter will
identify with a party under either of two conditions: if she had partisan parents
or if he perceives party differences. In 1952, for example, the appropriate bet-
ting odds would be between 2:1 and 3:1 under either condition. That year,
either a voter with partisan parents, or a voter perceiving party differences, would
be between two to three times more likely to be a partisan identifier than either
one whose parents were not partisan or one who did not perceive differences.

(These ratios are calculated with controls for age, sex, race, education, income, and region.)

There is a clear trend in the relative importance of these two factors in predicting partisan identification (Fig. 10.3). Perception of party differences has increased greatly in its predictive power, becoming the better predictor in the 1970s. From that time, even as overall partisanship declined, the odds grew to better than 5:1 that cognitive partisanship would predict attachment to the parties. In contrast, the effect of affective partisanship varies considerably but slowly declines.

To reinforce these trend findings more specifically, we predicted the direction of party identification on a five-point scale, from strong Republicans to strong Democrats. There is a significant difference between the two end periods. Affective partisanship has diminished considerably over the decades, as the Report's authors would probably wish. Parental partisanship continues to have a significant impact, but its contribution is now dominated by the effect of perceived party differences.

Strong Republicans and strong Democrats are particularly interesting, because these most committed voters are most likely to reflect systemic influences. The results for strong Republicans are provided in Figure 10.4, which displays the cumulative probability of partisanship as more cues are introduced. At the base of each bar is the proportion of partisanship that can be predicted blindly, when there are no cues available to a respondent, that is, when partisanship is completely absent from the parental home and the respondent also perceives no party differences. The next segment is the additional probability of the

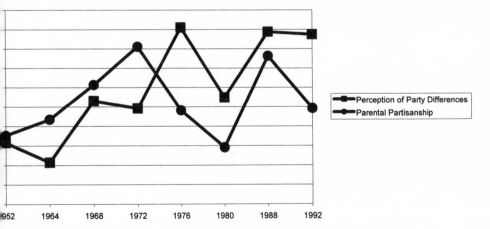

Figure 10.3. Relative effect of parental partisanship and perception of party differences on the probability that respondent will be a partisan identifier (3-point, nondirectional ordinal model)

respondent's present strong Republican identification that can be attributed to parental loyalty, followed by the additional probability attributable to the respondent's perception of party differences.

The trend is clearly toward increased impact by perceived party differences, with the change coming about 1970. The temporal endpoints show the pattern. In 1952, with no political cues, the probability of strong Republican partisanship among these voters is quite low, about 5 percent being strong identifiers. When cues are provided, that of parental partisanship is far more important in raising this probability than the cue of perceived party differences. Even at this time and even among the most committed, however, partisanship could not properly be considered an unthinking adoption of family tradition. Then, or later, "it is not something learned at mommy's knee and never questioned thereafter" (Fiorina 1981, 102).

In 1992, effects change. With no political cues, the probability of strong Republican partisanship continues low. However, in contrast to the earlier time, the parental cue has declined considerably. The cue of party difference is now predominant, close to twice as great in its effect as parental loyalty. (The results for Democrats are quite similar.) These voters still find reasons to be strong partisans, but they are learning less at their mothers' knees while getting more lessons from the combat of parties.

Party loyalty surely combines affective and cognitive partisanship in an interaction that reflects socialization by partisan parents who also commu-

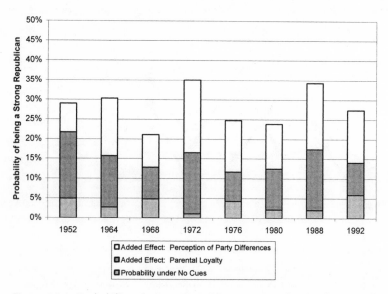

Figure 10.4. Probability of strong Republican partisanship (multinominal model)

nicate a perception of party differences. Such interaction is found in other recent research showing the development of issue-based partisanship (Miller and
Shanks 1996, 178–182). This effect is fully consistent with the programmatic
partisanship urged by the Committee on Political Parties. Inherited partisanship that interacts with perceived differences underlines Fiorina's portrait "of
the voter as a reasonably rational fellow" (1981, 200) and his conclusion, "controversies about issue voting versus party identification miss the point: the
'issues' are in party identification."

CHANGED PERCEPTIONS: SOCIAL CHANGE AND POLITICAL EFFECTS

The increase in cognitive partisanship now requires explanation. From 1960 to
2000, the proportion of citizens perceiving important party differences rose,
more or less steadily, from 53.8 percent to 68.6 percent. Theoretically, there
are two possible kinds of explanations for the increase. First, the mass public
may now be better able to perceive differences. Second, actual interparty differences may have increased. We contend that the dominant cause was changes
in the real world of politics rather than more general social trends.

Education is the most prominent social change over this period. The average respondent's schooling has risen from about tenth grade in high school to
about two years of college. As academic political scientists, we would expect—
or hope—that the added years in classrooms would also open the voters' minds
to an increased perception of party differences. Moreover, education might also
increase citizens' individual capabilities; they might feel an increased personal
efficacy, and they might be better able to use the mass media to further their
political education.

There is no doubt that the increase over time in the mean level of education has enhanced cognitive proficiency and sophistication in individual citizens in an absolute and additive fashion (Nie, Junn, and Stehlik-Barry 1996,
108). Indeed, the more educated that individual citizens are, the more likely they
are to be able to understand the positions of the parties and, in turn, the presence—or absence—of important differences in the parties' stances.

For our purposes, the vital characteristic of education is that it is distinct
from the world of politics itself. Whatever Democrats and Republicans were
doing, people got more schooling. Although politics may have contributed to
that change, it was a change in society, distinct from any structural changes in
the parties. We can consider the increase in the level of education as an independent, nonpolitical influence.

Yet we find education alone an unsatisfactory explanation. Political change
without politics? To capture the impact of political changes, we turn to our
political institutions. The collective Congress reifies the world of political ab-

stractions through political engagement. Through their behavior, congressional parties tell voters what "Republican" and "Democratic" mean—what the parties stand for, whether they are different, how they differ. The clash of the parties in Congress provides dramatic lessons for voters on the content of politics and stimuli for the perception of party differences. As Bagehot (1928, 119) said of parliamentary debate, "It makes us hear what otherwise we should not."

From the early 1960s through 2000, the parties in Congress became more ideologically distinct (for this trend through 1996, see Fleisher and Bond 1996, Figure 2), more unified, and more polarized in their roll-call voting. We use House and Senate party unity as a measure of real-world political change. The substantive meaning of the parties becomes clearer to voters when parties are unified and when these unified parties are different from each other.

For the relative trends of the two influences, education and party unity, see Figure 10.5. Both have increased steadily over the period, and each bears a striking similarity to the trend in the perception of party differences. We believe the political indicator is more meaningful. Education may increase, as it has, even in the absence of party differences, but greater ability to perceive differences is meaningless in the absence of such differences. We contend that although education is a necessary but not sufficient condition, this change in the political environment is an absolutely necessary condition to account for voters' perceiving party differences. We expect that the level of party differentiation will have a distinct effect on mass perceptions.

One could eliminate either predictor, standing alone, and still generate the trend line in the perception of party differences in Figure 10.5. Analysts then

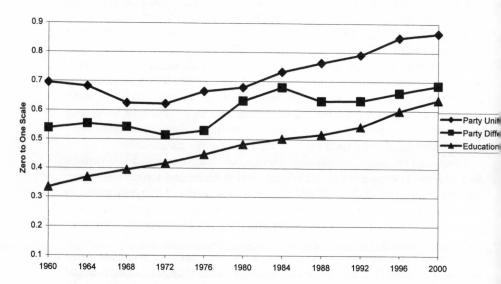

Figure 10.5. Comparison of trends (change in education and party unity relative to change in perception of party differences)

could easily (albeit atheoretically) conclude that the increase in education was irrelevant to political change. Or they could conclude conversely that changes in political parties were unnecessary for understanding political change. We now seek to show that change in the perception of differences between the parties cannot be adequately explained solely on the basis of nonpolitical factors.

CHANGED PERCEPTIONS: THE CENTRALITY OF POLITICS

We justify the centrality of political change through three statistical tools. First, we examine the direct relationship in each election year between the perceptions of important party differences and two possible explanations, the mean levels of education and party unity, using Spearman's rho as a measure of association. These results support our inference. Although both relationships are high, the relationship between perceived party differences and party unity is higher ($.83$, $p = .0017$) than it is for education ($.78$, $p = .0045$).

Next, we try to explain the changes over time in the proportion of people who perceive important differences between the parties. Our premise is that we must look beyond individual characteristics for explanation. Instead, theory compels us also to look outside at the real political world. In this model, we measure the extent to which real-world aggregate level influences—specifically, party unity—combine with individual level effects, particularly education. For this analysis, we combine survey responses over the entire period, creating a pooled cross-sectional time-series.

As control variables, we include individual-level measures of age, sex, and race. We include age to take account of the speculation that the "greening" of the electorate has brought a new youthful perceptiveness into politics. In 1972, eighteen-year-olds were admitted to the franchise. Furthermore, the electorate was transformed by the addition of the massive baby-boom generation. Just as these cohorts have changed American music and lifestyles, they once gave promise of transforming political consciousness (for example, recall Reich 1970). It is certainly conceivable that the changes in party perceptions that become manifest in the 1970s simply reflect the simultaneous enfranchisement of these young and restless voters.

Sex and race are included as basic demographic controls. We might hypothesize that the great social movements of these decades, by blacks and women, leading to new racial and feminist consciousness, might also be the source of new party perceptions. We note, but dismiss, these arguments as tendentious and untestable with the data at hand. For temporal control, we include dummy variables to capture variation over time unrelated to the other included variables (Beck, Katz, and Tucker 1998). (We would have liked to include media exposure as another control variable, but these data were not available in the relevant data sets for 1988 and 2000.)

The most common and most efficient statistical technique to test the relative importance of the political and nonpolitical factors would be to compare standardized coefficients from an ordinary least squares regression. But because these data are both individual level and aggregate, and because the dependent variable is binary, that method is inappropriate here. Thus, we used the indirect strategies of first differences analysis[3] and comparison of predictions.

First differences analysis: We examine the total effect of changes in party unity, and then education, on the perception of party differences. As party unity increased, so did the perception of party differences. When we compare the low and high points of this measurement of the real world, the proportion of the sample perceiving party differences increased by 15.2 points, or approximately 27 percent. As party unity increased over this time period, so did perceived party differences, but the pace of change was not evenly spaced over time. The greatest part of the change came in the 1980s, with half of the total relationship coming from 1980 to 1992.[4]

In comparison, education also increased the proportion of the sample perceiving party differences, with a maximum change of 25 points, or approximately 42 percent. The difference between those with a high school education or less and those with some college training produced the larger share of this change, increasing the proportion perceiving important party differences by 16 points, or 27 percent.

Let us restate this comparison more clearly. The largest possible change in education—for all respondents to increase their educational level from high school or less, to college or more—effects a 42 percent change in the perceptive proportion of the sample; the largest possible change in party unity—from the real-world low to the real-world high—effects a change of 27 percent. Despite the larger value for the change in education, these results support our inference that party unity is a more significant explanation of the change over time in the perception of party differences. This is because a change in the levels of education for all respondents from the lowest to the highest is a profoundly unrealistic hypothetical statistical construct. The changes in the level of party unity, in contrast, are real.[5]

Explanation from prediction: In our final test, we infer explanation from statistical prediction. A good statistical model will have fewer errors in predicting a result such as perceived party differences. When we use the model including both education and party unity (as well as all control variables), our predictions are fairly accurate: the mean error in prediction was .00094 with a standard deviation of .01725. Omitting party unity from the model increased the mean error in prediction considerably, by 25 percent to .0012, and increased the standard deviation by roughly 20 percent to .0207 (for both models $N = 15,485$). Predictions under the full model closely track the actual observed proportion perceiving important differences between the parties, but excluding the political variable is simply less accurate. This disparity is especially evident after Ronald Reagan's transformation of the Republican Party in 1980.

The events of American politics at the end of the twentieth century illuminate the statistical results. Voters unfamiliar with regression analyses still could hardly ignore the party differences, often rancorous, within Congress. Voters inattentive to party platforms could still respond to tense conflicts of emblematic party leaders such as Gingrich and Clinton. Voters unversed in the constitutional separation of powers could still learn that the government had shut down after a partisan dispute over the federal budget and, later, that a Republican majority in Congress was seeking to remove a Democratic president from elected office.

Voters have come to see greater party differences for a simple reason. The parties have been emphasizing their differences in dramatic and obvious fashion, in their roll-call voting in Congress, including their responses to the president's program (and dalliances with interns). Education has helped people to understand, younger people have been more prone to comprehend, and media users have consumed this information better. But the character of the political world has been the great teacher of all Americans, whether in or out of the classroom, whether wizened or apple-cheeked, whether couch potatoes or hermits.

VOTERS AND PARTY RESPONSIBILITY

Politics matters. That is our most basic conclusion, and our research conveys a testament to the authors of the Report, scholars who cared about the real world of parties and elections. Politics affects the existence of partisanship in parents and in children, and it affects the direction of partisanship across generations. More specifically in our analysis, it affects the perception of party differences and, to close the circle, those perceptions affect partisanship itself.

We go beyond our detailed data and technical analyses to speculate on past and future trends in American politics. To begin, let us quickly review what we know about trends in partisanship. Over the past four or five decades, partisanship declined somewhat, and the strength of party identification declined considerably for most of the period. The effect of partisanship on the vote lessened for a time but has now become as strong as at the beginning of the era (Bartels 2000). Partisan-elite conflict has become elevated and intense. The voters came to perceive greater differences between the parties, these perceptions became more important sources of their partisanship, and traditional loyalties became less important.

These trends are probably interrelated. Without attempting to test it, we suggest this explanation. The decline of the strength and extent of party identification made the remaining strong partisans more ideologically coherent. Elected officials became more overtly committed to their distinctive ideological programs, providing new cues for mass polarization (Carmines and Stimson 1989, chap. 7). Party elites became more coherently ideological because of the growing influence of programmatic interest groups; the policy commitments of rising leaders, such as Gingrich; and the decline of moderating influences within the congressional parties, such as southern Democrats and liberal Republicans. In an important new analysis that parallels—and broadens—our own study, Hetherington aptly summarizes these developments: "Greater ideological polarization in Congress has clarified public perceptions of party ideology, which has produced a more partisan electorate" (2001, 629).

Elite conflicts communicated party differences to the general public, and these new perceptions made the mass base of the parties more homogeneous in their policy preferences, more cognitive in their partisanship, and more apt to follow their issue-based party loyalties in casting votes. "Once citizens moved toward greater polarization, elites seemed to have taken sustenance from this, and polarized even more. Thus, there may be . . . a relatively simultaneous influence of mass and elite polarization in which each actor's more partisan attitudes reinforced the other" (Fleisher and Bond 1996, 17).

Until the tragedy of September 11, 2001, intensified partisanship seemed likely to increase as a result of the elections of 2000. The long ballot recount in Florida was notable for the fierce party divisions displayed, extending even to the Supreme Court, and for the complete absence of any efforts at moderate resolution by any national leaders. George W. Bush faced four years of attacks on the legitimacy of his presidency, as Democrats formed battles lines for the campaigns of 2002 and 2004. This partisanship promised to be further exacerbated by the even division of Senate seats and the thin Republican margin in the House. Public attitudes toward the postelection events also mirrored partisan loyalties, and the coming conflict of party elites would most likely have reinforced these mass sentiments.[6]

The world and American politics were surely transformed by the terrorist attacks on the nation, and the ultimate consequences cannot be predicted at this writing and perhaps not for many years. In the immediate aftermath, partisanship was invisible, George Bush achieved a presidential legitimacy through foreign attack that he lacked through domestic elections, and the congressional parties united to pass new security laws and appropriations. Yet even as the nation's politicians were muted and shocked, partisan differences remained and were likely to be voiced in the coming elections, even if in softer words and accompanied by patriotic melodies. Party differences had already emerged on such new issues as federal employment of airport security workers and the content of an economic stimulus package, and they continued on such old issues as social security reform. The parties would not battle over Afghanistan, but they were preparing to compete vigorously the impending elections. Voters were likely to perceive the continuing party differences.

These developments bring us back to the future envisaged in the Report.

The Committee on Political Parties saw the development of coherent and distinct parties as the elite stimulus of a responsible two-party system. We now have such parties. The Report expected voters to respond to this stimulus by choosing leaders on the basis of their own issue preferences and the performance of the parties. Decades of electoral studies verify the development of issue-based voting as well as the continuing importance of performance judgments (Key 1966; Pomper 1975; Nie et al. 1979; Fiorina 1981; Popkin 1991; Miller and Shanks 1996).

These elements of the doctrine of responsible parties, however, lacked a vital link between parties and voters. Coherent issue-based parties and issue-based voting could exist independently of one another. It is at least theoretically possible that the parties could present coherent issue alternatives that are also not salient to the issue concerns of the voters. Indeed, some of the sharpest issue differences between the party elites today (estate taxes and even abortion) may concern only small fractions of voters, and the parties may be very similar on issues (free trade is one example) that do concern large numbers of voters.

To link the two elements of the theory of responsible parties, voters must perceive that there are important differences between the parties—important to the perceiving voters, not only to the policy analyst and the party activist. We now have evidence that voters do indeed more fully perceive such party differences and link that perception to their partisanship. Even if our politicians often fail in their jobs, the voters have become more responsible. To that extent, we have come closer to realizing the goals of the political scientists who dared, half a century before our time, to dream of a new American politics.

METHODOLOGICAL APPENDIX

1. *Data Sets*. All data for this analysis were drawn either from the 1998 edition of the American National Election Studies (ANES) (1948–1997) CD–ROM, or from the ANES cumulative data file (1948–2000). The critical ANES question focuses on the "perception of important differences in what the parties stand for." Because this question was not asked in 1956, we were unable to use that year for any purpose.

   For Figure 10.1, we used 1952 through 2000, with the exception of 1956. For Figure 10.2, and the first part of the research (generating Figures 10.3 and 10.4), we had to further omit 1960 and 1984, because the parental partisanship questions were not asked in those years. For the aggregate measures shown in Figure 10.5, we were able to add 1960 and 1984, and to include 1996 and 2000; but not having the party unity data for 1952, we had to drop that year.

2. *PDIFF*. In general, this binary variable is a simple yes/no dichotomy to

the following question: "Do you think there are any important differences in what the Republicans and Democrats stand for?" Contrary to the NES coding, we consider responses of "don't know," "depends," and "yes, a difference but don't know what," as indicating substantively negative responses.

3. *PPSHIP*. This variable, which measures the respondent's parental partisanship, was coded in two different ways. Initially, it was coded as a binary variable. Regardless of the year, if the respondent reported that either or both parents belonged to a major political party, then PPSHIP was scored as partisan; if neither parent belonged to a major political party or if the respondent answered "don't know," then PPSHIP was scored as nonpartisan. PPSHIP was also coded by direction of parental party identification. Under that scheme, if, for example, both parents identified as Democrats, or if one parent identified as a Democrat and the other as "other," "none," or "apolitical," that respondent was coded as having a Democratic parental influence. PPSHIP was used in its more differentiated form to generate Figure 10.2 and in its binary form for the ordered logit analysis that generated Figure 10.3. For the multinomial logit analysis that generated Figure 10.4, PPSHIP was used in its more differentiated form but was converted to a set of dummy variables.

4. *Control Variables*. For the ordered and multinomial logit analyses, control variables included age, anchored such that 0 represented the voting age; sex, with 0 indicating male; and, race, with 0 indicating white. Additionally, we included education, following the NES's cumulative data file's four-point coding, and income, also following the cumulative data file's coding convention of a five-point percentile spread. Finally, in order to control for southern politics, we included a region variable where 1 indicated the former Confederate states. For the pooled time-series cross-section data, we included as control variables only sex, race, and age. In that model, education became a primary explanatory variable, and income and region were theoretically unhelpful; for a discussion of our desire to include a measure of media exposure, see note 5.

5. *Ordered Logit Model*. To generate an over-time analysis of the comparative effect of the odds ratios for PDIFF and PPSHIP, we specified an ordered logit model with the dependent variable as a three-point, non-directional measure of party identification. Under that coding, 0 represented "true independents," 1 represented "wary partisans" composed of "independent leaners" and "weak partisans" (of both parties), and 2 reflected "strong partisans" (again, of both parties). We included as explanatory variables a set of dummy variables to capture PDIFF and PPSHIP alone and in interaction (dropping, so as to prevent collinearity, the combination reflecting "no–PDIFF and no–PPSHIP"), as well as age, sex, race, education, income, and region for control variables. Using Stata

Version 6, ordered logit coefficient estimates were obtained for each available year and, using the conventional formula, those coefficients were converted to odds ratios. All of the dummy variables for PDIFF–PPSHIP combination were statistically significant at $p>|z| = 0.000$, with the sole exception of the PDIFF dummy variable in the 1964 equation, with $p>|z| = 0.010$. We used Stata's specification link-test in order to examine model goodness-of-fit for the ordered logit equations.

6. *Multinomial Logit Model.* The dependent variable for the multinomial model that generated Figure 10.4 was a five-point directional measure of party identification. The midpoint, which served as the comparison group, was "true independents," surrounded by "wary Republicans" and then "strong Republicans" on the right, and "wary Democrats" and "strong Democrats" on the left. As before, "wary" partisans included "independent leaners" and "weak partisans." The control variables were included in this model as they were in the ordered logit model. PDIFF remained a binary measure, but PPSHIP was expanded to a four-point factor in order to include directionality. A multinomial logit regression was run for each available year. From those regression results, we held the control variables at their sample means for the given year and generated probabilities that the respondent would fall into each response category under each of the eight different conditions of the combined PDIFF–PPSHIP variable. From those probabilities we extracted the incremental probability increases that constitute Figure 10.4. We conducted likelihood ratio tests to confirm that these sets of predictors were statistically significant.

7. *Party Unity Scale.* This variable is a summative scale composed of unstandardized measures of four *Congressional Quarterly* indexes for the two-year Congress preceding the presidential elections from 1960 through 2000. These indexes are the average party unity score for each party in each chamber. This scale performs well (Chronbach's $\alpha = .9613$).

8. *Spearman's rho.* The choice of Spearman's rho as a measure of correlation was compelled by the small size of the aggregate data set. For aggregate measures, we had only eleven years, that is, presidential election years from 1960 through 2000. As a nonparametric measure, rho is particularly appropriate for small sample sizes.

9. *Binary Dependent Variable Time-Series Cross-Section Model.* We seek to model changes over both "space and time," which is methodologically difficult (Stimson 1985; and see, for example, Markus 1988 and Kramer 1983). Although the political variable does vary over the eleven available year-points, within each year it is constant. A further complication is that the only measure of perception of party differences we have at the individual level is the binary individual response to the party differences question. Beck, Katz, and Tucker (1998) have dubbed this type of model the "binary time-series-cross-section model."

Given our desired inference, the problem with this data set is twofold: first, though we seek to draw an inference about a continuous aggregate measure, the only indicator of the concept underlying that aggregate measure is a binary individual level measure. Second, the independent variables are of two kinds: individual and aggregate. The constancy of the political variable within a given year prevents us from using the earlier relative odds ratios analysis.

In three preliminary tests, we found that the temporal dummy variables are necessary; that—as predicted—each of the explanatory variables presents net effects and that the model performs admirably (with ten groups ordered on the predicted probabilities at N = 15,485 the Hosmer-Lemeshow $\chi^2(8) = 8.85$, $p > \chi^2 = .3547$).

Within the confines of a given sample, the most efficient way to show the relative importance of the variables is to display the standardized coefficients from an ordinary least squares (OLS) regression. Unfortunately, the only continuous measure we have of the relevant dependent variable is limited to eleven cases, which rules out any meaningful use of OLS. We instead use a two-part indirect analysis.

First, using King and associates' bootstrapping software, Clarify (Tomz, Wittenberg, and King 1999; see King, Tomz, and Wittenberg 2000), we ran the model with one thousand resampling (with replacement) iterations to generate a nonparametric distribution of the model parameters. We then used the mean value for each parameter to generate the first differences produced by relevant changes in the explanatory variables. Those first differences quantify the increase or decrease in the proportion of the sample perceiving important party differences.

For the second analysis, we ran the model twice, first without the political variable and then with the political variable. From each run, we predicted,

Table 10.1. Logit Estimates

PDIFF	Odds Ratio	Std. Err.	z	P>|z|	[95% Conf. Interval]	
Puscale	1.881474	.5008823	2.374	0.018	1.1165	3.1703
E3	1.923574	.0850445	14.797	˙0.000	1.7639	2.0976
E4	2.949158	.1446382	22.052	0.000	2.6788	3.2467
Age	1.003413	.0009824	3.480	0.001	1.0014	1.0053
Sex	0.737350	.0250259	−8.977	0.000	0.6898	0.7880
Race	1.018815	.0225702	0.841	0.400	0.9755	1.0640

Number of obs = 15485; LR chi2(12) = 974.46; prob > chi2 = 0.000.
Log likelihood = −10112.049 where:
PUSCALE = the party unity score, scaled from 0 to 1; E3 = dummy variable for "some college (thirteen grades or more but no degree)"; E4 = dummy variable for "college or advanced degree"; Age = respondent's report age; Sex = dummy variable for sex, male = 0, female 1; Race = dummy variable for race, white = 0, nonwhite = 1; (Consistent with convention, the values for the temporal dummy variables are suppressed.)

by year, the proportion of the sample perceiving important differences between the parties and compared those results to the observed proportions. For ease of interpretation, we scaled party unity so that 0 represented the real-world low (62.25) and 1 reflected the real-world high (86.625). We then assessed the change in predicted values in the binary dependent variable from 0 to 1 (that is, whole range) change in party unity. Expressed in the more comprehensible odds ratios, the logit estimates for the results for the full model are shown in Table 10.1.

NOTES

1. We extend grateful appreciation for advice from Richard R. Lau, Beth L. Leech, and Jane Junn, all of Rutgers University, and to Germán Rodríguez of Princeton University. Replication data sets are available from the authors, <MDWEINER@PRINCETON. EDU>.

2. The average age of respondents in any given year is forty-two to forty-six. If we assume that meaningful political socialization takes place during the ages of fourteen to eighteen, then the benchmark for remembered parental partisanship would be the presidential election about twenty-eight years earlier. The remembered Democratic upturn in 1964 would then reflect the high-water mark of the New Deal in 1936, and the remembered downturn in 1980 would reflect the movement toward Eisenhower Republicanism. These patterns are consistent with Andersen's reconstruction (1976, 83) of party identification in pre-NES years.

3. First differences analysis holds all other variables at some set value—typically their sample mean—while examining the effect resulting in the dependent variable from changes in the independent variable of immediate interest.

4. We can also make finer distinctions about the effect of changes in party unity by dividing the total change into four equal increments, each of approximately 6.25 points of change in the unity scale. The first difference change in the first increment (from the lowest level of party unity, 62.25, to 68.25) increased the proportion of difference-perceiving respondents by .0394 (6.88 percent of the observed proportion). This is roughly equal to the effect in the change in party unity from 1972 (62.25) to 1980 (67.9). The second incremental change, from about 68.25 to 73.25 on the real scale, corresponds roughly with the change from 1980 (67.9) to 1984 (73.3). This change increased the relevant proportion by .0389, 6.79 percent. The third incremental change, from about 73.25 to 79.125, matches the change from 1984 (73.3) to 1992 (79.1), a change in the relevant proportion of .0376, 6.58 percent. Finally, the change from about 79.1 to the real-scale high of 86.6, matching the change from 1992 (79.1) to 2000 (86.6), increased the proportion by .0358, 6.26 percent.

5. The development of the mass media is clearly a social trend that could affect perceptions of politics. Television became ubiquitous in the United States in the last half of the twentieth century, cable television vastly multiplied the number of outlets, print media became more numerous and more specialized, and the Internet has provided detailed guides for media consumers. This enriching of the information envi-

ronment could also prompt voters to an increased perception of party differences. We would have liked to have controlled for this possibility by including an additive measure of individual media exposure in the model, and we argue that although including a measure for media exposure clearly improves the model, omitting it does not fatally flaw our analysis. Spurred on by curiosity, however, we did run the model with the measure of media exposure included but with the data for 1988 and 2000 omitted. Under that model, which makes our case even more strongly, the real-world increase in the perception of respondents perceiving important party differences increases by 30.36 percent when the party unity score moves from its real-world low to its real-world high. The movement in the percentage of respondents perceiving party differences attendant to the maximum, albeit unrealistic, increase in education, is a nearly equal 31.94 percent.

6. See, for example, the CBS News/New York Times Poll of November 20, 2000.

11

A Persistent Quest

Leon D. Epstein

Among this book's authors, I am probably alone in having begun a career in political science as far back as the 1940s. With this dubious distinction goes an awareness of the party responsibility doctrine before the publication of the Report by the Committee on Political Parties of the American Political Science Association (1950a) and a recollection of the political context in which it was written and received. I had read Schattschneider's *Party Government* (1942) while pursuing graduate work at Chicago in 1946, and I remember how persuasive I then found the case for responsible parties. Even now, long after I have ceased to be so fully persuaded, Schattschneider's book strikes me as more cogent than the subsequent Report. Although he chaired the Committee on Political Parties and served on its drafting committee, the Report's style might be more readily attributable to the chair of the drafting committee, Fritz Morstein Marx, who was a specialist in public administration. On matters of substance, the most striking difference from Schattschneider's prior work was the Report's emphasis on a participatory policymaking party membership—even though party membership was not precisely defined. Schattschneider's own version of majoritarian party government depended on an effective policymaking leadership of a largely unorganized electoral following. On this score as on some others it is fair to assume that he went along with a rough consensus or compromise typical of committee work. To be sure, the Report rested squarely on Schattschneider's principal argument for a party representing majority opinion as a counter to interest-group politics, and its authors also shared his belief that such a party could be developed at the national level in the United States without a constitutional amendment to establish parliamentary government. That belief was a central feature of the Report's responsible party advocacy, distinguishing it from plans to achieve cabinet government, British style, by disposing of the constitutionally mandated separation of powers.

To seek responsible party government within the established constitutional structure was not an entirely new idea in the 1940s. Many years earlier, Woodrow Wilson pursued a similar scholarly line after first contemplating fundamental constitutional change as a means to establish something like the British cabinet government that he admired (Ranney 1954, chap. 3). As Ranney reminds us, Wilson was one of several American scholars who advocated, in varying ways, more responsible party government long before the Report, Schattschneider's work, and the rest of the post–New Deal discussion. The quest is so old that it coincides with the late-nineteenth-century origins of American political science and precedes the formation of our association by a few decades. During this long history, "party responsibility" has been understood in different ways. As is evident from the preceding chapters, perspectives vary regarding the nature and degree of policymaking responsibility and the locus of responsibility—in an organized activist membership, a loosely defined electoral following, a legislative caucus, or an executive leadership.

The Report's appeal rested at least in part on its authors' hopes to achieve in the U.S. Congress some of the cohesion of British parliamentary parties without trying to overcome the formidable obstacle of formal constitutional change. For anyone interested in that kind of cohesion, it was tempting to regard many of the proposals in the Report, as well as in Schattschneider's own work, as feasible within our political system. And because they were proposals to strengthen parties, they were especially attractive to the parties' specialists, most of whom tended, like Schattschneider, to believe generally in the importance of their subject matter and, in particular, to regard parties as significant causal factors. Moreover, as White and Mileur note in chapter 2, the proposals were made in circumstances that enhanced their appeal to liberal Democrats, then as now numerous in our profession. Between 1938 and 1950, despite Democratic majorities in Congress in all but two of those years, along with Democratic presidents, liberal Democrats had little success in enacting their domestic legislative proposals. Most recently, they had failed to secure congressional support for President Harry Truman's Fair Deal program, despite Democratic electoral victories in 1948. The conservative coalition of Republicans and mainly southern Democrats often prevailed, as they had in the last six years of Franklin Roosevelt's presidency and as they did for a few more decades.

This is not to suggest that liberal Democrats were the only advocates of the responsible parties doctrine in 1950. One can identify a few Republicans on the Committee on Political Parties, and some Republican members of Congress probably shared their views. But liberal Democrats had special reasons to champion the doctrine. They operated on the assumption, widely held at the time, that they could mobilize an electoral majority, mainly in northern states, for a party committed to a liberal program. On this same assumption, an important Republican leader explicitly rejected the ideological alignment accompanying the responsible party doctrine. In 1950, when the "C" word, conservatism, was less popular than the now often shunned "L" word, Thomas Dewey is reported to have said, in a lecture at Princeton University, that there were impractical theorists who wanted "to drive all moderates and liberals out of the Republican Party and then have the remainder join forces with the conservative groups of the South. Then they would have everything neatly arranged, indeed. The Democratic party would be the liberal-to-radical party. The Republican party would be the conservative-to-reactionary party. The results would be neatly arranged, too. The Republicans would lose every election and the Democrats would win every election" (quoted by Key 1964, 220–221). Although Dewey probably had presidential and statewide elections principally in mind, his views were also relevant to congressional contests.

Adding to the attraction of the responsible party doctrine for liberals in the late 1940s was the British Labour government's use of a cohesive parliamentary party majority to enact the legislative program that it had offered in its 1945 general election manifesto. Perhaps that experience was particularly salient for me because I had just begun to teach British politics and was impressed by Labour's legislative accomplishments. I may not yet have understood how much of that success depended on a parliamentary system. Possibly, too, I still tended, like certain other American observers, to overstate and overvalue the influence of a British party's mass-membership organization in committing elected legislators to a set of policies. In that light, the Report's proposal to develop mass-membership parties looked like a means to help achieve programmatic party cohesion. But with or without emphasis on a mass membership, many American political scientists admired the effectiveness of British party government. Not unexpectedly, therefore, we learned later from a participant in the Committee on Political Parties that "the British model was significant for a number of its members" (Kirkpatrick 1971, 974 n. 29).

Yet the Report hardly suggests that its authors expected to do any more than approximate some aspects of that model. They recognized the limitations imposed by the American constitutional system and the need to make proposals that would not override those limitations, although they might push hard against them. The modesty of the Report is most clearly evident when its recommendations are compared with recurrent schemes to establish parliamentary government by means of constitutional change, as proposed, for example, by Charles Hardin (1974). But the Report is also less radical than plans to achieve party government under a strong president (Burns 1963). Not surprisingly, therefore, several—though by no means all—of the Report's proposals were so feasible that they have been implemented, in substance, during the last half century. We remain well short of full responsible party government, as I suspect we always will (and probably should). Nevertheless, American parties have become somewhat more ideologically cohesive and also strengthened in certain organizational respects, even if suffering from well-publicized signs of electoral decline. No doubt, parties would have thus responded to broad social forces without the advice of the political scientists who wrote the Report. But since we are now commemorating the Report, I shall review what has happened to American parties in the context of its recommendations, taking into account developments at odds with the Report as well as those that loosely resemble the suggestions of our scholarly predecessors. In light of the more specialized and detailed topical chapters in this book, my review will be relatively brief and will often refer to earlier chapters. My views of the Report fall between those of the most admiring and the most adversely critical writers, and are, I believe, a little less rejectionist in tone than what I had to say on the subject in the 1960s and 1970s.

ELECTORAL BASE

American voters have continued to be divided principally between Republicans and Democrats, as they were when the Report explicitly built its recommendations on the traditional two-party system (Committee on Political Parties 1950a, 18). Then and subsequently, third and minor parties have had some impact, notably in presidential contests, but few of their candidates have been elected to office. The occasional success, like the 1998 election of Minnesota's Reform party governor, seems so far to have been no more significant a deviation than the election of a few third-party governors in the 1930s. And Congress has been even more fully dominated by Republicans and Democrats in the last fifty years than it was earlier in the century. Nor have other parties secured durable party identifiers in such numbers as to rival those that appear in surveys as Republicans and Democrats or that are registered as Republicans and Democrats in states with provisions for party registration. Plainly, a multiparty system has not replaced the two-party system that the Report understandably regarded as fundamental in its advocacy of majoritarian party government.

As Weisberg writes in chapter 9, the authors of the Report did not examine what political scientists began to call the party in the electorate and were soon to analyze by means of increasingly sophisticated survey-research methods. Rather, they seem to have assumed, consistent with such data as were then available, that most voters tended to be loyal to Republican or Democratic tickets. Indeed, the strength of electoral partisanship was widely taken for granted, even when parties were regarded as weak in other respects.

Now, however, although we know more about electoral parties, there is less assurance that the continuing two-party division of voters is as meaningful as it was forty or fifty years ago. Even without growing attachments to other parties, larger proportions of the electorate have evidently ceased identifying as Republicans and Democrats, especially as strong Republicans and strong Democrats, and more often cast split-ticket ballots. During much of the last half century, as the numbers of professedly independent voters increased and as even self-identified Republicans and Democrats voted in greater numbers for candidates carrying a party label different from their own, the evidence pointed toward electoral party decline (Wattenberg 1984). The decline can be observed in a careful comparison between voters from 1952 to 1960 and voters from 1988 to 1996 (Mayer 1998, 212). Though party identification and partisan presidential voting are only modestly lowered, the comparison shows a significant growth in split-ticket voting. Surely, that change, closely associated with the candidate-centered campaigns, works against responsible party government by increasing the likelihood of electing a president of one party and a Congress in which the other party controls one or both houses. Presidential coattails do not seem as important as they were before campaigns became as heavily candidate-centered as other contributors to this book have shown them to be.

Yet there is considerable dispute about the extent and significance of the decline in electoral parties. Even when acknowledging the disruption of party loyalties in the 1960s and 1970s, a leading study of voting behavior described party affiliation as a thread that was "frayed" rather than broken (Nie, Verba, and Petrocik 1979, 73). Partisanship, though diminished, remained the principal determinant of voting behavior. Most of the electors classified as Independents, having told pollsters they were neither Republicans nor Democrats, were found to lean toward a major party (earning labels as Independent Republicans or Independent Democrats) and to vote heavily for that party's candidates (Keith et al. 1986). Moreover, it is now argued that the decline of partisanship has been reversed since 1976 so that by the 1990s a larger proportion of voters were party identifiers than in immediately preceding decades and that more of these identifiers voted for their party's presidential and congressional candidates than had done so in the earlier decades (Bartels 2000). To be sure, the partisan revival was not sufficient in 1996 to produce unified party control of presidency and Congress. And when it briefly did in 2000, party control was so remarkably narrow and tenuous as to fall well short of the kind of mandate for majoritarian party government sought by its advocates.

IDEOLOGICAL NATIONALIZATION

The programmatic coherence that the Report's authors wanted in national party policies is arguably closer to attainment at the start of the twenty-first century than it was in 1950. However often candidates appeal to moderate and centrist voters in closely contested general election campaigns, the Republican Party looks more preponderantly conservative and the Democratic Party more preponderantly liberal than fifty years ago. I use the "L" word though aware that many Democrats seek to avoid it, perhaps substituting "progressive," and that the political spectrum has shifted so much to the right on economic issues that Democrats are generally associated with more moderate positions than those held by some of their predecessors in the 1960s or even in the 1930s. Thus, economic policy differences between Republicans and Democrats are still further removed from those formerly expected of European parties. Compared with a conflict between a socialist party of the left and a capitalist party of the right, American Republicans and Democrats hardly reflect any deep ideological disagreement. Nevertheless, each party, though far from monolithic and often only incrementally different from its opposition, appears to have less internal dissent from its prevailing tendency than was once the case. And a nearly similar intraparty consensus has developed on social issues, as on matters of economic policy. Indeed, in the late 1990s and in the election of 2000, the differences between Republicans and Democrats were often sharper on increasingly salient social issues (notably but not only abortion, affirmative action, gay rights, sectarian school vouchers, and gun control) than on economic questions. The culture wars of the Clinton era may well persist and even assume greater importance in interparty competition. At the same time, however, the parties surely continue to be identified with contrasting policies on taxes, spending priorities, labor legislation, business regulations, and other economic issues. The significance of these alignments, social and economic, is illustrated by the way successful candidates in presidential primaries have lately appealed to their party's distinctive ideological electorate (see Pomper and Weiner in chapter 10).

Most readily observable is the diminution, if not complete extinction, of the once substantial bloc of conservative southern Democrats and the slow but steady decline of northern liberal Republicanism. The Republican Party's ascendance in southern states has transformed American politics. Not only has it enhanced the conservatism of Republican membership in Congress and in presidential candidate selection, but it also has made for a fuller northern liberal dominance in the Democratic Party. The still significant numbers of southern Democrats, though often less overtly liberal than northern Democrats, tend to be less conservative than southern Republicans. No doubt, racial issues played a part in this transformation, as many white southerners reacted against civil rights legislation championed by Democratic national leaders, while newly enfranchised black southerners entered Democratic ranks. But the Republican Party is now linked to the South's relatively conservative preferences on many economic as well as various social issues, in addition to those related to race. At the same time, the Democratic Party, with a considerably smaller and less traditional southern conservative contingent (and with little lingering conservative support elsewhere) has a greater degree of coherence than in the past. The coherence may be enhanced by the decline of the essentially nonideological big-city machines that once played a larger part in Democratic politics. Admittedly, the changes in party alignment do not preclude deviations from each party's ideological positions by politicians seeking to represent regional and local interests. Thus, some suburban Republican representatives are likely to remain pro-choice, and some Democratic representatives from hunting districts are likely to remain opposed to gun control. Our system of separated branches of government readily allows such deviations, even as party ideologies have become more fully distinguishable. At most, one might look for a somewhat greater partisan cohesion.

CONGRESSIONAL PARTIES

Looking for that cohesion in Congress takes one to the familiar measure based on party unity scores—the mean of party members voting with their own party when party majorities oppose each other in the House of Representatives and Senate—despite doubts about the significance of these scores (Krehbiel 2000). Tabulations for the 1980s and 1990s show substantial increases in overall party unity as well as increases specifically among southern Democrats, after low points in the 1960s and 1970s (Strahan 1998, 28–29; *Congressional Quarterly* 1999, 2993). The data thus confirm expectations based on the new politics of the South, which elected to Congress fewer but often more liberal Democrats than in the past. The tabulations also reinforce impressions of a rising congressional partisanship associated with the Reagan years, Gingrich's Contract with America in 1994, and other events linked to the conflict between a Republican Congress and the Clinton administration in the late 1990s. That conflict can be seen in the decline in presidential support scores—recording the percentage of contested votes on which the president's known position prevailed. Clinton's score was over 86 percent in his first two years with a Democratic Congress, but it dropped to a record low of 36 percent in 1995, rose only to 50 to 55 percent from 1996 to 1998, and dropped again to 37.8 percent in 1999. The lowest of these scores was not much below the lowest for Reagan (43.5 percent) and Bush (43 percent), when they faced opposition party majorities in Congress, but the numbers differed more substantially from scores for Eisenhower, Nixon, and Ford, none of whom dropped below 50 percent when facing an opposition-controlled Congress in the 1955–1977 era (*Congressional Quarterly* 1999, 2987). Plainly, the greater party unity of the 1980s and 1990s accounts for the contrast to the immediately preceding decades.

It must be noted, however, that the party unity scores even in the 1990s were no higher than they had been in the late 1940s (Strahan 1998, 28–29). Further, the scores appear a little lower than they were between 1890 and 1910 (Schneier and Gross 1993, 434). Still, it should be emphasized that recent roll-call voting numbers no longer suggest, as they did in the 1960s and 1970s, that congressional parties are moving further away from the Report's objectives. Significantly, party unity scores have risen, despite candidate-centered campaigns in which congressional members have been perceived as seeking their own re-election mainly by serving their constituents' interests. Such motivations, it turns out, appear compatible with party loyalty insofar as each party's constituencies tend to resemble each other more than they did a few decades ago (Rohde 1991, 170–171).

Organizational developments in congressional parties, like changes in intraparty policy agreement, are relevant to the Report's advocacy. Particularly in the House, as Sinclair more fully shows in chapter 7, both Republicans and Democrats have in certain respects developed structurally in directions consistent with recommendations found in the Report. Especially in the last few decades, House party organizations have been strengthened. There are more deputy whips and larger staffs. It is true that such developments may be at least partly offset by the decentralizing effects of more powerful subcommittees and by the increased electoral independence of many members. Or perhaps the growth in House party organizations has reflected an effort to respond to the decentralization. Nevertheless, the party developments seem significant. Most striking were the changes instituted by the new Republican House majority elected in 1994. These included term limits for committee chairs and for the Speaker, along with a different management of other House affairs. Moreover, Speaker Gingrich exercised his power in a substantially new way when he skipped over senior members in naming three committee chairs and most aggressively promoted his party's program (Strahan 1998, 28). Earlier, in the 1970s, Democrats in the House had modified the seniority principle for selecting committee chairs by permitting their party caucus to reject, in secret ballot, the most senior member of a committee. At the same time, House Democrats restricted a chair's powers within a committee and the chair's ability to block legislation. Along with these changes went enhanced powers for the Democratic leadership in assigning members to committees and in referring bills to more than one committee (Rohde 1991, 11–12).

Another relevant organizational development is the observably increased fund-raising of campaign committees in the Senate as well as in the House. These committees are of long standing (originating in the House in 1866), and their activities have waxed and waned over the years. But in the last twenty years, for reasons Frank Sorauf explains in chapter 5, the officeholder committees have become regularly more significant in collecting large sums and distributing them strategically to help candidates in crucial early stages of campaigns in marginal seats. Hence, even though candidates generally raise most of their funds on their own, some of them may well be particularly indebted to party leaders and be more open than otherwise to appeals for party unity in congressional roll calls.

Even with consequential organizational developments added to ideological nationalization and greater party cohesion on roll-call votes, no one suggests that they have reduced the congressional roles of interest groups, as the Report's authors, and most explicitly Schattschneider, had sought. Possibly, particular interest groups have become more closely linked with one or the other party, but it is doubtful that their effort to influence individual members has thereby diminished. They appear to flourish, along with greater partisanship, and thus to remain at least as much of an obstacle to the kind of responsible party government that the Report's authors wanted when they so emphatically looked to Congress, rather than to the presidency, to achieve their purpose.

EXTRAGOVERNMENTAL PARTY ORGANIZATIONS

The congressional campaign committees should be counted among extragovernmental party organizations. Although headed by senators and representatives, their activities are conducted outside their chambers. The same can be said for legislative caucus campaign committees in the states. Plainly, however, officeholder committees like these, or a president's reelection campaign committee, are not what advocates of responsible party government usually have in mind when they recommend that parties build more effective organizations. The Report, for example, does not include such committees in its proposals for strengthening extragovernmental parties. Its recommendations concerned national party committees (RNC and DNC) and conventional state and local party organizations, through which it was hoped that a national issue-oriented rank-and-file membership would help formulate party policies.

Nevertheless, congressional campaign committees, in particular, are decidedly relevant to the objectives of the Report. Understandably, they might not have seemed so in the early postwar years when their staffs were small, their funds limited, and their operations almost entirely concentrated on helping incumbents. They were not the major actors that they became during the 1980s and 1990s when, as observed, both Republican and Democratic campaign committees in the House and Senate raised and distributed substantial sums while also providing significant services for candidates (Bibby 1998, 146, 163–166). Moreover, they helped to recruit candidates. Similarly, legislative campaign committees have emerged in many states, first mainly as fund-raisers but then additionally as service providers and candidate recruiters (Bibby 1999a, 203–205). It is true that these officeholder committees can be viewed merely as accommodations to candidate-centered campaigns. They do not ordinarily substitute party management for candidate management of campaigns.

The same can be said for the greatly enlarged and now regularly active Republican and Democratic National Committees. They, however, are among the party organizations that the Report wanted to strengthen, in line with its pursuit of a more nationally oriented politics. And just as our national parties do seem more distinct ideologically than they were fifty years ago, so do certain changes in the RNC and DNC appear consonant with the Report's recommendations—so much so, as Maisel and Bibby write in chapter 4, that they serve as the prime fulfillment of the Report's hopes. Both national committees are more fully staffed, between as well as during presidential election years, and both raise large sums on their own rather than depending on state parties. They have even been able to distribute nationally raised funds to state parties. Especially in the last decade, the national committees, in addition to their successful money raising under the federal campaign finance laws, have also collected massive amounts of so-called soft money that cannot be contributed directly to candidates but that can be spent for party purposes indirectly helping candidates, particularly presidential candidates. Campaign finance reforms might well prohibit or restrict soft money contributions and thus curtail party organizational roles. Even without soft money, however, national committees could remain major financial players because of their capacity, demonstrated in the last twenty years, to raise large amounts of hard money. And these amounts might readily increase if present legal limits were raised as part of a congressional measure that banned soft money contributions. In any case, the RNC and the DNC, no longer exclusively concerned with presidential campaigns, are likely to continue to work closely with congressional campaign committees. Together, they represent a considerable, though not an overwhelming, party-driven nationalization of political campaigns in a direction favored by the authors of the Report (Herrnson 1988, 128).

Structurally, the RNC and DNC are still federations of state parties, although they act like national organizations; notably, when fortified by court decisions, they impose their rules on state parties (Bibby 1998, 144–145, 160–168). Neither national committee has an individual dues-paying membership. The "membership card" given to a contributor provides no role for its holder in deciding party policy or candidate selection, beyond that of any voter in party primaries. Without a truly participatory membership base, these party organizations may well appear to lack electoral roots of the kind desired by responsible party advocates. And because their development coincides with a perceived decline in the partisanship of voters, they have been described as elements of a "base-less party system" (White and Shea 2000, 302–314).

State party developments of the last half century have paralleled those at the national level in more ways than the ones noted with respect to the resemblance of legislative campaign committees to congressional campaign committees. The conventional extragovernmental state parties have become professionalized service providers (Bibby 1999a, 198–205). And as Magleby, Patterson, and Thurber note in chapter 6, professional campaign consultants have largely replaced traditional party officials in campaigns. Open to question is whether these are as potent as the old state and local machines, more of which survived in 1950 than today, but there is no doubt that the new-style party organizations are closer to the purposes of the Report. Their contributors and activists tend to be much more issue-oriented than were the precinct captains in the old patronage organizations. In some states, there is a regularized dues-paying membership. Hence, individuals are available for personalized get-out-the-vote efforts even in election campaigns dominated by mass-media advertising and news coverage. Nevertheless, party activists, like party supporters generally, are probably more important as financial contributors than as canvassers. Modern party organizations, like the candidate-centered organizations that they supplement, tend to be capital-intensive rather than labor-intensive. A question that remains is the extent to which party activists, be they dues-paying members or only informally affiliated, have come to influence their party's policy commitments, as the Report suggested. Fragmentary evidence points toward such influence, in developing party platforms, by social conservatives on the Republican side and by left-of-center groups on the Democratic side. There are also indications that candidates resist identification with such platforms and that they often do so successfully.

NOMINATING PROCESS

To achieve the Report's objectives, its authors depended on party members to play important roles in determining party nominations as well as party platforms. For this purpose, however, the Report accepted the characteristically loose American definition that counts as "members" all those eligible to vote in a party's primary. Such members might or might not be activists, issue-oriented or otherwise, and most of them would have no involvement in party affairs beyond voting. Understandably, therefore, the Report regarded preprimary endorsements by "responsible party committees or party councils" as "a healthy development" (Committee on Political Parties 1950a, 10). Here, presumably, policy-oriented activists would prevail and subsequently expect to influence primary outcomes. So modest a development is far from the candidate-selection practices in nations whose parties fit the responsible party model. Not only in Britain but also almost everywhere else, party candidates are chosen by organized members, ordinarily dues payers, or by their chosen representatives. Apart from possible recent exceptions in a few countries, only in America have laws required party nominations to be determined by party voters rather than by party organizations. Realistically, the Report accepts the direct primary, which, by 1950, was a well-established twentieth-century American progressive reform already used in varying forms in most states for nominating U.S. senators and representatives as well as for most state and local offices. And it became even more fully established in the next three decades as its preferential variant came to dominate the process of nominating presidential candidates. Generally, too, after 1950, as old-time party organizations lost power, primaries became increasingly candidate centered.

No alternative to the direct primary is proposed in the Report, despite the obvious difficulties that it poses for responsible party advocacy. Instead, the Report's authors seek the kind of direct primary that best suits their purposes. Troubled by the variety of state laws, they see advantages in national regulation but put that aside as impractical (Committee on Political Parties 1950a, 70).

Hence, the arguments for closed rather than open primaries are addressed to the states. The open primary, the committee asserts, "tends to destroy the concept of membership as the basis of party organization" (71). And the "Washington blanket primary corrupts the meaning of party even further by permitting voters at the same primary to roam at will among the parties" (72). These words (italicized in the Report) reflect strong preferences not popularly shared during the last half century. Closed primaries, requiring preelection party registration or enrollment, have not become more numerous. The old open-primary states remain; and some other states, once classified as having closed primaries because they required meaningful party declarations at the polls, now seem either semiopen or semiclosed, as it has become easier for voters to change such declarations and for independent voters to declare their party preference at the primary election. Still worse, for later advocates of the Report, was the adoption of the blanket primary in subsequent decades by California and Alaska, in addition to its continued use in Washington. But that development appears to have been reversed in June 2000 by the U.S. Supreme Court (*California Democratic Party v. Jones,* 530 U.S. 567 [2000]). In a decision that would have delighted, but also surprised, the authors of the Report, the Court ruled that California's blanket primary violated the associational rights of the state's political party organizations. The party organizations, accustomed to a closed primary over several decades and preferring to limit primary participation, had appealed to the Supreme Court after losing in lower federal courts.

So notable a judicial decision against the blanket primary would have seemed most unlikely in 1950. Only later did the U.S. Supreme Court emphasize associational rights under the First Amendment and in the 1970s and 1980s begin to uphold party assertions of such rights against state primary laws and against certain other state regulations of parties. Summarizing a portion of what I have written at length elsewhere (Epstein 1989, 1999), I emphasize here that the U.S. Supreme Court has held that the national Democratic Party can refuse to seat presidential nominating delegates chosen by a state's open-primary process and that a state party can determine who is eligible to vote in its state-office primaries rather than having to abide by the state's definition. The latter ruling, though it actually led to opening a party primary that had been legally closed, has now in effect been followed in upholding the rights of California's parties against their state's wide open blanket primary. Whether parties in traditionally open (but not blanket) primaries could also succeed if they were to seek similar judicial invalidation of their state laws is not yet clear. Nor is it clear that parties in states with long-established open primaries would want to risk popular disapproval by seeking to bar independents and crossover voters from participating in the selection of candidates.

Public opinion, to be sure, did not deter California's parties; they went to court even though almost 60 percent of the state's voters chose the blanket primary in a 1996 referendum. But it is still uncertain how closed they will choose to make their primaries now that they are rid of the blanket method. A few months after the Supreme Court decision, the state enacted a "modified closed-primary law" to allow unaffiliated voters (about 2 million Californians who choose not to register by party) to select a party ballot at a primary election polling booth, provided that parties agreed to allow such voters in their primaries along with registered party members (see chapter 4). This legislative adaptation to the Court decision is much more moderate than an option favored by the original backers of California's blanket primary. Immediately after the Court decision, they were reported to want a variant of Louisiana's open-election system that would probably be as safe from constitutional challenge as the modified closed primary actually adopted (*Los Angeles Times* 2000). In the Louisiana system, there is no party primary but simply an election to determine, regardless of party, the two top vote getters for each office, who then run against each other in a second election (unless one has over 50 percent of the votes in the first election). Used during the last two decades, the Louisiana system resembles a nonpartisan election except that candidates may (and usually do) put their party affiliation beside their names on the ballot. Moreover, party organizations often endorse candidates (Hadley 1986). Of course, the system can produce two Democrats or two Republicans running against each other in the second election. Partly because of that possibility, responsible party advocates may well regard the Louisiana system as even worse than the blanket primary. On the other hand, the system can be seen as consistent with a tendency to free parties from state control of their candidate-selection process. Thus freed, American parties would no longer be treated as state agencies, as they have been for nearly a century, but more like parties in other democratic nations.

Yet despite the new freedom of parties fostered by the U.S. Supreme Court, it is hard to imagine the demise of the American party primary. Major parties themselves, like responsible party advocates in our academic ranks, are unlikely to prefer the Louisiana system since it looks so much like a nonpartisan election, even though party labels can be attached to candidates' names. And its openness to all voters could make it harder than in party primaries for party associations to secure support for their endorsed candidates. Given characteristically low turnouts in party primaries, except for certain presidential preference primaries and a few other unusual contests, a party's own most zealous voters—conservative Republicans and liberal Democrats—can be numerous enough to produce the results desired by activist party membership organizations and thus reflect the kind of issue-oriented politics sought by responsible party advocates. Again, it is reasonable to assume, with the authors of the Report, that closed primaries are more conducive to such results than are open primaries.

Whether closed party primaries can prevail strikes me as less likely than the durability of party primaries in one form or another. As I have suggested, popular support for relatively open primaries may well discourage parties from using the new legal opportunities to change from open to closed primaries. Insofar as more voters choose to consider themselves independents, closed primaries appear increasingly unappealing politically, even as the Supreme Court has made it possible for parties at least to challenge open primaries in a way that authors of the Report would have appreciated.

SUMMARY REFLECTIONS

Institutionalization of the direct primary has been nearly as intractable an obstacle to full-blown responsible party government, British style, as has the constitutional separation of powers. Both foster increasingly candidate-centered electoral competition to which new-style party organizations adapt by developing professional staffs and fund-raising capacities. Even together, however, these distinctively American fixtures have not discouraged persistent proposals, like those in the Report, to make our parties stronger and more responsible. Nor have the obstacles precluded modest changes in accord with some of those proposals. I am not alone in observing ways in which parties have adopted practices resembling those recommended in the Report. The point was made over thirty years ago by Gerald Pomper (1971). More recently, Baer and Bositis (1993, 204–243) published a detailed scorecard showing a remarkably large number of changes implementing at least partially what the Report proposed (see also Green and Herrnson in chapter 3 for a similar scorecard over a longer period of time). One may welcome many of these changes while rejecting, as I do, the possibility or desirability of anything like British-style responsible party government in the United States. This is to say that parties can be usefully strengthened without becoming so cohesive as to produce stalemate, or otherwise to make for ineffective government, when different parties often control different branches of the national government. Believing, however, that we reached that stage in 1998, one of our esteemed colleagues, Nelson Polsby, declared, "The trouble began when we political scientists finally got our wish— 'responsible' political parties instead of broad, nonideological coalitions. The idea was, of course, completely nuts from the start" (quoted by Klein 1998). Most of us proparty political scientists might well think that Polsby overstates the consequences of our now more ideologically cohesive national parties, but his remark is a useful reminder of the limits that the American system imposes on advocates of stronger parties.

On the other side, I grant, true believers in responsible party government hope to transcend the apparent limits through elections that produce single-party control of the presidency and Congress. Often, proponents of this doctrine depend on presidential leadership both to elect and subsequently to influence congressional party majorities. The authors of the Report, while explicitly putting aside any such dependence on presidential power, could well have assumed that the same party would ordinarily control both executive and legislative branches. That had been the case in all but four years between the elections of 1920 and 1954. The problem was disunity within the majority party. Now, of course, we are accustomed to divided government, since in thirty-two of the fifty years before 2001, including twenty-six of the thirty-two years after 1968, the president's party did not control at least one house of Congress and often controlled neither. The briefly and barely unified government produced by the election of 2000 did not lead observers to predict the beginning of a new era in which one-party control would again become the norm.

Furthermore, an impressive case has been made for the legislative productivity of divided government, compared with unified government, between 1946 and 1990 (Mayhew 1991). Responsible party advocates, however, are not thus readily discouraged. Even during the Clinton presidency, when cross-party majorities were needed (and often obtained) for passage of legislation, especially after 1994, they could point to the passage of the administration's crucial legislative accomplishment, the tax-raising budget of 1993, solely by congressional Democrats when they still controlled both houses. The responsible party school can also draw comfort from a highly sophisticated analysis of "significant legislation" that finds unified government to be associated with more such enactments (Coleman 1999). Still, we can hardly be certain that the quest will continue in the twenty-first century as it has since the beginnings of American political science in the late nineteenth century.

Not only might the quest for more responsible parties diminish, so might the use of responsible party government, more or less British-style, as an analytical model. For until now, party specialists, if not political scientists more generally, have often described American parties by indicating the extent to which they approximated that model or deviated from it. Not all of us who did so were advocates of the model. Some were even critics of attempts to establish anything like British parties in American circumstances. Now, however, the model itself may be challenged, as it is by Charles Jones in chapter 8, where he suggests a "government of parties" as a substitute. Perhaps a new generation of political scientists will prefer it or another model to the one we have so often used for over a century.

About the Authors

John F. Bibby is professor emeritus of political science at the University of Wisconsin–Milwaukee. He is the author of *Politics, Parties, and Elections in America* and a co-author of *Party Organizations in American Politics* and *Two Parties—Or More?* (with Sandy Maisel). His experience in practical politics has included service on the staff of the Republican National Committee during the chairmanship of Ray C. Bliss.

Leon D. Epstein is professor emeritus of political science at the University of Wisconsin–Madison. His books include *Political Parties in the American Mold, Political Parties in Western Democracies, Governing the University,* and *Politics in Wisconsin.*

John C. Green is director of the Ray C. Bliss Institute of Applied Politics and professor of political science at the University of Akron. He is an editor of *The State of the Parties* and *Financing the 1996 Elections* and an author of *The Bully Pulpit* and *Religion and the Culture Wars.*

Paul S. Herrnson is director of the Center for American Politics and Citizenship and professor of government and politics at the University of Maryland. He is the author of *Congressional Elections: Campaigning at Home and in Washington* and *Party Campaigning in the 1980s.* His edited books include *Playing Hardball: Campaigning for the U.S. Congress.*

Charles O. Jones is professor emeritus of political science at the University of Wisconsin–Madison. His books include *Clinton and Congress, 1993–1996; Separate but Equal Branches: Congress and the Presidency; Passages to the Presidency; The Presidency in a Separated System; The United States Congress: People, Place, and Policy;* and *The Minority Party in Congress.*

David B. Magleby is dean of the College of Family, Home, and Social Sciences and Distinguished Professor of Political Science at Brigham Young University. His books

217

include *Direct Legislation: Voting on Ballot Propositions in the United States; The Money Chase: Congressional Campaign Finance Reform;* and *Outside Money.*

L. Sandy Maisel is the William R. Kenan Jr. Professor of Government at Colby College. A former candidate for Congress and a Democratic Party activist, he is the author of *From Obscurity to Oblivion: Running in the Congressional Primary; Parties and Elections in America: The Electoral Process;* and *Two Parties—Or More?* (with John Bibby). He is the editor of *The Parties Respond: Changes in American Parties and Campaigns* and *Jews in American Politics.*

Jerome M. Mileur is professor of political science at the University of Massachusetts–Amherst. His edited books include *The Liberal Tradition in Crisis; American Politics in the Sixties; Progressivism and the New Democracy; Parties and Politics in the New England States; America's Choice: The Election of 1996;* and *Challenges to Party Government* (coedited with John Kenneth White).

Kelly D. Patterson is associate professor of political science at Brigham Young University. He is the author of *Political Parties and the Maintenance of Liberal Democracy* and coeditor of *Contemplating the People's Branch: Legislative Dynamics in the Twenty-First Century.*

Gerald M. Pomper is professor emeritus of political science at Rutgers University. His books include *Passions and Interests; Voters, Elections, and Parties;* and *Elections in America.* He is coeditor of *The Election of 2000* and related volumes dating back to 1976.

Barbara Sinclair is Marvin Hoffenberg Professor of American Politics at the University of California, Los Angeles. Her books include *Unorthodox Lawmaking: New Legislative Processes in the U.S. Congress; Legislators, Leaders, and Lawmaking: The U.S. House of Representatives in the Post-reform Era; The Transformation of the U.S. Senate;* and *Congressional Realignment, 1925–1978.*

Frank J. Sorauf is Regents' Professor Emeritus of Political Science at the University of Minnesota. His books include *Party Politics in America; Money in American Elections; Inside Campaign Finance: Myths and Realities;* and *What Price PACs?* He is coauthor of *Campaign Finance Reform: A Sourcebook.*

James A. Thurber is professor of government and director of the Center for Congressional and Presidential Studies at American University. His edited books include *The Battle for Congress: Consultants, Candidates, and Voters; Campaign Warriors: The Role of Political Consultants in Elections; Crowded Airwaves: Campaign Advertising in Elections;* and *Rivals for Power: Presidential-Congressional Relations.*

Marc D. Weiner is the assistant director of the Princeton University Survey Research Center. He holds a JD from Widener University and is a doctoral candidate at Rutgers University. His forthcoming dissertation is "The Bureaucratic Effect: Toward a More Comprehensive Measure of Party Responsibility."

Herbert F. Weisberg is professor of political science at Ohio State University. He is coauthor of *An Introduction to Survey Research, Polling, and Data Analysis* and an editor of *Democracy's Feast: Elections in America; Classics in Congressional Politics; Controversies in Voting Behavior;* and *Classics in Voting Behavior.*

John Kenneth White is professor of politics at the Catholic University of America. His books include *The Values Divide: American Politics and Culture in Transition; Still Seeing Red: How the Cold War Shapes the New American Politics; The New Politics of Old Values;* and *Challenges to Party Government* (coedited with Jerome M. Mileur).

References

Abramson, Jill, and Leslie Wayne. 1997. "Democrats Used the State Parties to Bypass Limits." *New York Times,* October 2, A1, A8.

Aldrich, John H. 1995. *Why Parties? The Origin and Transformation of Political Parties in America.* Chicago: University of Chicago Press.

Aldrich, John H., and Richard G. Niemi. 1996. "The Sixth American Party System: Electoral Change, 1952–1992." In *Broken Contract?* ed. Stephen C. Craig. Boulder, Colo.: Westview Press, 87–109.

Alexander, Herbert E. 1984. *Financing Politics.* 3d ed. Washington, D.C.: CQ Press.

Allen, Mike. 2000. "House GOP Goes Within for Money." *Washington Post,* June 14.

American Political Science Review (APSR). 1947. "News and Notes." 41: 101–128.

———. 1948. "News and Notes." 42: 91–115.

———. 1949. "News and Notes." 43: 107–128.

———. 1950. "News and Notes." 44: 154–176.

———. 1951. "News and Notes." 45: 158–184.

Andersen, Kristi. 1976. "Generation, Partisan Shift, and Realignment," in *The Changing American Voter,* ed. Norman Nie et al. Cambridge: Harvard University Press, 74–95.

Baer, Denise L., and David A. Bositis. 1993. *Politics and Linkage in a Democratic Society.* Englewood Cliffs, N.J.: Prentice-Hall.

Bagehot, Walter. 1928. *The English Constitution.* London: Oxford University Press.

Bailey, Stephen K. 1959. *The Condition of Our National Political Parties.* New York: Fund for the Republic.

Bartels, Larry M. 2000. "Partisanship and Voting Behavior, 1952–1996." *American Journal of Political Science* 44: 35–50.

Bass, Harold F., Jr. 1998. "Partisan Rules, 1946–1996." In *Partisan Approaches to Postwar American Politics,* ed. Byron E. Shafer. New York: Chatham House, 220–270.

Beck, Nathaniel, Jonathan N. Katz, and Richard Tucker. 1998. "Taking Time Seriously: Time-Series–Cross-Section Models with a Binary Dependent Variable." *American Journal of Political Science* 42: 1260–1288.

Belknap, George, and Angus Campbell. 1952. "Political Party Identification and Attitudes Toward Foreign Policy." *Public Opinion Quarterly* 15: 601–623.

Bibby, John F. 1981. "Party Renewal in the National Republican Party." In *Party Renewal in America: Theory and Practice*, ed. Gerald M. Pomper. New York: Praeger, 101–115.

———. 1994. "Party Leadership, the Bliss Model, and the Development of the Republican National Committee." In *Politics, Professionalism, and Power*, ed. John C. Green. Lanham, Md.: University Press of America, 19–33.

———. 1998. "Party Organizations, 1946–1996." In *Partisan Approaches to Postwar American Politics*, ed. Byron E. Shafer. New York: Chatham House, 142–185.

———. 1999a. "State and Local Parties in a Candidate-Centered Age." In *American State and Local Politics*, ed. Ronald E. Weber and Paul Brace. New York: Chatham House, 194–211.

———. 1999b. "Party Networks: National-State Integration, Allied Groups, and Issue Activists." In *The State of the Parties*, ed. John C. Green and Daniel M. Shea. Lanham, Md.: Rowman and Littlefield, 69–85.

———. 2000. *Politics, Parties, and Elections in America*. 4th ed. Belmont, Calif.: Wadsworth.

Bibby, John F., and Thomas M. Holbrook. 1999. "Parties and Elections." In *Politics in the American States: A Comparative Analysis*, ed. Virginia Gray, Russell L. Hanson, and Herbert Jacob. 7th ed. Washington, D.C.: CQ Press, 66–112.

Binder, Sarah, and Steven S. Smith. 1997. *Politics or Principle? Filibustering in the United States Senate*. Washington, D.C.: Brookings Institution Press.

Bohren, Oyvind. 1988. "The Agent's Ethics in the Principal-Agent Model." *Journal of Business Ethics* 17: 745–755.

Bolling, Richard. 1965. *House Out of Order*. New York: E. P. Dutton.

Bond, Jon R., and Richard Fleisher. 1999. "The Disappearing Middle and the President's Quest for Votes in Congress." *PRG Report* (fall): 6–9.

Brennan, Geoffrey, and Alan Hamlin. 1999. "On Political Representation." *British Journal of Political Science* 29: 109–127.

Broder, David S. 1972. *The Party's Over: The Failure of Politics in America*. New York: Harper and Row.

Brooks, Robert C. 1923. *Political Parties and Electoral Problems*. New York: Harper.

Bruce, John M., John A. Clark, and John H. Kessel. 1991. "Advocacy Politics in Presidential Parties." *American Political Science Review* 85: 1089–1106.

Bryce, James. 1889. *The American Commonwealth*. London: Macmillan.

Burns, James MacGregor. 1956. *Roosevelt: The Lion and the Fox*. New York: Harcourt, Brace, and World.

———. 1963. *The Deadlock of Democracy*. Englewood Cliffs, N.J.: Prentice-Hall.

Burton, David H. 1988. *The Learned Presidency*. Rutherford, N.J.: Farleigh Dickinson University Press.

Busch, Andrew E. 1996. "Early Voting: Convenient but . . ." *State Legislatures* 22: 8–24.

Calvert, Randall L. 1985. "Robustness of the Multidimensional Voting Model: Candidate Motivations, Uncertainty, and Convergence." *American Journal of Political Science* 29: 69–95.

Campbell, Angus, Gerald Gurin, and Warren E. Miller. 1954. *The Voter Decides.* Evanston, Ill.: Row, Peterson.

Campbell, Angus, and Warren E. Miller. 1957. "The Motivational Basis of Straight and Split Ticket Voting." *American Political Science Review* 51: 293–312.

Campbell, Angus, Philip E. Converse, Warren E. Miller, and Donald E. Stokes. 1960. *The American Voter.* New York: Wiley.

Canon, David T., and Kenneth R. Mayer. 1999. *The Dysfunctional Congress? The Individual Roots of an Institutional Dilemma.* Boulder, Colo.: Westview Press.

Carmines, Edward G., and James A. Stimson. 1989. *Issue Evolution.* Princeton: Princeton University Press.

Ceaser, James W. 1979. *Presidential Selection.* Princeton: Princeton University Press.

Chambers, William Nisbet. 1963. *Political Parties in a New Nation.* New York: Oxford University Press.

Charles, Joseph. 1956. *The Origins of the American Party System.* New York: Harper and Row.

Cheney, Richard B. 1989. "An Unruly House." *Public Opinion* 11: 41–44.

Clemens, Elisabeth S. 1997. *The People's Lobby.* Chicago: University of Chicago Press.

Cohen, Adam, and Elizabeth Taylor. 2000. *American Pharaoh.* Boston: Little Brown.

Coleman, John J. 1996. *Party Decline in America.* Princeton: Princeton University Press.

———. 1999. "Unified Government, Divided Government, and Party Responsiveness." *American Political Science Review* 93: 821–835.

Commission on Party Structure and Delegate Selection. 1970. *Mandate for Reform: A Report to the Democratic National Committee.* Washington, D.C.: Democratic National Committee.

Committee for Party Renewal. 1977. "Declaration of Principles." Committee for Party Renewal.

———. 1984. "Principles of Strong Party Organization." Committee for Party Renewal.

Committee on Political Parties. American Political Science Association. 1950a. "Toward a More Responsible Two-Party System." *American Political Science Review* 44. Supplement.

———. 1950b. *Toward a More Responsible Two-Party System. A Report of the Committee on Political Parties of the American Political Science Association.* New York: Rinehart.

Congressional Quarterly. 1999. "Party Unity Background." *CQ Weekly Report* 57 (December 11): 2987–2993.

Connelly, William, and John Pitney. 1994. *Congress' Permanent Minority? Republicans in the U.S. House.* Lanham, Md.: Rowman and Littlefield.

Cook, Rhodes. 2000. *The Race for the Presidency: Winning the 2000 Nomination.* Washington, D.C.: CQ Press.

Cooper, Joseph, and David W. Brady. 1981. "Institutional Context and Leadership Style: The House from Cannon to Rayburn." *American Political Science Review* 75: 411–425.

Corrado, Anthony. 1997. "Money and Politics: A History of Federal Campaign Finance Law." In *Campaign Finance Reform: A Sourcebook,* ed. Anthony Corrado,

Thomas E. Mann, Daniel R. Ortiz, Trevor Potter, and Frank J. Sorauf. Washington, D.C.: Brookings Institution Press, 25–60.

Coser, Lewis. 1956. *The Functions of Social Conflict.* Glencoe, Ill.: Free Press.

Cotter, Cornelius P., James L. Gibson, John F. Bibby, and Robert J. Huckshorn. 1984. *Party Organizations in American Politics.* Pittsburgh: University of Pittsburgh Press.

Cox, Gary W., and Mathew D. McCubbins. 1993. *Legislative Leviathan: Party Government in the House.* Berkeley: University of California Press.

Croly, Herbert. 1988. *Progressive Democracy.* New Brunswick, N.J.: Transaction Press.

Crotty, William. 1983. *Party Reform.* New York: Longman.

———. 1991. "Political Parties: Issues and Trends." In *Political Science: Looking to the Future,* ed. William Crotty. Vol. 4. Evanston, Ill.: Northwestern University Press, 137–201.

David, Paul T. 1992. "The APSA Committee on Political Parties." *Perspectives on Political Science* 21: 70–79.

Davis, James W. 1992. *The President as Party Leader.* New York: Praeger.

DeSart, Jay A. 1995. "Information Processing and Partisan Neutrality: A Reexamination of the Party Decline Thesis." *Journal of Politics* 57: 776–795.

Dionne, E. J., Jr. 1999. "Construction Boon: It's No Accident That the GOP Is Being Rebuilt by Its Governors." *Washington Post,* March 14.

Downs, Anthony. 1957. *An Economic Theory of Democracy.* New York: Harper and Row.

Dulio, David A. 2001. "For Better or Worse? How Political Consultants Are Changing Elections in the United States." Ph.D. dissertation. American University.

Dulio, David A., Candice J. Nelson, and James A. Thurber. 1999. "Campaign Elites: The Attitudes and Roles of Professional Political Consultants." Paper presented at the 1999 Annual Meeting of the Western Political Science Association, Seattle, Washington, March 25.

Dulio, David A., and James A. Thurber. 2000. "America's Two-Party System: Friend or Foe?" *Administrative Law Review* 52: 769–792.

Dwyre, Diana. 1996. "Spinning Straw into Gold: Soft Money and U.S. House Elections." *Legislative Studies Quarterly* 21: 409–424.

Eisenhardt, Kathleen M. 1989. "Agency Theory: An Assessment and Review." *Academy of Management Review* 14: 57–74.

Eldersveld, Samuel J. 1964. *Political Parties: A Behavioral Analysis.* Chicago: Rand McNally.

Enelow, James M., and Melvin J. Hinich. 1984. *The Spatial Theory of Voting.* Cambridge: Cambridge University Press.

Epstein, Leon D. 1967. *Political Parties in Western Democracies.* New York: Praeger.

———. 1975. "Political Parties." In *The Handbook of Political Science,* ed. Fred I. Greenstein and Nelson W. Polsby. Vol. 4. Reading, Mass.: Addison-Wesley, 229–277.

———. 1983. "The Scholarly Commitment to Parties." In *Political Science: The State of the Discipline,* ed. Ada W. Finifter. Washington, D.C.: American Political Science Association, 127–153.

———. 1986. *Political Parties in the American Mold.* Madison: University of Wisconsin Press.

———. 1989. "Will American Parties Be Privatized?" *Journal of Law and Politics* 5: 239–274.

———. 1999. "The American Party Primary." In *On Parties: Essays Honoring Austin Ranney,* ed. Nelson W. Polsby and Raymond E. Wolfinger. Berkeley: Institute of Governmental Studies Press, University of California, Berkeley, 43–71.

Federal Election Commission. 1999. "FEC Issues Report on Impact of National Voter Registration Act." Press release, July 7.

———. 2000. "Party Fundraising Escalates." Press release, November 3.

Fenno, Richard F., Jr. 1978. *Home Style: House Members in Their Districts.* Boston: Little, Brown.

———. 1982. *The United States Senate: A Bicameral Perspective.* Washington, D.C.: American Enterprise Institute Press.

———. 1996. *Senators on the Campaign Trail: The Politics of Representation.* Norman: University of Oklahoma Press.

———. 2000. *Congress at the Grassroots.* Chapel Hill: University of North Carolina Press.

Fiorina, Morris. 1981. *Retrospective Voting in American National Elections.* New Haven: Yale University Press.

———. 1996. *Divided Government.* 2d ed. Boston: Allyn and Bacon.

Fleisher, Richard, and Jon R. Bond. 1996. "Why Has Party Conflict Among Elites Increased If the Electorate Is Dealigning?" Paper presented at the Annual Meeting of the Midwest Political Science Association, Chicago.

Flemming, Gregory. 1999. *An Agenda-Setting Model of Congressional Campaigns.* Ph.D. dissertation. University of Wisconsin–Madison.

Foley, Michael. 1980. *The New Senate.* New Haven: Yale University Press.

Ford, Henry Jones. 1967. *The Rise and Growth of American Politics.* New York: Da Capo Press.

Frantzich, Stephen E. 1989. *Political Parties in the Technological Age.* New York: Longman.

Frendreis, John, and Alan R. Gitelson. 1999. "Local Parties in the 1990s: Spokes in a Candidate-Centered Wheel." In *The State of the Parties,* ed. John C. Green and Daniel M. Shea. Lanham, Md.: Rowman and Littlefield, 135–153.

Galloway, George B. 1946. *Congress at the Crossroads.* New York: T. Y. Crowell.

Gamm, Gerald, and Steven S. Smith. 1999. "Emergence of Senate Party Leadership." Paper presented at the Conference on Senate Exceptionalism, Vanderbilt University, Nashville, Tenn., October 21–23.

Garvey, Gerald. 1966. "The Theory of Party Equilibrium." *American Political Science Review* 60: 29–39.

Geer, John G. 1998. *Politicians and Party Politics.* Baltimore: Johns Hopkins University Press.

Gierzynski, Anthony. 1992. *Legislative Party Campaign Committees in the American States.* Lexington: University of Kentucky Press.

Gimpel, James G. 1996. *Fulfilling the Contract: The First 100 Days.* Boston: Allyn and Bacon.

Glendon, Mary Ann. 1991. *Rights Talk.* New York: Free Press.

Goldberg, Cary. 2000. "Vermont's 'Clean Money' Law Will Finance Underdog's Campaign." *New York Times,* June 15.

Goldman, Ralph M. 1951. "Party Chairmen and Party Factions, 1789–1900." Ph.D. dissertation, University of Chicago.

Gorman, Siobhan. 2000. "Florida Times 50." *National Journal* (December 12): 3720–3725.

Green, John C., and Daniel M. Shea, eds. 1996. *The State of the Parties.* 2d ed. Lanham, Md.: Rowman and Littlefield.

Green, John C., John S. Jackson, and Nancy L. Clayton. 1999. "Issue Networks and Party Elites in 1996." In *The State of the Parties,* ed. John C. Green and Daniel M. Shea. Lanham, Md.: Rowman and Littlefield, 105–119.

Guth, James L., and John C. Green. 1996. "Balance Wheels: Minor Party Activists in the Two-Party System." In *The State of the Parties: The Changing Role of Contemporary American Parties,* ed. John C. Green and Daniel M. Shea. 2d ed. Lanham, Md.: Rowman and Littlefield.

Hadley, Charles D. 1986. "The Impact of the Louisiana Open Elections System Reform." *State Government* 58: 152–157.

Hamilton, Alexander. 1961. "Federalist no. 68," *The Federalist Papers,* ed. Clinton Rossiter. New York: New American Library.

Hardin, Charles E. 1974. *Presidential Power and Accountability: Toward a New Constitution.* Chicago: University of Chicago Press.

Heard, Alexander. 1960. *The Costs of Democracy.* Chapel Hill: University of North Carolina Press.

Herring, Pendleton. 1940. *The Politics of Democracy.* New York: Norton.

———. 1965. *The Politics of Democracy.* New edition. New York: Norton.

Herrnson, Paul S. 1986. "Do Parties Make a Difference? The Role of Party Organizations in Congressional Elections." *Journal of Politics* 48: 589–615.

———. 1988. *Party Campaigning in the 1980s.* Cambridge: Harvard University Press.

———. 1992. "Why the United States Does Not Have Responsible Parties." *Perspectives on Political Science* 21: 91–99.

———. 1993. "Political Leadership and Organizational Change at the National Committees." In *Politics, Professionalism, and Power,* ed. John Green. Lanham, Md.: University Press of America, 186–202.

———. 1995. *Congressional Elections: Campaigning at Home and in Washington.* Washington, D.C.: CQ Press.

———. 1998. *Congressional Elections: Campaigning at Home and in Washington.* 2d ed. Washington, D.C.: CQ Press.

———. 2000. *Congressional Elections: Campaigning at Home and in Washington.* 3d ed. Washington, D.C.: CQ Press.

Herrnson, Paul S., Kelly D. Patterson, and John J. Pitney. 1996. "From Ward Heelers to Public Relations Experts: The Parties' Response to Mass Politics." In *Broken Contract? Changing Relationships Between Americans and their Government,* ed. Stephen C. Craig. Boulder, Colo.: Westview Press, 251–267.

Herrnson, Paul S., and John C. Green. 2001. *Multiparty Politics in America.* 2d ed. Lanham, Md.: Rowman and Littlefield.

Hetherington, Mark J. 2001. "Resurgent Mass Partisanship: The Role of Elite Polarization." *American Political Science Review* 95: 619–631.

Himes, David. 1995. "Strategy and Tactics for Campaign Fundraising." In *Campaigns and Elections American Style,* ed. James A. Thurber and Candice J. Nelson. Boulder: Westview Press, 62–77.

Hofstadter, Richard. 1972. *The Idea of a Party System.* Berkeley: University of California Press.

Howell, William, Scott Adler, Charles Cameron, and Charles Riemann. 2000. "Divided Government and the Legislative Productivity of Congress, 1945–1994." *Legislative Studies Quarterly* 25: 285–312.

Huitt, Ralph. 1961. "The Outsider in the Senate: An Alternative Role." *American Political Science Review* 55: 566–575.

Huntington, Samuel P. 1950. "A Revised Theory of American Party Politics." *American Political Science Review* 44: 669–677.

Jacobson, Gary C. 1992. *The Politics of Congressional Elections,* 3d ed. New York: HarperCollins.

Jackson, Brooks. 1988. *Honest Graft.* New York: Knopf.

Jackson, John S., Barbara L. Brown, and David Bositis. 1982. "Herbert McClosky and Friends Revisited: 1980 Democratic and Republican Party Elites Compared to the Mass Public." *American Politics Quarterly* 10: 158–180.

Janda, Kenneth. 1993. "Comparative Political Parties: Research and Theory." In *Political Science: The State of the Discipline II,* ed. Ada W. Finifter. Washington, D.C.: American Political Science Association, 163–191.

Jeter, Jon. 1998. "Campaign Reform Helped 'The Body' Slam Rivals." *Washington Post,* November 5.

Jewell, Malcolm E., and Sarah M. Morehouse. 1999. "State Political Party Endorsements: Continuity and Change." Paper presented at the Annual Meeting of the Midwest Political Science Association, Chicago.

———. 2000. *Political Parties and Elections in American States.* 4th ed. Washington, D.C.: CQ Press.

Johnson, Dennis W. 1998. "Political Consulting: The Making of a Profession." Paper presented at conference, "The Role of Political Consultants in Elections," Washington, D.C.

———. 2000. "The Business of Political Consulting." In *Campaign Warriors: Political Consultants in Elections,* ed. James A. Thurber and Candice J. Nelson. Washington, D.C.: Brookings Institution Press, 37–53.

Jones, Charles O. 1994. *The Presidency in a Separated System.* Washington, D.C.: Brookings Institution Press.

———. 1999a. *The Speculative Imagination in Democratic Lawmaking.* Oxford: Oxford University Press.

———. 1999b. *Separate but Equal Branches: Congress and the Presidency.* New York: Chatham House.

Karp, Jeffrey A., and Susan A. Banducci. 2001. "Absentee Voting: Mobilization and Participation." *American Politics Research* 29: 183–195.

Kayden, Xandra, and Eddie Mahe, Jr. 1985. *The Party Goes On.* New York: Basic Books.

Keith, Bruce E., David B. Magleby, Candice J. Nelson, Elizabeth Orr, Mark C. Westlye, and Raymond E. Wolfinger. 1986. "The Partisan Affinities of Independent 'Leaners.'" *British Journal of Political Science* 16: 155–185.

Kessel, John H. 1984. *Presidential Parties.* Homewood, Ill.: Dorsey Press.
————. 1988. *Presidential Campaign Politics.* 3d ed. Chicago: Dorsey.
Key, V. O., Jr. 1942, 1947, 1952, 1958, 1964. *Politics, Parties, and Pressure Groups.* 1st, 2d, 3d, 4th, and 5th eds. New York: Crowell.
————. 1956. *American State Politics: An Introduction.* New York: Knopf.
————. 1966. *The Responsible Electorate.* Cambridge: Harvard University Press.
Kiewiet, Roderick A., and Mathew D. McCubbins. 1991. *The Logic of Delegation: Congressional Parties and the Appropriations Process.* Chicago: University of Chicago Press.
Kimball, David E., and Chris T. Owens. 2000. "Where's the Party? Eliminating One-Punch Voting," Paper presented at the Annual Meeting of the Midwest Political Science Association, Chicago, April 26–30.
King, Gary, Michael Tomz, and Jason Wittenberg. 2000. "Making the Most of Statistical Analyses: Improving Interpretation and Presentation." *American Journal of Political Science* 44: 341–355.
Kirkpatrick, Evron M. 1971. "Toward a More Responsible Two-Party System: Political Science, Policy Science, or Pseudo-Science?" *American Political Science Review* 65: 965–990.
Kirkpatrick, Jeane. 1976. *The New Presidential Elite.* New York: Russell Sage Foundation and Twentieth Century Fund.
Klein, Joe. 1998. "The Town That Ate Itself." *New Yorker* 74: 79–87.
Klingemann, Hans-Dieter, Richard I. Hofferbert, and Ian Budge. 1994. *Parties, Policies, and Democracy.* Boulder, Colo.: Westview Press.
Klinkner, Philip A. 1994. *The Losing Parties: Out-Party National Committees, 1956–1993.* New Haven: Yale University Press, 1994.
Kolodny, Robin. 1998a. *Pursuing Majorities: Congressional Campaign Committees in American Politics.* Norman: University of Oklahoma Press.
————. 1998b. *Electoral Partnerships: Political Consultants and Political Parties.* Monograph from the Improving Campaign Conduct series. Washington, D.C.: Center for Congressional and Presidential Studies.
————. 2000. "Electoral Partnerships: Political Consultants and Political Parties." In *Campaign Warriors: Political Consultants in Elections,* ed. James A. Thurber and Candice J. Nelson. Washington, D.C.: Brookings Institution Press, 110–132.
Kolodny, Robin, and Angela Logan. 1998. "Political Consultants and the Extension of Party Goals." *PS: Political Science and Politics* 31: 155–159.
Koopman, Douglas L. 1996. *Hostile Takeover: The House Republican Party, 1980–1995.* Lanham, Md.: Rowman and Littlefield.
Kramer, Gerald H. 1983. "The Ecological Fallacy Revisited: Aggregate- Versus Individual-level Findings on Economics and Elections, and Socio-tropic Voting." *American Political Science Review* 77: 92–111.
Krasno, Jonathan, and Daniel Seltz. 2000. *Buying Time: Television in the 1998 Congressional Elections.* New York: Brennan Center, NYU Law School.
Krehbiel, Keith. 2000. "Party Discipline and Measures of Partisanship." *American Journal of Political Science* 44: 212–227.
La Raja, Ray. 2001. "State Parties and Soft Money: How Much Party Building?" Paper presented at conference, "State of the Parties: 2000 and Beyond," Ray C. Bliss Institute of Applied Politics, University of Akron, Akron, Ohio, October 17–19.

Ladd, Everett Carll. 1992. "Political Parties, 'Reform,' and American Democracy." In *Challenges to Party Government,* ed. John Kenneth White and Jerome M. Mileur. Carbondale: Southern Illinois University Press, 22–39.

Lapinski, Daniel. 1999. "Communicating the Party Record: How Congressional Leaders Transmit Their Messages to the Public." Paper presented at the Annual Meeting of the American Political Science Association, Atlanta, Ga., September 2–5.

Little, Thomas H. 1997. "An Experiment in Responsible Party Government: National Agenda Setting and State Replicas of the Contract with America." *American Review of Politics* 18: 1–24.

Los Angles Times. 2000. "Primary Reform Won't Die." July 3.

Lowi, Theodore J. 1985. *The Personal President: Power Invested, Promise Unfulfilled.* Ithaca, N.Y.: Cornell University Press.

———. 1998. "Toward a Responsible Three-Party System: Prospects and Obstacles." In *Republic of Parties: Debating the Two-Party System,* ed. Theodore J. Lowi and Joseph Romance. Lanham, Md.: Rowman and Littlefield, 3–21.

———. 1999. "Toward a Responsible Three-Party System: Plan or Obituary?" In *The State of the Parties,* ed. John C. Green and Daniel M. Shea. Lanham, Md.: Rowman and Littlefield, 171–189.

Luntz, Frank I. 1988. *Candidates, Consultants, and Campaigns: The Style and Substance of American Electioneering.* New York: Basil Blackwell.

Madison, James. 1987. "Federalist no. 10," *The Federalist Papers,* ed. Isaac Kramnick. New York: Penguin.

Magleby, David B. 1998. "Outside Money: Soft Money and Issue Ads in Competitive 1998 Congressional Elections." In *Outside Money: Soft Money and Issue Advocacy in the 1998 Congressional Elections.* Provo, Utah: Center for the Study of Elections and Democracy, Brigham Young University.

Magleby, David, and Kelly Patterson. 1998. "Consultants and Direct Democracy." *PS: Political Science and Politics* 31: 160–164.

Main, Jackson Turner. 1973. *Political Parties Before the Constitution.* Chapel Hill: University of North Carolina Press.

Maisel, L. Sandy, 1999. *Parties and Elections in America: The Electoral Process.* 3d ed. Lanham, Md.: Rowman and Littlefield.

———, ed. 1990. *The Parties Respond: Changes in the American Party System.* Boulder, Colo.: Westview Press.

———, ed. 1991. *Political Parties and Elections in the United States: An Encyclopedia.* New York: Garland.

Malbin, Michael, and Thomas L. Gais. 1998. *The Day After Reform: Sobering Campaign Finance Lessons from the American States.* Albany, N.Y.: Rockefeller Institute Press.

Maltzman, Forrest. 1995. "Meeting Competing Demands: Committee Performance in the Postreform House." *American Journal of Political Science* 39: 653–682.

Marcus, Ruth. 1996. "DNC Finds Easy Way to Save Hard Money." *Washington Post,* July 1.

Markus, Gregory B. 1988. "The Impact of Personal and National Economic Conditions on the Presidential Vote: A Pooled Cross-Sectional Analysis." *American Journal of Political Science* 32: 137–154.

Martinez, Michael D., and David Hill. 1999. "Did Motor Voter Work?" *American Political Quarterly* 27: 296–315.

Mattei, Franco, and Richard G. Niemi. 1991. "Unrealized Partisans, Realized Independents, and the Intergenerational Transmission of Partisan Identification." *Journal of Politics* 53: 161–174.

Matthews, Donald E. 1960. *U.S. Senators and Their World.* New York: Vintage.

Mayer, William G. 1998. "Mass Partisanship, 1946–1996." In *Partisan Approaches to Postwar American Politics,* ed. Byron E. Shafer. New York: Chatham House, 186–219.

Mayhew, David R. 1974. *Congress: The Electoral Connection.* New Haven: Yale University Press.

———. 1986. *Placing Parties in American Politics.* Princeton: Princeton University Press.

———. 1991. *Divided We Govern: Party Control, Lawmaking, and Investigations, 1946–1990.* New Haven: Yale University Press.

McCloskey, Herbert, Paul Hoffman, and Rosemary O'Hara. 1960. "Issue Conflict and Consensus Among Party Leaders and Followers." *American Political Science Review* 54: 406–427.

McGovern, George S. 1977. *The Autobiography of George McGovern.* New York: Random House.

McJimsey, George. 2000. *The Presidency of Franklin D. Roosevelt.* Lawrence: University Press of Kansas.

McKean, Dayton D. 1949. *Party and Pressure Groups.* Boston: Houghton Mifflin.

McKelvey, Richard D. 1976. "Intransitivities in Multidimensional Voting Models and Some Implications for Agenda Control." *Journal of Economic Theory* 12: 472–482.

McSeveney, Samuel T. 1994. "The Fourth Party System and Progressive Politics." In *Parties and Politics in American History,* ed. L. Sandy Maisel and William G. Shade. New York: Garland, 157–178.

Medvic, Stephen K. 1997. "Is There a Spin Doctor in the House? The Influence of Political Consultants in Congressional Campaigns." Ph.D. dissertation, Purdue University.

———. 1998. "The Effectiveness of Consultants as a Campaign Resource." *PS: Political Science and Politics* 31: 150–154.

Medvic, Stephen K., and Silvo Lenart. 1997. "The Influence of Political Consultants in the 1992 Congressional Elections." *Journal of Legislative Studies* 22: 61–72.

Merriam, Charles E. 1922. *The American Party System.* New York: Macmillan.

———. 1924. *The Convention and the Primary.* Washington, D.C.: National League of Women Voters.

Merriam, Charles E., and Louise Overacker. 1928. *Primary Elections.* Chicago: University of Chicago Press.

Merriam, Charles E., and Harold F. Gosnell. 1929. *The American Party System.* New York: Macmillan.

Milkis, Sidney M. 1993. *The President and the Parties: The Transformation of the American Party System Since the New Deal.* New York: Oxford University Press.

———. 1999. *Political Parties and Constitutional Government.* Baltimore: Johns Hopkins University Press.

Miller, Warren E. 1953. "Party Preferences and Attitudes on Political Issues." *American Political Science Review* 47: 45–60.

Miller, Warren E., and J. Merrill Shanks. 1996. *The New American Voter.* Cambridge: Harvard University Press.

Mitchell, Greg. 1992. *The Campaign of the Century: Upton Sinclair's Race for the Governor of California and the Birth of Media Politics.* New York: Random House.

Mockabee, Stephen T. 2001. "Party Polarization in American Politics." Ph.D. dissertation. Ohio State University.

Moe, Terry M. 1984. "The New Economics of Organization." *American Journal of Political Science* 28: 739–777.

Mutch, Robert E. 1988. *Campaigns, Congress, and Courts.* New York: Praeger.

Neustadt, Richard E. 1960. *Presidential Power: The Politics of Leadership.* New York: John Wiley.

Nie, Norman H., Sidney Verba, and John R. Petrocik. 1979. *The Changing American Voter.* Cambridge: Harvard University Press.

Nie, Norman H., Jane Junn, and Kenneth Stehlik-Barry. 1996. *Education and Democratic Citizenship in America.* Chicago: University of Chicago Press.

Niemi, Richard G., and Herbert F. Weisberg, eds. 2001. *Controversies in Voting Behavior.* 4th ed. Washington, D.C.: CQ Press.

Nimmo, Dan D. 1970. *The Political Persuaders.* Englewood Cliffs, N.J.: Prentice-Hall.

Ornstein, Norman, Thomas Mann, and Michael Malbin. 1996. *Vital Statistics on Congress, 1995–1996.* Washington, D.C.: American Enterprise Institution Press.

Overacker, Louise. 1932. *Money in Elections.* New York: Macmillan.

Owens, John. 1998. "Taking Power? Institutional Change in the House and Senate." In *The Republican Takeover of Congress,* ed. Dean McSweeney and John E. Owens. London: Macmillan, 33–70.

Patterson, Kelly D. 1996. *Political Parties and the Maintenance of Liberal Democracy.* New York: Columbia University Press.

Patterson, Stephen E. 1973. *Political Parties in Revolutionary Massachusetts.* Madison: University of Wisconsin Press.

Peltason, Jack W. 1999. "Constitutional Law of Parties." In *On Parties: Essays Honoring Austin Ranney,* ed. Nelson W. Polsby and Raymond E. Wolfinger. Berkeley: Institute of Governmental Studies Press, University of California, 9–42.

Pennock, J. Ronald. 1952. "Responsiveness, Responsibility, and Majority Rule." *American Political Science Review* 46: 790–807.

———. 1972. "Comments on Gerald M. Pomper's "Toward a More Responsible Two-Party System? What, Again?"" *Journal of Politics* 34: 952–955.

Pollock, James K. 1926. *Party Campaign Funds.* New York: Knopf.

Polsby, Nelson W. 1983. *Consequences of Party Reform.* New York: Oxford University Press, 1983.

Pomper, Gerald M. 1971. "Toward a More Responsible Two-Party System? What?, Again?" *Journal of Politics* 33: 916–940.

———. 1975. *Voters' Choice.* New York: Dodd, Mead.

———. 1992. *Passions and Interests: Political Party Concepts of American Democracy.* Lawrence: University Press of Kansas.

————. 1999. "Parliamentary Government in the United States." In *The State of the Parties,* ed. John C. Green and Daniel M. Shea. 3d ed. Lanham, Md.: Rowman and Littlefield, 251–270.

————. 2000. "Inside the Party Platforms." *The World and I* (October): 22–27.

————. 2001. "Party Responsibility and the Future of American Democracy." In *American Political Parties: Decline or Resurgence?* ed. Jeffrey E. Cohen, Richard Fleischer, and Paul Kantor. Washington D.C.: CQ Press, 162–183.

————, ed. 1980. *Party Renewal in America: Theory and Practice.* New York: Praeger, 159–175.

Pomper, Gerald M., and Susan Lederman. 1980. *Elections in America.* 2d ed. New York: Longman.

Popkin, Samuel L. 1991. *The Reasoning Voter.* Chicago: University of Chicago Press.

Price, David E. 1984. *Bringing Back the Parties.* Washington, D.C.: CQ Press.

Ranney, Austin. 1951. "Toward a More Responsible Two-Party System: A Commentary." *American Political Science Review* 45: 488–499.

————. 1954. *The Doctrine of Responsible Party Government.* Urbana: University of Illinois Press.

————. 1968. "The Concept of 'Party.'" In *Political Research and Political Theory,* ed. Oliver Garceau. Cambridge: Harvard University Press, 143–162.

————. 1975. *Curing the Mischief of Faction.* Berkeley: University of California Press.

————. 1978. "Political Parties: Reform and Decline." In *The New American Political System,* ed. Anthony King. Washington, D.C.: American Enterprise Institution Press, 213–248.

Ranney, Austin, and Willmoore Kendall. 1956. *Democracy and the American Party System.* New York: Harcourt, Brace.

Redfield, Kent D. 1995. *Cash Clout.* Springfield: University of Illinois Press.

Reich, Charles R. 1970. *The Greening of America.* New York: Random House.

Rieselbach, LeRoy N. 1994. *Congressional Reform: The Changing Modern Congress.* Washington, D.C.: CQ Press.

Roberts, George C. 1994. "Paul M. Butler and the Democratic Party: Leadership and New Directions in Party Building." In *Politics, Professionalism, and Power,* ed. John C. Green. Lanham, Md.: University Press of America, 93–104.

Robinson, Edward E. 1924. *The Evolution of American Political Parties.* New York: Harcourt, Brace, and World.

Rohde, David W. 1991. *Parties and Leaders in the Postreform House.* Chicago: University of Chicago Press.

Rohde, David, Norman Ornstein, and Robert Peabody. 1985. "Political Change and Legislative Norms in the U.S. Senate, 1957–1974." In *Studies of Congress,* ed. Glenn Parker. Washington, D.C.: CQ Press, 147–188.

Rohde, David W., and Kenneth W. Shepsle. 1987. "Leaders and Followers in the House of Representatives: Reflections on Woodrow Wilson's *Congressional Government.*" *Congress and the Presidency* 14: 111–133.

Romano, Lois. 1998. "Growing Use of Mail Voting Puts Its Stamp on Campaigns." *Washington Post,* November 29.

Roosevelt, Theodore. 1994. "Speech Before the National Convention of the Progressive Party." In *The Essential Theodore Roosevelt,* ed. John Gabriel Hunt. New York: Gramercy.

Rusk, Jerrold. 1970. "The Effect of the Australian Ballot Reform on Split Ticket Voting." *American Political Science Review* 64: 1220–1238.

Sanchez, Rene. 2000. "Oregon Vote-by-Mail Delivered, but It Wasn't Letter Perfect." *Washington Post,* November 29.

Sapiro, Virginia, Steven J. Rosenstone, Warren E. Miller, and the National Election Studies. 1998. *American National Election Studies, 1948–1997* (CD–ROM). ICPSR ed. Ann Arbor, Mich.: Inter-University Consortium for Political and Social Research.

Scammon, Richard M., and Ben J. Wattenberg. 1970. *The Real Majority.* New York: Coward-McCann.

Scarrow, Harold A. 1983. *Parties, Elections, and Representation in the State of New York.* New York: New York University Press.

Schattschneider, E. E. 1942. *Party Government.* New York: Rinehart.

———. 1948. *The Struggle for Party Government.* College Park: University of Maryland Press.

———. 1975. *The Semi-Sovereign People.* Hinsdale, Ill.: Dryden.

Schlesinger, Arthur M., Jr. 1949. *The Vital Center.* Boston: Houghton Mifflin.

Schlesinger, Joseph A. 1991. *Political Parties and the Winning of Office.* Ann Arbor: University of Michigan Press.

Schneier, Edward V., and Bertram Gross. 1993. *Congress Today.* New York: St. Martin's Press.

Sellers, Patrick J. 1999. "Leaders and Followers in the U.S. Senate." Paper presented at the Conference on Senate Exceptionalism, Vanderbilt University, Nashville, Tenn., October 21–23.

Shafer, Byron E., ed. 1998. *Partisan Approaches to Postwar American Politics.* New York: Chatham House.

Shea, Daniel M. 1995. *Transforming Democracy: Legislative Campaign Committees and Political Parties.* Albany: State University of New York Press.

Shea, Daniel M., and John C. Green, eds. 1994. *The State of the Parties.* 2d ed. Lanham, Md.: Rowman and Littlefield.

Sinclair, Barbara. 1982. *Congressional Realignment.* Austin: University of Texas Press.

———. 1983. *Majority Leadership in the U.S. House.* Baltimore: Johns Hopkins University Press.

———. 1989. *The Transformation of the U.S. Senate.* Baltimore: Johns Hopkins University Press.

———. 1995. *Legislators, Leaders, and Lawmaking.* Baltimore: Johns Hopkins University Press.

———. 1997. *Unorthodox Lawmaking: New Legislative Processes in the U.S. Congress.* Washington, D.C.: CQ Press.

———. 1999. "Transformation Leader or Faithful Agent? Principal-Agent Theory and House Majority Party Leadership." *Legislative Studies Quarterly* 24: 421–449.

———. 2000a. "Hostile Partners: The President, Congress and Lawmaking in the Partisan 1990s." In *Polarized Politics: Congress and the President in a Partisan Era,* ed. Jon Bond and Richard Fleisher. Washington, D.C.: CQ Press, 134–153.

———. 2000b. *Unorthodox Lawmaking.* 2d ed. Washington, D.C.: CQ Press.

Smith, Steven. 1989. *Call to Order: Floor Politics in the House and Senate.* Washington, D.C.: Brookings Institution Press.

Songer, Donald R., Jeffrey A. Segal, and Charles M. Cameron. 1994. "The Hierarchy of Justice: Testing a Principal-Agent Model of Supreme Court–Circuit Court Interactions." *American Journal of Political Science* 38: 673–696.

Sorauf, Frank. 1980. "Political Parties and Political Action Committees: Two Life Cycles." *Arizona Law Review* 22: 445–464.

———. 1988. *Money in American Elections.* Glenview, Ill.: Scott, Foresman.

———. 1999. "What Buckley Wrought." In *If Buckley Fell,* ed. E. Joshua Rosenkranz. New York: Century Foundation Press, 11–62.

Sostek, Anya. 2000. "Vote Naked? Not Yet." *Governing* (October): 38, 50.

Special Committee on Congressional Reapportionment. American Political Science Association. 1951. "The Reapportionment of Congress." *American Political Science Review* 45: 153–157.

Spitzer, Robert J. 1997. "Multiparty Politics in New York." In *Multiparty Politics in America,* ed. Paul S. Herrnson and John C. Green. Lanham, Md.: Rowman and Littlefield, 125–140.

Stanley, Harold W., and Richard G. Niemi. 1995. "The Demise of the New Deal Coalition: Partisanship and Group Support, 1952–1992." In *Democracy's Feast: Elections in America,* ed. Herbert F. Weisberg. Chatham, N.J.: Chatham House, 222–240.

———. 1999. "Party Coalitions in Transition: Partisanship and Group Support, 1952–96." In *Reelection 1996: How Americans Voted,* ed. Herbert F. Weisberg and Janet M. Box-Steffensmeier. New York: Chatham House, 162–180.

———. 2001. "Partisanship, Party Coalitions, and Group Support, 1952–2000." Paper presented at the Annual Meeting of the American Political Science Association, San Francisco.

Stimson, James A. 1985. "Regression in Space and Time: A Statistical Essay." *American Journal of Political Science* 29: 914–947.

Stokes, Donald E. 1963. "Spatial Models of Party Competition." *American Political Science Review* 57: 368–377.

Strahan, Randall W. 1998. "Partisan Officeholders, 1946–1996." In *Partisan Approaches to Postwar American Politics,* ed. Byron E. Shafer. New York: Chatham House, 5–40.

Sundquist, James. 1968. *Politics and Policy: The Eisenhower, Kennedy and Johnson Years.* Washington, D.C.: Brookings Institution Press.

———. 1988. "Needed: A Political Theory for the New Era of Coalition Government in the United States." *Political Science Quarterly* 103: 613–635.

———. 1992. *Constitutional Reform and Effective Government.* Rev. ed. Washington, D.C.: Brookings Institution Press.

Taft, William Howard. 1913. *Popular Government.* New Haven: Yale University Press.

———. 1921. *Representative Government in the United States.* New York: New York University Press.

Taylor, Michelle M. 1992. "Formal Versus Informal Incentive Structures and Legislator Behavior: Evidence from Costa Rica." *Journal of Politics* 54: 1055–1073.

Thurber, James A. 1995. "The Transformation of American Campaigns." In *Campaigns and Elections American Style,* ed. James A. Thurber and Candice J. Nelson. Boulder: Westview Press, 1–13.

———. 1998. "The Study of Campaign Consultants: A Subfield in Search of a Theory." *PS: Political Science and Politics* 31: 145–149.

———. 1999. *National Survey of Professional Campaign Consultants: Who Are They and What Do They Believe?* Washington, D.C.: Center for Congressional and Presidential Studies.

———. 2000. "Introduction to the Study of Campaign Consultants." In *Campaign Warriors: Political Consultants in Elections,* ed. James A. Thurber and Candice J. Nelson. Washington, D.C.: Brookings Institution Press, 1–10.

Thurber, James A., and Candice J. Nelson, eds. 2000. *Campaign Warriors: Political Consultants in Elections.* Washington, D.C.: Brookings Institution Press.

Thurber, James A., Candice J. Nelson, and David A. Dulio, eds. 2000a. *Crowded Airwaves: Campaign Advertising in Elections.* Washington, D.C.: Brookings Institution Press.

———. 2000b. "Portrait of Campaign Consultants." In *Campaign Warriors: Political Consultants in Elections,* ed. James A. Thurber and Candice J. Nelson. Washington, D.C.: Brookings Institution Press, 10–37.

———. 2000c. *Political Consulting: A Portrait of the Industry.* Washington, D.C.: Center for Congressional and Presidential Studies.

Tocqueville, Alexis de. 1954. *Democracy in America,* ed. Phillips Bradley. New York: Vintage.

Tomz, Michael, Jason Wittenberg, and Gary King. 1999. "CLARIFY: Software for Interpreting and Presenting Statistical Results." Version 1.2.1. Cambridge: Harvard University, June 1. *<http://gking.harvard.edu/>.*

Turner, Julius. 1951a. "Responsible Parties: A Dissent from the Floor." *American Political Science Review* 45: 143–152.

———. 1951b. *Party and Constituency Pressure on Congress.* Baltimore: Johns Hopkins University Press.

Vega, Arturo, and Ronald M. Peters, Jr. 1996. "Principal-Agent Theories of Party Leadership Under Preference Heterogeneity: The Case of Simpson-Mazzoli." *Congress and the Presidency* 23: 15–32.

Walker, Jack L. 1966. "Ballot Forms and Voter Fatigue: An Analysis of the Office Block and Party Column Ballots." *Midwest Journal of Political Science* 10: 448–463.

Wallas, Graham. 1921. *Human Nature in Politics,* New York: F. S. Crofts.

Ware, Alan. 1985. *The Breakdown of Democratic Party Organization, 1940–1980.* New York: Oxford University Press.

Washington, George. 1958. "Farewell Address." In *Documents of American History,* ed. Henry Steele Commager. New York: Appleton-Century-Crofts.

Wattenberg, Martin P. 1984. *The Decline of American Political Parties, 1952–1980.* Cambridge: Harvard University Press.

———. 1996. *The Decline of American Parties: 1952–1994.* Cambridge: Harvard University Press.

Wayne, Leslie. 2000. "Popularity Is Increasing for Balloting Outside the Box." *New York Times,* November 4.

Wayne, Stephen J. 2000. *The Road to the White House 2000.* Boston: Bedford/St. Martin's.

Weber, Ronald E. 1980. "Gubernatorial Coattails: A Vanising Phenomenon." *State Government* 53: 153–156.

Weisberg, Herbert F. 1998. "The 1996 Election: Independents on the Decline." *Votes and Opinions* (March/April): 14–15.

West, Darrell M., and Burdett A. Loomis. 1998. *The Sound of Money: How Political Interests Get What They Want.* New York: W. W. Norton.

Weyl, Walter Edward. 1912. *The New Democracy.* New York: Macmillan.

White, John Kenneth. 1991. Testimony of John Kenneth White Before the House Task Force on Campaign Finance Reform, May 28.

———. 1992. "Responsible Party Government in America." *Perspectives on Political Science* 21: 80–90.

———. 1998. *Still Seeing Red.* Boulder, Colo.: Westview Press.

———. 2001. "Reviving the Political Parties: What Must Be Done?" In *The Politics of Ideas,* ed. John Kenneth White and John C. Green. Albany, N.Y.: SUNY Press.

White, John Kenneth, and Daniel M. Shea, 2000. *New Party Politics.* Boston and New York: Bedford/St. Martin's.

White, Theodore H. 1969. *The Making of the President, 1968.* New York: Atheneum.

Wiebe, Robert H. 1967. *The Search for Order, 1877–1920.* New York: Hill and Wang.

Wildavsky, Aaron B. 1979. *Speaking Truth to Power: The Art and Craft of Policy Analysis.* Boston: Little, Brown.

Wilson, James Q. 1960. *The Amateur Democrat.* New York: Basic Books.

Wilson, Woodrow. 1908. *Constitutional Government.* New York, Columbia University Press.

———. 1913. Inaugural Address, Washington, D.C.

Wittman, Donald. 1983. "Candidate Motivation: A Synthesis of Alternate Theories." *American Political Science Review* 77: 142–157.

Index

National Voter Registration Act (NVRA;
motor voter bill; U.S., 1993), 63–
64
Neustadt, Richard E., 148
New Deal, 20–24, 168
Nie, Norman H., 169–171
Niemi, Richard G., 168
Nixon, Richard M.
contributions to campaigns of, 84
in election of 1960, 153
resignation of, 29
*Nixon v. Shrink Missouri Government
PAC* (U.S., 2000), 99n
Nominating process, 211–214
Nonvoters, 182
North American Free Trade Agreement
(NAFTA), 137

O'Connor, John, 22–23
Office bloc ballot forms, 79–80
Open primary elections, 54, 66–68, 74–
75, 212–213
Oregon, 64
Oregon v. Mitchell (U.S., 1970), 62

Paine, Thomas, 34
Partisanship, 167, 205
in congressional parties, 138–139
party realignment and, 168–169
among voters, 185–189
among voters, increase in, 189–191
voting and, 169–170
Party-centered politics, 7
Party columns, on ballot forms, 79–80
Party councils, 48–49, 57, 145–146, 150
Party whip system, 130–132
Patronage, 16, 46
Patronage parties, 13–14, 16, 34, 41
Patterson, Kelly D., 11, 210
Pendleton Act (U.S., 1883), 16
Perot, H. Ross, 8, 78, 170
Petrocik, John R., 169–171
Platforms, 46, 50, 54
APSA Report on political parties on,
38–40
congressional parties and, 135–136

Political Action Committees (PACs), 55,
85–88, 94
Political consultants. *See* Campaign
consultants
Political conventions
APSA Report on political parties on, 39
changes in, 48
Committee for Party Renewal on, 30
decline in importance of, 57
in early twentieth century, 45
in late twentieth century, 52
McGovern-Fraser Commission on
delegate selection for, 24–28
new rules on delegate selection to, 70
party registration for voting in, 46
presidential primary elections and, 76–
77
Political Organizations and Parties (POP;
APSA section). *See* Committee on
Political Parties
Political parties
APSA Report on, 2–5, 38, 40–41, 141–
144, 203
campaign consultants to, 102–105
Committee for Party Renewal on, 28–33
congressional, 121–123, 135–140,
207–209
congressional, at beginning of twenty-
first century, 129–131
congressional, changes in, 123–129
congressional, legislative agendas set
by, 133–135
congressional, legislative coordination
of, 131–133
congressional, organization of, 11
constitutional law on, 65–69
decline in identification with, 205
differences between, 183–184, 206
differences in goals between
consultants and, 110, 114–115
in early twentieth century, 41–47
in electorate, 161
in electorate, historical development of,
162–165
in electorate, responsible parties and,
176–177

Referendums, 17, 18
Reform Party, 78, 79, 204
Registration for voting
  changes in procedures for, 63–64
  by party, 46
  Voting Rights Act on, 63
Rehnquist, William, 69
Republican National Committee, 70–71,
  209–210
  Committee to Reelect the President
  and, 84
Republican Party
  Committee to Reelect the President
  and, 84
  in Congress, at beginning of twenty-
  first century, 130–131
  conservative takeover of, 28
  differences between Democratic Party
  and, 183, 206
  in election of 1994, 55–56
  fund raising by, 86
  in House of Representatives, 128–129
  in House of Representatives,
  organization of, 208
  new rules of, 70
  during Roosevelt's New Deal, 21
  selection of convention delegates in,
  76–77
  soft money spent by, 90
  in South, 206
Republican Party of Connecticut v.
  Tashjian (U.S., 1986), 67, 68, 75
Residency requirements for voting, 63
Responsible party model, 107–109
Riemann, Charles, 159n
Rieselbach, LeRoy, 158n
Robinson, Edward E., 162
Roosevelt, Franklin Delano, 9, 15
  New Deal administration of, 20–24,
  47–48, 50–51
Roosevelt, Theodore, 17–19, 26, 45
  party government under, 47
Rosario v. Rockefeller (U.S., 1973), 68
Rules Committee (House of
  Representatives), 123, 124, 126–
  127, 131

Scalia, Anton, 67, 68
Schattschneider, Elmer E., 23, 121
  on active role for political scientists,
  33
  Committee on National Parties and
  Elections chaired by, 14–15
  Committee on Political Parties chaired
  by, 2
  on divided and unified government,
  159n
  on governmental burdens, 16
  on intraparty democracy, 6
  on party loyalty, 162
  on responsible parties, 201, 202
Schlesinger, Joseph A., 161
Seltz, Daniel, 91
Senate (U.S.)
  at beginning of twenty-first century,
  130–131
  changes in (1960s–1970s), 125–126
  changes in (1980s–1990s), 129
  Federal Election Campaign Act on
  campaign finances for, 85
  legislative leadership of, 132–133
  liberal Democrats in (late 1950s), 124
  parties in, 122, 123
  responsibility of members of, 150
  Seventeenth Amendment on direct
  election to, 17
Seniority, in Congress (U.S.), 122–123,
  208
September eleventh terrorist attacks, 194
Shays, Chris, 10
Sinclair, Barbara, 11, 208
Sinclair, Upton, 103
Smith, Alfred E., 21, 22
Smith v. Allwright (U.S., 1944), 62
Social Security Act (U.S., 1935), 23
Soft money, 89–90, 210
  corporate donations of, 94
  legislation on, 10–11
  spending for election of 2000, 54
  spent by state party organizations, 72
  Supreme Court on, 73
Sorauf, Frank J., 10, 96, 208
Souter, Anthony, 97